WILL BRITAIN MAKE IT?

THE RISE, FALL AND FUTURE OF BRITISH INDUSTRY

WILL BRITAIN MAKE IT?

THE RISE, FALL AND FUTURE OF BRITISH INDUSTRY

RICHARD MORRIS

The
History
Press

Jacket illustration: Old BP fuel sign, Norfolk (Eric Farrelly/Alamy)

First published 2022

The History Press
97 St George's Place, Cheltenham,
Gloucestershire, GL50 3QB
www.thehistorypress.co.uk

British Library Cataloguing in Publication Data.
A catalogue record for this book is available from the British Library.

ISBN 978 0 7509 9992 2

Typesetting and origination by The History Press
Printed and bound in Great Britain by TJ Books Limited, Padstow, Cornwall.

Trees for Life

Contents

Introduction

About the Book

For a lot of people it seems as though engineering and manufacturing in Great Britain ended about twenty years ago with the belief that all production shifted to China. There seems to have been a collective British shrug about this, as if there was an inevitability to it as low-cost Asian economies started to develop but, never mind, the creative, financial and service sectors have risen to fill the gap. Recent years have indeed witnessed a quite remarkable collapse of British industry and with it some of the country's biggest and best-known companies. However, it is not true that low-cost economies were solely to blame for this demise and many of the great names of British business ceased to exist in their recognised form long before the exodus of manufacturing overseas. Britain's collapse from Industrial Revolution pioneer and leader to industrial also-ran was due to a heady mix that included myopia, duplicity and stupidity. You only have to look at the health of industry in Germany – a nation devastated by the Second World War – to see what could have been avoided and what should have been possible. Nor is it true that the rise of Britain's service sector will compensate for the loss of its industrial base, making this collapse a national tragedy even if the British can't quite acknowledge it. It would be possible to write about this collapse and its effects using pure statistics, but this seems a rather dry approach. This book instead simply provides some initial political and economic context in Chapters 1 and 2. For simplicity, I've generally referred to 'Britain' rather than the 'United Kingdom'. The United Kingdom, or UK, would be the more correct as it includes Northern Ireland, whereas Britain refers only to England, Scotland and Wales, but 'Britain' is I think how most overseas readers recognise the national identity. It's also easier to write about 'Britons' and the 'British' rather than 'United Kingdomers' or the 'United Kingdomish'. Please also note that I've deliberately tried not to riddle the book with academic footnotes and references, or frequent deferment to 'ibid.', simply to make it more readable but would refer you instead to the sources listed in the bibliography.

From Chapter 3 onwards, the book views the industrial decline from the inside, from the perspective of what were some of Britain's – and the world's – greatest companies. These chapters tell the stories of how these companies started, how they became great and seeks to understand why they failed and what happened to their business subsequently. The stories are compelling because many started from quite humble beginnings and went on to achieve greatness only to fail, and fail quickly, from positions that seemed invincible. If you think I have got these corporate facts wrong then I apologise. There are many sources of information about the histories of the companies and these are often conflicting. It's also difficult to encapsulate so much information in the shorter summaries that are provided here. For example, the government decision to invest or not in the ailing British motorbike industry involved several different departments, several potential funding policies and schemes, political divides, manifesto promises, election intrigues and multiple political personalities. In the book this is encapsulated in one short sentence (see p.88). Getting the history and nuance right in a few words across such a depth of material is challenging and inevitably different interpretations and opinions will be apparent. There are many books that do go into companies more deeply than I've been able to here and I would encourage you to investigate these more detailed company biographies. I am certainly indebted to the authors of these books, whose research I have drawn on extensively and whose passion for our cultural heritage leaves me much indebted and with much admiration. (And if you want a fuller understanding of the motorbike investment saga, Jock Bruce-Gardyne's 1978 book *Meriden: Odyssey of a Lame Duck* would be a good place to start.)

The majority of the companies looked at are or were involved in manufacturing, which is simply because this is the nature of business that arose out of the crucible of the Industrial Revolution and the power of Victorian industrial engineering that made Britain the 'workshop of the world'. Younger readers may be surprised at just how great these British companies were. The company names may provide a degree of nostalgia for older generations, who will remember them and who may well have worked for them, coupled with a gnashing of teeth at the passing of so many great British institutions. Chapters 12 and 13 may fuel that sadness, looking more holistically at the corporate and government mistakes that were made alongside the effects of the collapse. Despite these corporate losses, I hope that the biographies will yet be inspirational, with Chapter 14 looking at the things that were achieved, and at the surprising legacies that have been passed on.

I hope that this uniquely macro and micro look at British industry will give insights into the industrial past, and the future. Are the legacies and lessons learned enough to see Britain maintain an industrial presence? My views on whether Britain will 'make' it will need to be read in the final chapters. I hope that for readers – including those in business, as well as scholars and politicians – my collective analysis and overview for the future are thought-provoking. If you think I've got the analysis and predictions wrong then note that these are just my opinions. This is a book about lessons learned, however, rather than blame. I hope, too, you will forgive any factual errors made. The problem with writing about corporate ownerships, subsidiaries and business dynamics is that they are subject to such rapid change, and these changed even during the course of writing. The facts, therefore, were as accurate as I could make them at the time, which was prior to the outbreak of the Covid-19 pandemic.

About the Companies in the Book

There are some outstanding British inventors in British history, developing ideas that transformed this small, agricultural and wool-producing nation into an engineering powerhouse. Remarkably, there are some businesses that have survived from this era through to today, including Richard Carter Ltd, GB Kent & Sons Ltd, Jaques of London, Dudson Ltd and Ormiston Wire, which date back to the 1700s. Britain's oldest manufacturing company, the Whitechapel Bell Foundry, operated for nearly 450 years before closing in 2017.

For many pioneering names of the First Industrial Revolution, however, making a profit would prove to be more difficult than being inventive. James Hargreaves was embattled with industrial disputes, John Kay and Richard Arkwright would die as poor men, and even the great Victorian engineers of Brunel, Bessemer and Telford would not die as rich men. In most cases, successful early pioneers were themselves simply surpassed by new ideas, new ventures and new businesses in a process described in 1942 by the Austrian political economist Joseph Schumpeter as 'Creative Destruction'. The steam engine company founded by James Watt and his business partner Matthew Boulton, for example, operated with great success from 1775 but it was still out-produced by Newcomen's less efficient but cheaper engine and plagued with court cases from rival engineers. It would eventually be taken over in 1895 by the Avery Weighing Company to make scales instead of steam engines. Abraham Darby and his descendants operated their groundbreaking iron-making business for over two centuries before also closing in 2017. Darby's Coalbrookdale forge, however, had always had an erratic business life and its glory days were long since gone.

This book is intent on the study of companies whose flame burned brightest with visible impacts on today's society. It starts by looking at companies that did start life right at the very beginnings of the Industrial Revolution and which do have a story to tell right up to the present time. Courtaulds was established in 1794 and epitomises the story of the nation's industrial growth through textiles. Iron-makers Vickers was founded in 1828 and the machinery expert company founded by William Armstrong in 1847 were both at the start and very peak of Britain's First Industrial Revolution.

Other companies selected for examination are drawn mostly from the next generation of entrepreneurs and engineers who rose up through the eruption of new technologies and practices known as the Second and Third Industrial Revolutions. There are many British companies from this era with once great and familiar names that could be looked at: APV Ltd, Birmingham Battery and Metal Company, Bluebird Toys, Ever Ready, British Seagull, BTR Plc, Charles Churchill & Co., Crompton Parkinson, Dunlop Rubber, Ekco, Gerard Bros, Gillett & Johnston, Goblin Vacuum Cleaners, Greenwood & Batley, John Hetherington & Sons, Lucas Industries, Marshall, Sons & Co., Minimax Ltd, Muir-Hill, Murphy Radio, Northern Counties, Parnall & Sons, Patent Shaft, Plessey, Ransomes & Rapier, Silk Engineering, J.W. Spear, Strebor, Turner & Newell, Westclox and Yale & Valor.

Companies selected were considered to be 'successful', although defining 'success' can be a tricky business. If success is all about profit, then the value of money and profit can be equally problematic, particularly where values are compared over long periods of time. To say a company made a profit of £1 does not, of course, sound much today. Was it worth a lot 200 years ago? You could use a cost comparison, but it is difficult to say that £1 in 1800 would be equivalent to buying a car today – what sort of car (and, of course, you would not have been able to buy a car in 1800). Most representations of cost tend to look at the yearly increase on historical value through inflation as indicated by rises in the Retail Price Index (RPI), but the RPI has been a basket of ever-changing commodities and there are so many other factors that can influence the value such as income, availability and standards of living. A better estimate might not just look at RPI but also at Gross Domestic Product (GDP) and average earnings, although this approach tends to produce a wide range of possible values. For example, £1 in 1800 (noting that this would be in pre-metric imperial currency) might now be worth anywhere between £75 and £6,000. The lower value might represent the historical opportunity cost whereas the economic cost equivalent might be towards the higher value end.[1] Either way, just looking at the returns a company has made is not ideal for selection as criteria of success. Success has therefore been estimated subjectively in other ways using elements such as longevity, innovation, achievement and legacy. From this perspective, companies selected for examination from this period in time include Birmingham Small Arms, Morris Motors, the de Havilland Aircraft Company Ltd and International Computers Ltd.

For more recent companies still, businesses listed as public companies with tradeable share ownership, then the share values might be used as indicators of success. From 1935 onwards, business and finance professionals could look at the country's top-performing industrial and commercial sector companies via a new ratings table; the Financial News index, the oldest continuous share index in the UK and one of the oldest in the world. The index looked at the top thirty companies in the country and was originally known as the 'Financial News 30-share index' (FT 30). The *Finance News* merged with the *Financial Times* in 1945 and remained the barometer of investor sentiment until the FT Actuaries series was launched in 1962 followed by the Financial Times Share Index in 1984, known as the 'FTSE' or 'Footsie' (noting, of course, that the *Financial Times* itself, founded in 1888, is now owned by the Japanese company Nikkei). The FTSE now looks at the top 100, top 250, and all share companies, and is different to the original Financial News 30 index because it includes in its considerations market capitalisation (i.e. share value multiplied by the number of shares available). This means the FTSE 100 is more relevant to company size. It also means it is much more changeable than the FT 30 as companies shrink and grow in natural business cycles. Both indices, however, are indicative of the nature and value placed on leading UK-orientated companies.

For the FT 30, the original companies listed in 1935 are predominantly of an engineering or production nature: Associated Portland Cement, Austin Motors, Bass, Bolsover Colliery, Callenders Cables & Construction, J. & P. Coats, Courtaulds, Distillers, Dorman Long, Dunlop Rubber, Electrical & Musical Industries, Fine Spinners and Doublers, General Electric, Guest Keen & Nettlefolds, Harrods, Hawker Siddeley, Imperial Chemical Industries, Imperial Tobacco, International Tea Co. Stores, London Brick, Murex, Patons & Baldwins, Pincham Johnson & Associates, Rolls-Royce, Tate & Lyle, Turner & Newall, United Steel, Vickers, Watney Combe & Reid and F.W. Woolworth. From this esteemed FT 30 list, the General Electric Company and Imperial Chemical Industries are included in the company biographies that follow.

The companies chosen to have their stories told in the book have not therefore been selected through a particularly detailed analysis or model of financial success but have been chosen instead as being 'great', iconic British industrial companies spread over a period of time and embedded within British culture and the British economic and political landscape. Together they also represent a cross section of industrial sectors including textiles, iron-making, mechanical equipment, electrical equipment, armaments, transport and computing. Throughout the book, I've deferred to shortened versions of company names, a Midland and industrial custom that aids readability. Morris Motors, for example, is simply referred to as 'Morris', and Imperial Chemical Industrial by its acronym 'ICI'.

Acknowledgements

My thanks for their help and support to Amy Rigg at The History Press, Helen Jordan at BAE Heritage and the staff at Haywards Heath Library. Thanks also to the motivation from friends and colleagues interested in industry, history and Britain: Mark Milne, Tony Jacques, Andy Dunican and Mike Farmer. Especial thanks for the encouragement of Douglas, Sue, Barney and Seb Morris.

Part One

Industrialisation and Growth

1

The First Industrial Revolution

The Enlightenment

Seventeenth-century Britain was a troubled place. At the turn of the century, King James I of England had succeeded Queen Elizabeth I, but he was never likely to match the success of her long and mostly popular reign. The attempt on his life via the gunpowder plot of 1605 emphasised the religious disharmony that wreaked havoc throughout the land during his time. Both James I and his son Charles I also argued bitterly with the nation over the rights of kings to rule divinely, resulting in two bloody civil wars that tore the country apart and which ended particularly badly for Charles. There was also strife overseas with interminable European squabbling and trouble at home through the arrival of gin- and alcohol-infused depredation, compounded by plague, freak weather and the destruction of 13,000 houses in the Great Fire that swept the country's capital in 1666. Imagine an event today destroying nearly 90 per cent of homes in the capital city.

Eighteenth-century Britain was not without its troubles either. There was more overseas fighting with battles against France, Austria, Prussia, India and the states of America. There was more infighting too, notably this time with the Jacobite rebellions and recriminations over slave trading, and massive financial losses and instability arising from the 'South Sea Bubble' economic disaster. There was, however, a significant difference between seventeenth- and eighteen-century Britain through a series of underlying developments that would transform a relatively small and mediocre nation into a worldwide powerhouse.

One of these developments was the thirst for knowledge that would come to see the period labelled as the 'Age of Reason' or more simply, the 'Enlightenment'. The rediscovery of ancient scripts and knowledge is often cited as a reason for the new-found interest in learning during this period, a development of the earlier Renaissance period. There were other reasons too, however, including a movement towards questioning political and religious dogma, facilitated in some ways by the earlier civil war that had questioned the right to rule. Religious texts such as the Bible were wrested away by Lutherism from the Latin of the clergy to the language of English that everyday folk could read. Natural philosophy, or the study of nature, began to make inroads into quackery and superstition from which developed the evidence and analytics-based practice of science. Gresham College in London began to apply mathematics and science to shipbuilding and navigation, raising the standard of maritime Britain. In 1867, Isaac Newton's *Mathematical Principles of Natural Philosophy* (the *Principia Mathematica*) began to see some clear growth in the stature of British science. As Voltaire would exclaim to the Académi Française, 'We are all his disciples now.'

Such learning was only made wholly tacit by its transference across the nation's population rather than keeping it secure within academic cloisters. Clubs and learning groups grew, such as the 'Lunar Men' or the 'Invisible College', which included Christopher Wren and Robert Boyle and which would in time evolve into learned bodies such as the Geographic Society and the Royal Society. These societies took away the hidden, secret knowledge of artisans and trade societies and made them public and shared, written in everyday language that had hitherto been smothered by academic prose and jargon. Better medicinal practice also allowed people more time to pursue exploits and learning beyond mere existence. Museums started to appear, including the first British Museum founded by Sir Hans Sloane in 1753. People were also only too willing to share their new knowledge and demonstrate their development and thinking. Networking in coffee houses grew, with 551 such houses in London in 1734, five times as many as had been present seventy years previously.

The growing effect of the printing press also had a key role to play in the spread of knowledge through pamphlets, newspapers and magazines. Newspaper sales rose from 2.5 million in 1710 to 16 million a century later and the roots of *The Times* would make its first appearance in 1785. Popular learned books began to appear for the first time, including Doctor Johnson's *Dictionary of the English Language* in 1755 and the *Encyclopaedia Britannica* of Denis Diderot in 1768, while the polymath Joseph Priestley published over 150 science-based books. Six thousand books were produced in 1620 and this had risen to 56,000 in the 1790s, with the number of publishers outside London growing from none before 1710 to over 1,000 eighty years later. One of the world's oldest magazines, *The Spectator*, was started by Richard Steel and Joseph Addison in 1828.

The Enlightenment had a more profound effect, though, than just better informing and educating the populace. It led to a new breed of society, the middle class, sweeping away the medieval aristocracy and peasant boundaries. It also led to the challenging of societal and philosophic norms, generating a new culture of trust, hopeful virtue and a 'new world vision'. The 1700s became a period of radicals and parliamentary reformers. Thinkers and philosophers such as William Cobbet, Jonathan Swift, William Hazlitt and Thomas Malthus challenged the nation's rules and values. Immanuel Kant's essay on the role of government and free thinking, for example, became a worldwide bestseller, while campaigners such as Thomas Paine began to challenge the rights to rule of the incumbent autocracies. Instead they preferred to set forth the rights of individuals and laid the foundations of democracy, most notably in the United States but across Europe too, where it was epitomised by the French Revolution.

Britain's Leading Industry: Textiles

It was enlightenment in agriculture, and an Agricultural Revolution, that played a key initial role in the change of the nation's industrial fortunes, a revolution denoted by a procession of agricultural improvements from the Middle Ages onwards. Charles Townsend, the 2nd Viscount Townsend or popularly known as 'Turnip Townsend', popularised the use of turnips to enhance agricultural production in Britain. The deep roots of a turnip extract unused minerals from a field usually left fallow as part of a three-field crop rotation system, while growing clover enriched the soil in fallow fields for better production in the next year. Henceforth, 33 per cent of land usually left unused each year to recover could from now on be used for crop production. In 1700 Jethro Tull invented the horse-drawn seed drill to economically sow seeds in this new farming landscape, which alongside plough improvements, fertiliser development and the enclosure of common land all served to make farming more efficient. These changes increased the food supply and enabled population growth from 5.5 million in 1700 to 9 million by 1801. The population of Surrey alone then increased again by 65 per cent in the first three decades of the 1800s. This population growth provided a new labour force and, alongside improved roads and canals in a country that, unusually, developed toll- and tariff-free trade, enabled an increasingly large, coherent market to develop. These changes also benefitted Britain's main industrial business: textiles.

Over the course of time, the British Isles have coalesced, sunk and risen, and travelled to different geographic positions over the earth's surface, accumulating a rich tapestry of minerals and geological features. It has been rich in tin, lead, iron and coal, for example, which have all been used to good effect in industry. It is, however, the wet and green British environment that has made the country the ideal place to nurture sheep and process wool. Wool is an ideal clothing material. It is easily fashioned, easily washed, keeps wearers cool in summer and warm in winter and warmer than vegetable-based fibres such as hemp or cotton (or even many of today's synthetics). It is therefore desirable at both home and overseas, and wool has therefore formed the staple of British industry throughout the past two millennia. Up to the sixteenth century, every parish throughout the land had a thriving wool industry. That industry was based on wool production and processing producing long chains of wool thread known as yarn. It was, however, Flemish weavers in particular who were more adept at weaving and knitting yarn into high-value woollen cloth, from which clothing was made. The Englishman William Cockayne had tried to add value to

British-made cloth with a monopoly agreement to sell dyed and dressed wool abroad in the early seventeenth century but this failed and depressed the cloth trade for centuries. The one bright spot was the development of a lighter wool mix cloth that sold well to hotter, south European countries (paving the way for a more cordial relationship with Spain following the Armada invasion attempt of 1588).

The changes to Britain's traditional three-field rotation system not only changed human lives; it changed animal's lives too. It provided more winter fodder for an increasing number of farm animals, reducing the number of open-grazed sheep and increasing the number of farmyard-processed sheep. These different sheep grazed in different ways and fed on different food, and when raised through selective breeding by a process pioneered by Robert Bakewell, led to a change in the wool types available. British weavers were able to make smoother and silkier high-value wool products known as worsteds. Any idea that this was a pastoral industry with kindly shepherds passing tufts of wool on to gentle cottage weavers as per a Gainsborough or Constable painting would be very wrong. The wool and worsted industry was highly fractionalised, with regions competing with each other and with overseas countries to produce better and more innovative products more cheaply. Challis, felt, tweed, melton, loden, jersey, bustian, calimanco, camlet, cantillon, grogram, harrateen, mockado, prunella, sagathis, sateen, shalloon and serge are just some of the many hundreds of wool and woollen types (including the use of recycled wool known as 'shoddy', which is still known to us today as indicative of less than top-quality goods). British innovation in finer wools, dyestuffs and wool processing enabled the country to claim its place in the world as best in both the production of wool and the creation of woollens. By 1750, over 50 per cent of all British wool products were exported, and this accounted for around half of all British exports.[1] It was also the first British product to have an export charge attached to it, and likely to be the reason that smugglers evolved with the nickname 'owlers' derived from their trade in wool long before their association with tea, rum and brandy.

For thousands of years the weaving of cloth had been achieved by hanging threads vertically (the warp) from a high support and weighted at the bottom with loom weights. Through these vertical threads, a horizontal thread (the weft) would be passed in and out and backwards and forwards (the weave). Somebody clever but unknown in the mists of time had used two top bars to alternatively attach the vertical threads, allowing them all to be moved back and forth for the easier passage of the horizontal weft thread. Wool processing, particularly for fine wool and worsteds, was, however, still a slow, highly skilled and labour-intensive process, with around one in ten of the population working in the wool industry. It was the intensity of competition and concentration of labour that led producers to try and make efficiency savings, which in turn led to the explosion in equipment and operations that wrested cloth production away from Europe and into Britain, and would come to be known as the Industrial Revolution. In 1733, for example, the son of an English farmer called John Kay invented the flying shuttle, a wooden torpedo-shaped device that used wheels to carry the weft through the warp. Rather than being passed through by one weaver to another, it was propelled through the warp by flicking long leather straps at either end. This strap configuration meant that wider looms could be built, producing wider cloth (which would in time allow furniture makers to start to produce settees and sofas instead of armchairs) while doing this at a much faster rate. If the flying shuttle was twice as fast, and twice as wide, production would have quadrupled overnight, but it had the added advantage of enabling weaving machines to be operated by one person instead of two! Imagine companies today increasing their working practices eightfold overnight.

Cloth production in Britain was revolutionised, and if there was a drawback, it was that the suppliers of woollen thread and yarn needed by the weavers to make cloth could hardly keep up. Yarn production was the original cottage industry with spinners working at home producing wool on their spinning wheels – but they couldn't spin faster than they already did to match the new demand. The solution came via another innovation, the invention of the spinning jenny in 1764 by an illiterate weaver named James Hargreaves. Illiterate he may have been, but he had the insight and the ability to build a machine that could feed a number of spindles from one larger spinning wheel rather than one at a time. Unlike a traditional spinning wheel, the jenny also had a powered wheel that freed up the hands of the operators so that they could spin twice as fast. Richard Arkwright then took the process a step further in 1768. His invention of the water frame took Kay's and Hargreaves's designs to a higher level, with a bigger, more powerful and more automated weaving machine that needed to be powered by a water wheel in order to operate. Arkwright organised his production into a more factory-like mill. Once again production was revolutionised and textile mills would come to account for 40 per cent of Britain's exports.[2]

Power

Special-purpose machinery was one of the fundamentals of industrialisation, and through the ideas of Kay, Arkwright and Hargreaves it had now started to appear. The development of Britain's mill machinery brought with it demands for more power and this was in short supply. The predominant source of contemporary power was through water wheels, like the one still working today in the Styal Mill at the National Trust's Quarry Bank museum. The problem with water power is the uncertain flow of water driving it, often reduced or non-existent in summer, with the alternatives of wind or animal power being equally erratic. Enter now James Watt, a Scottish instrument maker working at the University of Glasgow trying to fix a small Newcomen engine. The Newcomen engine works by using steam power to lift a piston in a cylinder but it had to wait for the steam to condense in the cylinder before gravity returned the piston back to its starting position (essentially an atmospheric, rather than a true, fully steam-powered engine). Watt realised that the small model he was working on would not work properly because the ratio of the surface area to volume in this small model was different to that of larger Newcomen engines. Effectively it had less surface area so it was not able to radiate heat away as quickly, taking it longer to heat up and cool down and rendering it ineffective. He then realised through a moment of genius that the engine would work better if the whole cooling cycle was not actually taking place in the cylinder, and added a separate condensing cylinder. He then arranged for steam to be fed to the main drive cylinder not just at the bottom but alternatively via the top and bottom of the main cylinder, enabling steam pressure to drive the piston both up and down. By 1769 Watt had hence designed the world's first, true steam engine. What was needed now was a cheap material that enabled strength and accuracy in construction for steam engines to be reliable and affordable, and that material was developed by Abraham Darby.

Cast Iron

The 'makers and creators' of Britain engaged wholeheartedly in the heady mix of learning, exploration and optimism of the Enlightenment. Pivotal to their story is the work of a small-time farmer and locksmith called Abraham Darby. Darby wanted to make large quantities of high-quality cast iron, which would have been a strange thing to want to do at that time. If you had wanted a small metal object, such as a farm tool like shears or a household object like a candle holder, you turned to the black-smith, who would form them in his forge as 'wrought' iron. Wrought is the word used to describe the process of hammering and pounding hot molten iron to remove its impurities, leaving an iron with a low carbon content and making it both strong (resistant to deformation) and tough (resistant to breaking). Wrought iron was, however, of limited use in making large metal objects such as statues or cannon, which needed to be made by casting molten metal into moulds. The English gunsmith John Browne had proven that cast iron could be used for naval cannon but it was a costly and specialised process that required cannon to be annealed (heated and cooled at controlled temperatures) to give them wrought-like qualities. Bronze or brass, however, could be made liquid at lower temperatures than iron, and cast in thinner sections than iron, making it cheaper, lighter and more useful for large metal objects. Hence, iron was good for small, wrought items and bronze for large cast items, and there was no real reason why anyone would have wanted to change this status quo.

Abraham Darby thought otherwise and spent time and money on experiments, drawing on the experiences of his forbears and from his own familiarities working in the brewing industry, where coke – a type of high-carbon coal with fewer impurities – was used as a fuel in the brewing process. It would be this that would give him the breakthrough. By 1709 he had found that coke reduced the sulphur contamination of iron to produce a much higher-quality and purer metal that he could pour more easily into sand moulds to produce thin wall castings of good enough quality to be able to cast it in large volumes. Darby's work had profound effects. For a millennia since the Pax Romana, the centre of British industry had been in Sussex and the south of England, where thick Downland clay produced excellent bricks and tiles and Wealden oak provided the timber for ships, houses, furniture and for making charcoal used to smelt bronze and iron. Sussex was hence the world leader in cannon production and they had been used, for example, by the British navy against the Spanish Armada (who were also coincidentally armed with British cannon!). Darby's discovery moved the centre of British industry away from the wooded, charcoal areas of southern England into the coal- and coke-seamed areas of the Midlands and the North. His grandson, Abraham Darby III, built the world's first iron bridge in 1779, demonstrating the capabilities of cast iron. They would now supply a new material as the basis for either forge or large-scale casting work, which would become an ideal material for a whole host of other innovators who were emerging. Nobody would come to better demonstrate this than the great engineers Isambard Kingdom Brunel and Thomas Telford, whose innovations in suspension bridges, railways and ships would in due course stun the world and enable British-made goods to be transported internationally. Often overlooked in the role of this infrastructure revolution is the development of improved cement by James Parker (hydraulic, 1796) and William Aspdin (Portland, 1843).[3]

Britain Industrialises

Cast iron, however, was not limited to innovation in transport; it came to play a key part in the machinery and equipment that developed Britain's industry, aided by the superior manufacturing techniques established by the likes of Joseph Whitworth and John Wilkinson (whose accurate boring process enabled the cylinders for Watt's steam engines). The increasing ability to mechanise the reciprocating and linear motion machines and processes using power from fire and steam provided the platform for the Industrial Revolution and future British economic power. A new breed of entrepreneurial society and culture grasped the opportunities presented and energised the nation. The manufacturers of products and equipment in other sectors adopted the principles of a new way of working: specialist machinery, new materials, power, organised and larger factories. The term 'industry' would come to be defined by the engineering that created new goods and equipment, and engineers who could understand and apply new science and manufacturing techniques. They added their own innovations in due course. The number of patents per decade from 1760 through to 1790 was 365, five times greater than it had been in the century of preceding decades. One notable development was the generation of components that were interchangeable, which heralded another facet of industrialisation: the development of mass production with manufacturing tolerances. Eli Whitney and Marc Brunel (father of his more famous son Isambard) pioneered these practices through gun production and naval shackles.

It wasn't all about textiles and power though; it was about social change, too. A decline in agricultural work brought on by the newer farming methods and equipment, including threshing machines, coupled with an economic slump following the Napoleonic wars and long periods of poor weather meant that agricultural workers started to flock to the new forms of factory work and one-fifth of the country would come to work in the textile industry. This transformation of a medieval-type agrarian society into a factory-based one became known in a term affirmed by the economic historian Arnold Toynbee as the 'Industrial Revolution', and it really was a transformative revolution.

The resulting mixture of social change, education and ideas was commercially explosive. By 1851, Britain was mining half the world's coal, consuming ten times more than France and six times more than the fusion of states that would become Germany. It produced half the world's pig iron (the term for crude iron produced from furnaces), using three to four times more pig iron than anywhere else and with more train lines than Germany and France combined.[4] The British Gross National Product (GNP) rose from £452 million to £523 million between 1841 and 1851, 65 per cent higher than the German states and 30 per cent higher than the US.[5]

Britain Expands

Britain's industrial output was not just confined to British markets either and there was an overseas market for Britain's increasingly unique and low-cost goods. That market was growing, too. The European population alone grew from 150 million in 1800 to 400 million by 1914. Britain's markets were also expanding beyond just its closest European neighbours. James Wolfe had secured northern America for Britain in 1759, Captain James Cook claimed Australia for Britain in 1770 and Clive of India and the East India Company were at large in India. The total number of people who could be counted as being within the British Empire in 1900 was 436 million, a market over ten times that which the British market alone could provide.[6] In India alone exports rose around 20 per cent between 1796 and 1798 and contributed 40 per cent to Britain's Exchequer receipts during this period.[7] Between 1809 and 1839 British exports generally tripled from £25 million to £76 million, and exports were often nearly double the value of imports to the country. London and Liverpool had become the busiest ports in the world as early as the 1750s, with London including docks at St Katharine's, East and West India, Commercial, Tobacco, Shadwell, Victoria, and Wapping. The Wapping Docks built in 1799 with anchorage for 300 sailing ships and surrounded by 50 acres of warehousing, cost £5.5 million and was the world's most expensive building project at the time.

The peak of British industrial power is considered to be sometime between the 1830s and the 1850s when the country was reaping the benefits of innovations in iron- and steel-making, textile machinery, machine tools, chemicals, canals, steam engines and steam locomotives. The world's first Great Exhibition of 1851 in the Crystal Palace at Hyde Park further showcased Britain's industrial prowess to a staggered world. Britain had become the workshop of the world, with British industrial power accounting for nearly 30 per cent of all global manufacturing during the 1870s and this would come to account for over 9 per cent of the world's total Gross Domestic Product (GDP).

2

The Second and Third Industrial Revolutions

Industrial Problems

If Britain's Industrial Revolution was stunning, it would be wrong to view it as being utopian because that was far from the case. The dark, satanic, clanking, belching, roaring mills and increasing urbanisation brought disease and deprivation to the newly industrialised towns and cities. Average life expectancy during the Industrial Revolution remained the same, and even dropped for children, while average heights for the population as a whole dropped. Real wages barely rose and fell against the cost of food. Even at the height of this industrial period, the 1840s would become known as the 'Hungry Decade' as exports and output fell, wet and poor harvests hit food production and social unrest would arise in the face of growing slum developments. 'Luddite' craftsmen and workers fought against new technologies and ways of working, and farm workers rebelled through the Swing Riots.

One of the problems that Britain was facing was that although it was producing more, it was still paying for its conflicts, limiting its ability to generate sufficient profits. Its West Indian campaigns from 1793 to 1801 alone had probably cost around £30 million, while the Napoleonic wars cost the nation £831 million and the Crimean War a further £74 million.[1]

Under these restricted financial straits, Prime Minister Robert Peel repealed the Corn Laws in 1846, which abolished the tariffs on imported foodstuffs. These tariffs kept prices high for the vested aristocratic landowners and farmers but were indefensible given the state of the nation's starving citizens. The repeal enabled food prices to drop and helped industry to overcome desperate wage demands. It also started Britain on its drive towards being a free-trading, tariff-free world economy, a philosophical position that had first been advocated in Adam Smith's *Wealth of Nations* critique in 1776.

The adoption overseas of agricultural changes and mechanisation, along with cheaper global transport, brought cheaper agricultural products and foodstuffs into Britain but also its own problems. Imports rose. Grain imports to Britain, for example, were 2 per cent in the 1830s but by the 1860s stood at 24 per cent. The Agricultural Revolution that had fired up Britain now faced a terminal decline. The value of agriculture to the British economy dropped from 17 per cent to 7 per cent between 1871 and 1911. Agricultural unemployment skyrocketed, while agricultural land use and its value dropped and the 'Great' or 'Long Depression' followed between 1873 and 1896, with its apogee in 1879.

The Second and Third Industrial Revolutions

The First Industrial Revolution, which harnessed power, iron, machinery and mass production, was followed by the Second Industrial Revolution from 1870 onwards, which saw industrialists grasp the wondrous new technology of electricity emerging at the end of the nineteenth century to, quite literally, electrify the world. New factories started to appear across Britain away from the traditional heavy industry heartlands, including, for example, in the 'West London Industrial heartland'[2] along the A4 Great West Road, where the population grew from sixty in 1901 to 250,000 by 1956.

Some of these factories were not British owned, including US companies along the A4 like Sperry, Gillette, Hoover and Firestone, because if Britain's Industrial Revolution wasn't utopian, it wasn't omnipotent either.

Although Britain had advocated a free global market, other countries including the US and Germany maintained high tariffs and used these to protect their markets. Hence they were able to grow their own economies and press ahead in relative terms to the British economy. These would become increasingly industrialised economies that would benefit not only from greater protection but from new technological developments, too.

Entrepreneurs in the US were less constrained by Europe's social mores and castes, which in Britain tended to limit enterprise to enthusiastic gentry. They were often immigrants arriving from the old world, hungry to overcome the deprivations of migration in a 'land of opportunity'. The US would hence see electrical developments through the work of pioneers such as Thomas Edison and Nikola Tesla, and in flight through the Wright brothers. US companies were also run by technocrats rather than bureaucrats or the entitled vestiges of British aristocracy. Increasingly these US companies were large, vertically integrated organisations, while British companies were relatively late in growing large. By the time they achieved growth through a 'great merger' movement up to around 1905, US companies had grown big and powerful. Germany similarly forged ahead through technical developments that included the internal combustion engine and automobiles. Strong research, family cartels and tariffs also enabled German companies to grow stronger.

Cheap manufactured goods also now began to pour into Britain, while overseas orders began to suffer against tariffs in other countries. In 1886, a Royal Commission on Trade and Industry report noted this increasing competition and decline in the country's industrial leadership but refused to stray from free-market principles and the imposition of tariffs. Joseph Chamberlain, Colonial Secretary (1895–1903) and father of future Prime Minister Neville Chamberlain, also later noted the move in Britain away from the primacy of manufacturing and into banking.

Instead of implementing its own tariffs, the British response instead was to consolidate and bolster its colonial ambitions. It consequently descended into a number of expensive activities, including the Boer War (1899–1902), which cost it a further £222 million. The First World War would then see the world's largest industrial powers of the US, the UK and Germany slug it out together in a brutal, mechanised conflict that ran from 1914 to 1918. The war saw Britain's national debt rise from £677 million in 1910 to £7.8 billion by 1922, outstripping its Gross Domestic Product and without any easy option to reduce the debt as flu, poverty and depression swept the world. The hyperinflation in Germany that followed the war was due in part to war debts but also more largely attributable to the same global depression, rather than post-war reparations as is often cited. The bitterness towards reparations, however, combined with the dire economy enabled National Socialism to take a grip on the country. This led Germany to establish yet more tariffs and nationalistic approaches to ownership, leading to further industrial growth.

Not only was Britain's competition increasing, but its competitors were showing themselves to be more effective and adept at more efficient production. The development of enhanced and automated production lines with low-skilled and specialised workers overlapping with earlier industrial improvements, as well as with electrification reaching forward to computers and advances in internet communication, would collectively become known as the Third Industrial Revolution. This wide time span of development makes it difficult to date precisely, but many historians look at this period as starting from the mid-1900s onwards. The US mastered these efficiency progressions better than anyone else, with the most cited example being in the automobile production line techniques of Henry Ford and earning it the sobriquet of 'Fordism'. Fordism was, however, not restricted to Ford cars and would become endemic across vast swathes of US manufacturing, improved and refined further through pioneering management studies such as the time and methods approaches of Frederick Winslow Taylor. Germany similarly adopted US manufacturing techniques, enabling it to become efficient, and also able to join the US in surpassing British manufacturing before the turn of the twentieth century.

The Second World War

The Second World War played a further significant role in the decline of Britain's industrial status. The industrial base that had provided its finance and which was the means to recapitalise was in a desperate position at the end of the war, with material shortages and the need for extensive industrial re-tooling away from armaments. Markets were dire with rationing and a drop in consumer spending power both at home and overseas. Management expertise was also spread more thinly, while workers were tired, hungry and spread out. Yet there was no money to reconstruct and reinvest. In the 1930s Britain was the world's largest nation creditor but at the conclusion of the Second World War it was the world's biggest debtor, saddled with war debts of around £3,500 million. While it was faced with its own debts, it was also supporting post-war Germany, to the tune of £80 million during its first year of occupation.

At the same time, the US surprisingly withdrew its Lend-Lease support at the immediate conclusion of the war on 2 September 1945. There had been generous discounts under the scheme, but Britain had hoped for a gift from the US for the residues of this war trade agreement – some £1 billion at the time and around £40 billion in current terms – but instead it had to pay up in hard currency. It was forced to take from the US a £3,750 million loan at 2 per cent interest as described with the Lend-Lease successor, the Anglo-American Loan. The payment of interest alone in 1946 was £140 million and with a fifty-year term, and it took Britain until 29 December 2006 to make the final payment. It was a cruel blow to a nation that had at one time stood alone against the scourge of Nazism. Russia, by contrast, only part repaid its financial obligations to the US in grain, in shipments that never arrived, with around half the debt being written off.

British economist (Lord) John Maynard Keynes estimated that the results of Britain's financing meant it needed to increase exports from its pre-war figures by 175 per cent in order to maintain the same standard of living. Exporting hence became the government priority for industry, but the position was difficult because its main trading partner – Europe – was also in recovery. The terms of the Anglo-American Loan had also required Britain to allow sterling to become free floating. The post-war pound was therefore overvalued, making exports even harder. To make matters worse, the loan agreement also required Britain to forego its 'imperial preference' system, opening up its Commonwealth country trade. Its empire dominions were also now starting to gain their independence – a policy that was again led by the US and enforced upon the British as part of the 1941 Atlantic Charter, which the US President Roosevelt insisted upon as part of the deal for the US to enter the war. Barbados, Belize, Botswana, Cyprus, Fiji, Gambia, Ghana, Guyana, India, Israel, Jamaica, Jordan, Kenya, Kuwait, Malaysia Nigeria, Pakistan and Tanzania would be just some of the countries that gained independence from Britain in the post-war period. While this colonial end is to be supported, at the time it ended any natural proclivity to buy British and opened up new market blocs to the US. The US hence began not so much to take apart but to take over Britain's colonial customers.

As if these debts and loss of market weren't enough, Britain started to lose its global political status and with it its ability to manoeuvre and influence its position. The US was again at the heart of this development. During the Second World War, in 1944, national representatives from forty-four countries met in the US setting of Bretton Woods to plan for a post-war finance system that took its name from the setting. The lofty and laudable aim was to establish a system that would encourage economic co-operation and help to end the historic global cycle of conflict and war. Keynes, acting as Britain's Treasury Advisor, argued for a single world currency with the capacity of a central bank to expand the money supply and reflate the world economy. Trade and economic costs could be shared and adjusted more equitably with successful countries re-evaluating and deficient countries devaluating. It was instead the ideas of the US Treasury's Harry Dexter White and Henry Morgenthau that prevailed. The meeting set out a system of fixed exchange rates that were pegged to the dollar – itself pegged to the gold standard. This gave the US dollar a strong, global authority, allowing it to operate a trade deficit if necessary without having to devalue, and helped to open up new markets to the US, including Britain's own Commonwealth countries. A senior official at the Bank of England described the deal reached at Bretton Woods as 'the greatest blow to Britain next to the war'.[3] De Gaulle of France would also demur when faced with the same pressure to open up its imperial countries, but would also have to acquiesce in the face of its own financial needs.

The Bretton Woods system would also be regulated by a newly created International Monetary Fund (IMF), which could also offer short-term finance to help prevent countries having to devalue, while the International Bank for Reconstruction and Development (the World Bank) would offer longer-term finance for reconstruction. The US, which was one of the few nations to emerge better off from the war than when it entered it, provided majority funding to the IMF and World Bank, giving it at the same time the biggest voting rights alongside veto rights on policy decisions. A third institution, the International Trade Organisation, was intended to encourage free trade, although tariff reductions were enabled later by the General Agreement on Trade and Tariffs (GATT). GATT and its successor the World Trade Organization (WTO) are credited with reducing tariffs from around 22 per cent in 1947 to 5 per cent after 1999.[4] The newly freely convertible pound, however, immediately lost its status and a consequent run on the pound caused sterling to be devalued – adding to the woes of debt repayment. Later commentators have argued that any lofty principles first developed under Roosevelt were soon turned by Harry S. Truman and successive US leaders towards US hegemony.[5]

As sweeteners for their losses, both Britain and France received recovery funding. The US provided help to Europe after the war through a series of aid packages of around $41 billion, which was around one-sixth of its annual GDP, and this included the $13 billion European Recovery Program (ERP), better known today as the Marshall Plan. The support combined eventually with a bounce back from the war enabled Europe and the world to see a post-war economic expansion running from 1950 through to 1973, variously referred to as the 'Long Boom,' the 'Great Acceleration' or the 'Golden Age of Capitalism'. Britain secured a relatively high proportion of US aid and despite its troubles it did therefore thrive during the Long Boom with a period of high growth and low unemployment. Even at the end of the 1950s, industry still made up 48 per cent of the British economy, with one-quarter of the world's manufacturing still being British with products that could proudly display a 'Made in Great Britain' stamp. With the exception of food and oil, it was largely self-sufficient.

The trouble was that Britain did not necessarily benefit the most from the Long Boom, which may have obscured Britain's true trading position. It had emerged victorious from the Second World War but trashed resources, high debts, declining markets, reduced global status and the emergence of new industrial rivals would all ultimately have a disastrous effect on its economy. It was a perfect storm, into which were sailing British companies. Like the *Titanic*, many of them would find themselves at sea and heading for disaster – and displaying more than a fair amount of their own management incompetence.

Part Two

Britain's Leading Companies

3

Courtaulds

At the heart of Britain's historic textile industry is Courtaulds, one of the oldest companies in this book and once not only a giant of the natural fibres world but the world's leading producer of man-made fibres.

The fourth-century Roman Emperor Diocletian noted that British wool was the best, and it is wool that has for the best part of the past two millennia been the mainstay of British industry. As Daniel Defoe described, 'Let no man wonder that the Woollen Manufacture of England is arriv'd to such a Magnitude, when in a Word it may be said to cloath the world.' During the eighteenth century, however, a number of new materials were also beginning to appear, adding to the nation's commercial potential, and these included both cotton and silk.

Cotton is a fluffy fibre made from almost pure plant cellulose, which can be lighter, less absorbent and less irritating to the skin than wool. It can be twisted and spun into long threads and then woven into soft, light and breathable cotton cloth and its variants such as calico, chintz and muslin. It was carried from Asia to Britain by the East India Company originally as a novelty line, but it was cheap and colourful and by the late 1600s had become its most important commodity, exceeding even its trade in tea and spices. Cotton became so popular that it started to eat into Britain's wool trade and the government responded by introducing the Calico Acts from 1700 onwards. These Acts regulated that only raw cotton could be imported, in an attempt to enable British manufacturers to develop an

indigenous cotton-weaving industry. Pioneers like Arkwright began incorporating it into their mills and factories. Within three decades, production
of cotton had increased by 360 per cent.[1] The demand for cotton doubled
every decade for seven decades and while British manufacturers continued to be helped by both government tariffs on cotton textile imports and
East India Company's pressure on indigenous manufacturing industries, it
should also be noted that manufacturers were helping themselves by investing in new equipment and industrial ideas, including Lewis Paul and John
Wyatt's roller spinning machines and flyer-and-bobbin systems. Following
some dubious tariff and colonial practices, the Acts were partially repealed
from 1774, by which time the industry had proved capable of producing
cotton cloth of a quality and price that was the match of anywhere in the
world. In 1710, cotton provided 2.6 per cent added value to the economy
but by 1801 that reached 17 per cent. By 1831 it had reached 22 per cent, and
the country was processing half of the world's cotton. At the centre of this
was Manchester, or 'Cottonopolis' as it was nicknamed.

At the same time the cotton trade was growing, silk production was also
emerging in Britain. Silk is a strong, shimmering material made from the
sericin and fibroin proteins produced by insects such as the silkworm and
was then, as it still is now, a high-value cloth. China had held the monopoly
on silk production for centuries but knowledge of silk production had
moved slowly westwards across the Middle East and into Europe, quite
literally down the 'silk road'. Even with that knowledge, however, silk was
not easy to produce, requiring the elusive ability to cultivate the plants and
animals that could produce silk before it could be processed. James I of
England (who ruled from 1603 to 1625) was among the first to try and
introduced the mulberry trees needed for silkworms, but he and others
failed. Britain's silk industry hence grew only slowly during the late 1600s
and even stagnated during the first half of the 1700s. Gradually, however,
the experience needed to succeed began to accumulate, significantly more
so with the arrival of protestant immigrants (Huguenots) escaping religious
persecution in Europe. Successful silk businesses began to appear around the
towns of Stockport, Macclesfield, Congleton and particularly in London's
Spitalfields area. From 1750 onwards, the British silk trade began to bloom
through an increasing supply of raw silk from Asia, a rise in national

population and income, and the disruption of French silk production through the Seven Years' War.

Cotton and silk were both new, with desirable, fashionable properties, and they were unhindered by the long history and traditions of wool production. Manufacturers were hence more easily able to adopt the emerging production mechanisation, and the adoption of powered machinery is first noted effectively in the silk factory of the Lombe Brothers in 1719. Government actions, including the Spitalfields Act of 1773, also helped to stabilise the industry by setting prices, fixing wages and regulating apprenticeships. By 1770, wool exports only accounted for 34 per cent of British exports compared to the 50 per cent of twenty years earlier, and not because wool had contracted as an industry – between 1785 and 1800, British textiles exports as a whole doubled – but because other materials like silk and cotton had simply expanded. Textile entrepreneurs began to appear and the son of Britain's first cotton millionaire, (Sir) Robert Peel, would become a future prime minister.

It is against this background that the Courtaulds story began. George Courtauld was the son of an immigrant Huguenot goldsmith but had been apprenticed to fellow immigrant Huguenot silk throwers in Spitalfields, where he learnt the art of throwing silk. 'Throwing' was the process of cleaning, twisting, doubling and winding the silk fibres onto bobbins to make long silk threads, similar to the process of 'spinning' for wool. London-based silk throwing was, however, slow to adopt the newer production developments appearing elsewhere in the country and focused instead on the more time-consuming practice of decorative silk production perhaps associated with its nearby rich, court-based customers. George Courtauld became increasingly disenchanted with this slow pace of the London silk business. The Courtaulds were a Unitarian family; reformers and radical, open to new ideas and less taken with dogma, and this zeal may have been behind, and was certainly evident, in their enterprise, industrial drive and innovation. After a break overseas as a farmer, Courtauld returned in 1774, partly it was said because he hated farming, and partly because he and his wife hated each other and needed more sociable surroundings to escape being cooped up together in the US wilderness. As George would say, 'We lived miserably together for twenty-five years.'

He began work with Peter Nouaille in Sevenoaks, where he first saw the production of the wrinkled silk material known as crêpe. He left and experimented briefly with paper manufacturing before moving to Essex to run a silk mill for the London-based company Witts & Co. It was a comfortable living, but he could not secure from the company the promise of a long-term appointment, so he left to start his own business venture in 1782 in Pebmarsh with the finance of a London-based supplier of raw silk called Joseph Wilson. George was knowledgeable in the textile trade, experienced in business, law and contracts, and adept and keen on mechanical development, and this set the company going in the right direction. He invented a double spinning device that formed the basis of a partnership agreement between him and Wilson, with both investing further in the enterprise.

However, there were problems. These were generally troubled times for business, with the Napoleonic wars causing boom and bust cycles, coupled with poor harvests in 1816 and a collapse in earnings and business confidence. Finding labour was also difficult. In 1788, around two-thirds of people working in water-powered textile factories were children.[2] The 1802 Acts that would go on to become known as the Factory Acts started to reduce the ability to exploit children wholesale and since more businesses were starting up in the area, the demand for adult employees was outstripping supply and wages costs. As staff turned over and supervisors came and went, so quality failed. Half of the costs involved in production were rising in 1816, while retail prices dropped by 20 per cent at the same time.

These problems and the lack of returns soon became overwhelmingly problematic and led to bitter recriminations between Courtauld and Wilson. Wilson stopped supplying raw silk to the mill, leaving Courtauld with no production and thirty staff to pay. Courtauld began sourcing alternative raw silk, and the two men went to court amid a flurry of injunctions. In 1817, the court decided in favour of Courtauld, who received a lump sum payment but had to leave the plant and agree not to produce silk in the same area. This was a bitter business blow, coming on top of personal woes. However, his salvation came in the form of his son, Samuel, who was the third of his name in the family and is usually referred to as Samuel Courtauld III. George Courtauld was not noted as being unkind, but he had fallen out badly with his wife, his business partner and most of his children. George and Samuel's relationship had also been stormy, but the legal battle between George Courtauld and Joseph Wilson brought father and son together. The business restrictions on George allowed Samuel to head the business instead of his father and from 1818 onwards he became the boss of the Pebmarsh and Braintree silk businesses. Samuel Courtauld III was also as adept and as dynamic as his father and had even started his own small mill in Braintree in 1810 supplying raw silk to his father. George now departed from the stage. He vacillated between setting up new mills in England and trying new ventures in the US but achieved little more and died in 1823 from fever.

Like his father, Samuel also struggled with anxiety and financial worries, particularly for the first three years. The mills he had to work with were poor, and he had to buy and sell to get better plant. He also struggled with finding staff, and pulled his cousin Peter Taylor in from his own family's hardware business to help out, although this failed to work out. He even tried to sell the business but had few offers and these all eventually fell through. Gradually though, sales improved and he was joined by his younger brother and re-joined by Peter Taylor. His problem now was one of money. The silk industry was relatively easy to join, and mills in Manchester alone increased from three in 1820 to sixteen in 1832. Only those capable of investing, however, would grow and survive, and here Samuel now had some luck. His father, George, was the main company investor, and when he died the pressure to pay back eased off. Another investor also appeared, Stephen Beuzeville, who had a textile background from which Courtauld benefitted. He also got good support from his network of family and associates, including his good friend Stephen Newbury, who was helpfully relaxed over repayments. This financial structure enabled the company with lower-cost, long-term funding rather than high-cost, short-term borrowing that indebted so many other organisations.

At the start of the nineteenth century, the British government, inspired by the writings of Adam Smith and Jeremy Bentham, started to move more towards a free trade economy. This centred on food and the removal of trade tariffs and subsidies known as the Corn Laws (from 1815 onwards). The tariffs were fully repealed in 1846 but from 1824 the government had started by lowering the British silk tariffs from an average of around

30 per cent to 15 per cent. They also repealed the Spitalfields Law that regulated silk worker wages. The silk industry was worried by these actions, but it mainly caused problems for the older, more traditional and smaller organisations (as well as the poor workers who would be hit with lower earnings in response). The actions actually allowed an increase in raw silk production, which benefitted the business, including that now known as 'Courtaulds and Taylor'. With their solid financial base and eye for innovation, they were early adopters of water power and the advances in weaving as seen by the developments of Kay, Arkwright, Hargreaves and Jacquard, so that the company was not destined to stay as one of the smaller, cottage factories but to grow into a large and efficient business. It added more and more mills and was then an early adopter of steam-powered engines, buying a steam engine in 1826 just ahead of a cold winter that froze the water power of many other companies.

The company also started weaving silk cloth, as opposed to simply creating silk through the throwing process. It hence capitalised on the fashionable Victorian growth in silk's popularity, and it pioneered specialist silk such as 'organzine' and 'marabout'. Organzine had threads twisted in opposite directions and made excellent ribbon, while marabout was a hard silk ideal for making open cloth such as gauzes (the production difficulty of both of these materials allowed the company to quickly adopt power machinery and looms). When these trades began to wane, they started to produce through their own technical expertise the mechanised means of wrinkling silk to make the crêpe material that was also becoming increasingly popular. The crêpe fashion started with the judiciary and Church, particularly around black crêpe sashes at funerals, and the trend then seeped into mourning wear for the upper class and then voluminous general black attire for all sections of Victorian society. It had a cachet because it was hard to produce and required technical Victorian inventions in steam, power and gas, and it had a big market as an increasingly affluent Victorian population doubled in size between 1801 and 1849.

The company still struggled with cyclic demand, fluctuating supply prices, bad debts, failed forays (notably into machine production) and the permanent introduction of an income tax in 1846 (a forerunner to corporation tax), but the general upward trend in the demand for silk headed by a tight unit of partners who were family, jointly Unitarian, and all with complementary skills under the energetic Samuel Courtauld III, enabled the company to become one of the country's biggest silk firms with around 3,000 employees. It had 9,300 throwing spindles and 1,430 winding spindles at its Halstead plant alone, with another ten mills and 25,000 spindles dedicated to producing crêpe. By the time the Courtauld & Taylor partnership had run its course in 1849, profits had multiplied tenfold, and the return on capital averaged between 20 and 35 per cent. The now-named 'Samuel Courtauld & Co.' business continued to grow thereafter, helped by the opening of the Suez Canal in 1869 enabling the arrival of more raw silk at lower cost and increasing sales abroad to countries such as the US and France.

The departures and death of the close-working Peter Taylor, younger brother George (II) in 1861, and Samuel Courtauld III himself in 1881, saw a new generation of Courtauld family members take the reins. These arrived at one of the textile industry's down cycles, and a difficult trading time; a general economic depression was coming from the rising industrialisation and tariffs of the US, Germany and France. The American Civil War demand for cotton, for example, had led to overproduction, over-speculation and falling demand leading to the 1861–65 Lancashire cotton famine. At the same time, the cotton supply was restricted. US production stalled during the Civil War and Egypt became a main raw cotton supplier, increasing its production fivefold and turning it into a major industry for the country. When the US Civil War ended, however, Egypt was abandoned, and its investments led it to bankruptcy and takeover by Britain. In India, Mahatma Gandhi later railed against a system that saw millions of Indians paid pennies for backbreaking cotton work from which everyone else – mostly the British – benefitted. There was also a decline in the popularity of crêpe, possibly because of its gloomy association with the ever-in-mourning Queen Victoria. The subsequent fall in output between 1883 and 1894 was 45 per cent.

From the 1890s onwards, a number of new innovations helped the company pick itself up once again. One innovation was for ready-made, off-the-shelf clothing as opposed to the traditional linen, drapers and tailor-made clothing. Another was the development of waterproof and more coloured crêpe. Another was the replacement of old textile managers with a new generation of more engineering-savvy managers. Another was reform of the method of selling and marketing to improve overseas trade as well as bulk buying raw silk to get better discounts. Still another would be the installation of electric lighting throughout its factories. Yet another was the introduction of gas engines made by Crossley Brothers of Manchester under licence from the German Otto company to replace steam engines. The foremost innovation, however, was a period of consolidation in the industry. British textile production had always been a highly fragmented industry with different types and different levels of organisation working in different ways. It was, therefore, open to large-scale consolidation by entrepreneurs and often driven by early adopters of steam power, who would seek to maximise their financial investments by increasingly vertically integrating. Bigger firms were able to adopt the best practices of the concerns that were being integrated and so become more efficient. 'Newer' enterprises such as those run by Courtaulds were also able to adapt more easily than those 'older' organisations such as those working in wool where tradition, custom and practice were harder to overturn. Courtaulds picked up the slack from those companies that failed to change.

In 1856, the government had passed the legislation that allowed businesses to form limited liability joint-stock companies and Courtaulds adopted this new business form in 1891 as a precaution against the cyclical downturns it had seen in its history. Members of the Courtauld family would now remain at the highest level within the company for the next seventy years, but it now grew into the multinational public operation known as 'Courtaulds Ltd' or more simply 'Courtaulds'. For a twenty-five-year period Courtaulds ran smoothly under the management of H.G. Tetley and (Sir) Paul Latham. The senior management team also included Frederick Nettlefold, who had retired from the development of his own business (this business would become Guest, Keen and Nettlefolds, better known as GKN. GKN was one of the last of the great Victorian engineering companies to lose its name and place in the FTSE following the emotionally raw takeover by Melrose Industries in 2018).

The company generated steady profits from silk used in decorative edgings – galloons and tricots – that were trending in Edwardian times, but cotton sales were generally erratic, and sales of crêpe were still declining, so under Tetley and Latham's stewardship, with Nettlefold's support, Courtaulds sought to diversify risk away from being a manufacturer predominantly reliant on silk. To do this they turned to the research area of organic chemistry, which had been gathering pace towards the turn of the nineteenth century. Some of that research had focused on artificial fibres, particularly around cellulose; molecules of carbon, hydrogen and oxygen found in plant cells. Alfred Nobel had made an explosive example of what could be achieved with cellulose. He added nitric acid to cotton to make gun cotton and followed this by developing dynamite and evolving the explosives industry. Scientists such as Joseph Swan and Thomas Edison were searching for suitable fibres to act as filaments in light bulbs, and Swan dissolved nitro-cellulose in acetic acid and extruded the outcome under pressure to produce fine threads, which not only moved the lighting industry forward but showed the newer techniques for spinning artificial fibres (or more correctly 'extruding' fibres). German, French and Swiss scientists had also all manufactured fibres from nitro-cellulose in a variety of ways, producing the world's first man-made fibres, which they called artificial silk, but it was English chemists Charles Cross, Edward Bevan and Clayton Beadle who discovered and patented the most successful method of producing artificial silk in 1884. The process involved reacting the natural material cellulose produced typically from beech tree waste or cotton residue with a solution of carbon disulphide in sodium hydroxide to form a salt known as xanthate. When neutralised with sulphuric acid, the outcome is a thick, sticky, viscous liquid known as 'viscose', which can be drawn off as cellulose fibres known as 'artificial silk'.

Under Tetley's lead, Courtaulds bought the UK patents for the viscose process in 1904. Even though the chemistry looked promising, it was still a bold move. The process was still highly flawed, and numerous competitors had tried and failed to make the process technically robust and commercially viable. By 1906 the Courtaulds investment had reached a colossal £190,000 but still without any profit, and the company relied on capital accrued from a flotation to keep going. The Courtaulds team, however, were backed by numerous useful acquaintances that added engineering, chemical, and research expertise to its own spinning know-how, including

that from the Pears soap dynasty, paper, lighting and glass-blowing industries. Courtaulds also developed a European-wide research and business
collaboration that helped to move the process forward. Eventually they
developed a viable process for producing this 'artificial silk' in a cheaper
and more consistent quality than its rivals could achieve by spinning fibres
from wood pulp treated with caustic soda.

The company then stimulated interest and demand for artificial silk by
experimenting and demonstrating its properties from within their own
textile mills. It proved to be perfect for mixing with other materials. It
was cheaper and easier to work than many natural fibres and was at home
in clothing, where its moisture-wicking property was perfect. 'Rayon'
was chosen as the brand name because of the material's bright 'ray'-type
qualities, although it would also confusingly be known again as 'viscose'
when weaved into a fabric form. Courtaulds were soon producing the
first large-scale commercially successful rayon and by 1912 sales of rayon
thread had outstripped the profits made from the company's traditional
silk production. They paid out a dividend of 50 per cent to shareholders
who had supported the investments. By 1913 Courtaulds was easily the
world's largest producer of man-made fibres, producing 3 million lb
(1.3kg) of rayon yearly from its Coventry factory. It also bought the US
rights to rayon production and established a monopoly subsidiary, the
American Viscose Corporation (AVC). By 1915, AVC – operating inside
US trade tariffs – was outproducing its UK parent company. The now
consolidated, efficient and innovative British textile industry boomed,
and the First World War then stimulated the industry further still through
the need for textile war materials of all types.

However, the war would play a duplicitous role in first seeing a trade
boom and then generating problems for industry afterwards. This boom
and bust cycle was seen most prevalently in the armaments industry, but
it played havoc in textiles, too. Dundee, for example, was an area that specialised in jute production, needed in vast quantity for the sandbags used
in the war. When post-war demand crashed, the city's workforce moved
to a three-day week and by 1921 wages were cut by 22 per cent. Some of
the underemployed jute workers from Dundee went overseas to India and
began to develop a cheaper jute industry, which then started to erode,

and would eventually end entirely, the Dundee jute industry. By 1932 Britain was still the world's largest textile industry, processing one-fifth of its wool, but the rising level of competition was becoming a widespread problem across the sector. Between 1919 and 1939, 43 per cent of Britain's cotton spinning looms disappeared and the country's biggest cotton manufacturer, John Ryland, despaired at the lack of government support during a period when both tax and unionisation were increasing. However, even when introduced, national tariffs failed to stop the increasing inbound flow of cheaper materials. In 1936 and then 1939, the government passed the Cotton Industry (Reorganisation) Acts, which introduced a scheme to reduce surplus capacity and established a controlling cotton industry board to try and rescue the cotton spinning industry.

Courtaulds' silk production suffered similarly in the general British textile decline, but its rayon business continued to boom. The production of rayon outstripped the average industrial output of the country tenfold.[3] World consumption rose from 32 million lb in 1920 to over 2.8 billion lb in 1941 as demand for stockings, underwear, furnishing fabrics and dress materials grew. On Taylor's death in 1921 the leadership of Courtaulds passed into the hands of Samuel Courtauld IV, the great-nephew of Samuel III who had helped to found the original family business, and he would continue working together with H.G. Tetley. A £1 Courtauld share at the start of Tetley's involvement would be worth £6,250 by the time Tetley and Samuel Courtauld IV's reign concluded.

It was, as ever, not plain sailing though as the post-First World War period coincided with the cessation of Courtaulds' basic rayon patents, allowing more companies to compete in this rising global business. Accordingly, as the level of competition increased, the value of the Courtaulds product decreased, and rayon prices fell sharply, much more than those of silk, cotton, or wool. Another problem was that Courtaulds had grown from a small to a large company but had not made the organisational transition. It had grown into a company with a variety of products, yet it failed to organise into divisions in a way that US companies were. It had no committee structure, so that middle managers without a global view would make decisions, or senior directors (just five of them) became bogged down with detail.

Its directors also lacked the entrepreneurial drive that George Courtauld or H.G. Tetley had and only tended to see itself as a yarn company. In fact, rayon was perceived as an industrial fibre by its management board, and its use as a textile fibre was only of secondary interest until it was advocated by the scientific team. Its responses were therefore conservative and based around trying to maintain its position rather than continuing to drive forward. It tried price-cutting to try and fend off competitors but failed to predict demand elasticity, that is to generate enough additional sales to cover the cuts, and lost revenue as a consequence. It also responded by building new plants across the UK, in North America, Italy, Denmark, India and Spain, and establishing new joint enterprises in France and Germany. However, these developments were complex, legally messy affairs aimed at stabilising industry and maintaining margins. Its accounts around these deals might at best be described as 'furtive'. Courtaulds had also evolved from purely a silk producer into a man-made fibre maker but failed to recognise the value of its chemical knowledge, or even its weaving know-how. Its chemical domain was similarly seen only as a way to reduce costs rather than to generate radical new products. There were no chemists or researchers on the management board, so it was particularly backwards in its approach to investment in research. The company would develop a number of rayon variants over the next fifty years, working in association with the government's British Rayon Research Association. It made some advances, such as high-tenacity yarn (having a high strength to weight ratio), which opened up its use in tyre manufacture, but most of the bigger developments were restricted to continuous yarn production, the development of lucrative staple fibres and new textile materials.

As a result, Courtaulds' competitors started to innovate more effectively. Artificial silk, for example, was now being made cheaper by a number of companies through a lower-cost cellulose acetate process pioneered extensively following 20,000 experiments conducted by the Swiss Dreyfus brothers. Like viscose rayon, cellulose acetate was produced by spinning fibres out of cellulose from wood pulp, but it formed cellulose acetate chains rather than pure cellulose ones. The output fibre was similar to rayon and although it was less resistant to heat than rayon, it would become a cheap and more effective mix fibre. It was used extensively in the 'doping' of aircraft skins, with the curious situation arising of the British government funding these activities for the war effort but which helped boost foreign competition against their own British concern, Courtaulds. For example, British Celanese would start up with foreign ownership as a rival new venture.

In due course, rival company DuPont produced a new fibre in 1938, the world's first fully synthetic polymer called nylon. Nylon is made from repeating units of linked amides, so it is known as a polyamide. It can be formed in a number of ways and with varying properties so that it has come to be one of the world's most common polymers (engineers tend to refer to these materials as 'polymers' rather than the more common public form of 'plastic', because in engineering 'plastic' is a term that describes the property of a material to stretch under tension). Elsewhere, fibres from the polyester polyethylene terephthalate were produced by the Calico Printers' Association and known as Terylene in the UK or Dacron in the US (when used in the manufacture of modern-day recyclable drinks bottles, they are still referred to as polyethylene terephthalate or PET).

To try and keep abreast of developments, Courtaulds bought into these technologies as a licensee but often under quite complex arrangements. British Cellophane would be set up for the manufacture of transparent film. Courtaulds and ICI jointly created British Nylon Spinners (BNS) to exploit nylon within Britain and its empire. Courtaulds' profits were, however, hit by these costly licensing deals alongside poor trading conditions and increased competition, exacerbated by the 1929 stock market crash and the depression of the 1930s. Courtaulds' large financial reserves built on its rayon production helped it to weather the storm, but many investments had to be written down at huge cost, including the selling off of French, German and Canadian yarn processing mills following poor financial results. Dividends from its US subsidiary AVC dropped to nothing by 1938. An investigation showed that AVC was being poorly run by its British works manager Harry Johnson and US senior manager Samuel Salvage, and was in need of modernisation. Courtaulds had begun to invest when, for a second time, world war broke out.

Britain's fight with Germany during 1939 and 1940 was costing it everything, and its debts to the US for the munitions and materiel it was drawing on were escalating wildly. The argument to support Britain, or British democracy – or not – was not straightforward in the US, and Secretary to the Treasury Henry Morgenthau insisted that Britain would need to demonstrate its financial straits in order to persuade the US politicians to approve the supportive £7,000 million Lend-Lease and Appropriation Bills. This in turn meant the selling of British-owned assets in the US, and a number of company subsidiaries were in the frame for this. Lever Brothers were rejected because of some partial Dutch ownership that complicated matters but Courtaulds' US AVC business, with its poor management, hint of tax avoidance, cartel operation and secretive accounts, fitted the bill. It was, therefore, Courtaulds' AVC business that became the sacrificial lamb. The British government compulsorily purchased AVC shares under wartime regulations, and these were sold to an American banking consortium in March 1941 for just £32 million, of which bankers Morgan Stanley and other selling agents would receive a hefty £2 million commission. Morgenthau would claim, 'I consider this a great New Deal victory.' From this fire-sale price, Courtaulds, however, received just £27 million. When it appealed against the loss of half its business (it had 20,000 US employees and 20,000 UK employees) for measly recompense, the government drew on AVC's poor performances around the 1938 period, ignoring the massive profits and value the company had previously as a cash cow, and the £38 million that Courtaulds had invested in modernisation from 1936 to 1940. In the end, no further British company assets were sold and they were instead used as collateral against loans.

After the Second World War, Courtaulds re-engaged with the modernisation programme of its now solely British business under the chairmanship of Sir John Hanbury-Williams, who succeeded Samuel Courtauld (IV) in 1947. Its financial policy was still considered to be conservative, but it nevertheless invested in new directors, new plants (including a new rayon plant in the US) and reaffirmed its agreement with ICI for British Nylon Spinners (BNS), which proceeded to expand rapidly after the war, once released from producing parachutes. It also undertook new research, including acrylic fibres such as the synthetic wool known as 'Courtelle'. In many ways, however, the ship had already sailed. Du Pont, for example, while not a company with a textile background like Courtaulds, would share an interest in fibre chemistry and would produce in comparison Neoprene, Corian, Teflon, Mylar, Nomex, Lycra and Kevlar, in addition to its earlier nylon discovery.

From 1944 to 1954 Courtaulds' profits rose again, but thereafter began to slip as the loss of its US business and the impact of nylon and other synthetic fibres began to eat into its rayon and natural fibre businesses. The Courtaulds response was similar to that of other British companies in similar positions – instead of fighting and looking for new innovations in its core businesses, it sought to expand and diversify. Under the direction of Lord Frank Kearton, Courtaulds bought out five other rayon-producing companies, and also took over the main producer of acetate fibres, British Celanese. This latter acquisition included packaging and chemical interests. Courtaulds consolidated these interests with further acquisitions in packaging and chemicals, including International Paint and Pinchin, Johnson Ltd in 1960. International Paint was a major marine coatings specialist founded in 1888, and Pinchin, Johnson Ltd was a major coatings and paint business founded in 1834 and one of the original companies in the 1932 FT 30 index.

ICI, however, considered Courtaulds' position and responses as weak, while seeing opportunities in their growing chemical portfolio. In 1961 it launched Britain's biggest ever takeover bid with a grab for Courtaulds, prompting a three-month, high-profile battle. The bid failed, but ICI would secure 38 per cent of Courtaulds' equity, which Courtaulds would buy back in exchange for passing its share of BNS over to ICI. The battle can only have damaged the credibility of Courtaulds.

In 1965 and 1966, the last two family members of the Courtauld family to sit on the board retired and, now under Frank Kearton's chairmanship, the company embarked on more acquisitions to reduce its dependence on rayon and boost its weaker natural fibre area. This included acquiring more of the remaining British textile industry. In 1950, Britain had still been the largest producer of wool and the largest producer of rayon but textiles now only accounted for 5 per cent of the country's Gross Domestic Product (GDP). In 1910, for example, Britain exported 692 million lb of wool but by 1951 this was down to just 440 million. The wool yarn industry was struggling, and the big spinning company of Patons & Baldwins, with roots back to the Crompton spinning mules in the 1770s, would merge in 1961 with J. & P. Coats Ltd. Cotton was particularly in trouble and another Cotton Industry Act (1959) would attempt to consolidate 103 companies into a Lancashire cotton industry. This was the biggest market for Courtaulds fibre, but was s still declining in the face of cheaper imports despite rationalisation and, in an attempt to vertically integrate fibre and yarn with weaving, the cotton sector was largely bought out by Courtaulds in 1964. The same act brought hosiery into Courtaulds as an outlet for its acetate and nylon yarn. By 1968 then, the Courtaulds company controlled about 30 per cent of UK cotton spinning and 35 per cent of warp knitting.

Courtaulds was now the leading British textile company in what had for centuries been Britain's leading industry, but now this was really a case of last man standing as it accrued more and more lame ducks. It attempted modernisation, efficiency improvements, integration, sub-contracting, merging and reorganising but its actions, size and efficiency were no protection now against the continuing rise of cheaper imports. As the British government lost its influence and global control, these threats became more and more problematic, and the company struggled. Profits rose to a high point in 1975, then plummeted in 1976 as the oil crisis hit home. Inflation hit 20 per cent and in May 1975 the pound lost 25 per cent of its value against the dollar. In 1979, the succeeding chairman, (Sir) Christopher Hogg, invested in new machinery, but the company could not compete in the face of cheaper imports and falling overseas markets, and in 1981 profits reached their lowest point since the war. Plant closures followed and employee numbers halved from 100,000 in 1975 to 46,000 in 1988. In 1990, Courtaulds demerged itself into two parts. Courtaulds Plc became the fibre manufacture and chemicals businesses and Courtaulds Textiles Ltd became the yarn, fabric manufacture and clothing businesses, producing apparel and furnishing fabrics.

Thirty per cent of company profits came from Courtaulds Plc man-made fibre, with 33 per cent of these accrued from the paint businesses that had been bought and consolidated during the 1960s, '70s and '80s. The remaining income was realised through sundry chemical, packaging and speciality products such as Grafil carbon fibre and bulletproof armour. Retail businesses such as Salisbury and Sock Shop were sold off. Under a new CEO,

Sipko Huisman, the Courtaulds Plc business moved forward again with a programme of rationalisation, joint ventures and new product development. In 1991, it closed its viscose plan in France, allowing it to boost capacity in other plants and achieve efficiency gains. It also launched a soft, washable cellulosic fibre called Tencel Lyocell, which it made in the US and sold to Asia. The material was stronger than cotton or rayon, and much cheaper to produce as it recycled chemicals used in the production process. However, investment in Tencel of £100 million over ten years was heavy, while the returns were not as high as expected. In 1998 Courtaulds Plc was bought by AkzoNobel, which had worked with it on Tencel development. Its Lyocell division, which developed Tencel, was sold to private equity company CVC, who sold it on to the Austrian textile company Lenzing AG. The paint businesses bought and consolidated during the 1960s, '70s and '80s still operate as part of Akzo-Nobel under the 'International' brand. The Courtaulds aerospace business was sold to PPG Industries in the US and the Courtaulds Plc name disappeared.

Courtaulds Textiles employed around 20,000 people worldwide and was Britain's largest producer of underwear, including brands such as Berlei and Gossard. Much production was, however, overseas in plant that would become joint ventures. Forty per cent of its output was sold to Marks and Spencer, so its textile business was hit hard by the M & S decision to overthrow its 'Buy British' policy and start to buy cheaper clothes from abroad. Neither company would benefit from this. In 2000, the US Sara Lee Corporation launched a takeover battle, which it would eventually win. The Courtaulds name would survive as a division with Sara Lee, but the parent company would struggle to stem the decline of a brand that remained stubbornly British rather than global. It would struggle too to sell the business on because of a pension deficit the company had, but would eventually sell in 2006 to a Hong Kong-based Courtaulds supplier called PD Enterprise Ltd. Sara Lee CEO Brenda Barnes would say the company had effectively been given away. When Courtaulds customer BHS closed in 2016, PD Enterprises closed down the remaining Courtaulds operations and the remaining 380 UK-based staff were laid off.

Looking back, Courtaulds can be seen to have left an indelible mark on the nation. The production of low-cost cloth had enabled even the poorest margins of society to wear clothing rather than rags. It had manufacturing plants across Britain, including Coventry, Grimsby, Chorley, Derby, Trafford Park, Worksop, Middlesbrough and Somerset, and for decades it provided an income for the poorer sections of society, including women, albeit a hard-earned one. It was one of the earliest companies to establish an economics department, and following the end of the Second World War, this made notable contributions to the understanding of investment appraisal and the formulation of British – and later European – trade policy. Many of the Courtaulds spinning mills have become trendy places to live, while Eltham Palace – once owned by the Courtauld family – is now a pleasant place to visit. Samuel Courtauld (IV) became known to a wider public as a patron of the arts, and his collection of Impressionist paintings is the basis of the Courtauld Institute of Art, which he set up and endowed in 1931. It forms a college of the University of London in the heart of the capital and is the main centre for the study of art and architecture history in Britain, if not the world. The 530-piece Courtauld art collection forms the Courtauld Gallery in Somerset House.

4

W.G. Armstrong & Co.

William Armstrong and his Armstrong Company would, through innovation and acquisition, become one of Britain's greatest businesses, realising two breakthroughs in science and engineering that have left an indelible mark on how the world works.

1914 logo for Sir W.G. Armstrong, Whitworth & Co. Ltd, which combined the Armstrong Mitchell Company with the pioneering precision engineering company of Joseph Whitworth in 1897 to create an engineering powerhouse building armaments, ships, locomotives and, in due course, cars and aircraft. (© BAE SYSTEMS, courtesy BAE Systems plc)

William George Armstrong was born in Newcastle in 1810 to respectable parents, his father being a corn merchant who had risen to become the town mayor. Following his father's wishes, Armstrong trained and worked for eleven years as a solicitor. At the time, however, Britain was in the full throes of the Industrial Revolution and cast iron, steam power and railways were presenting powerful and exciting new technologies. It was in mechanical engineering that Armstrong's real interests lay. He indulged his interests by becoming a regular visitor to the engineering workshops of his old school friend Henry Watson, experimenting with steam boilers, the production of electrical discharges from rapid steam production, the move-ment of clear water through channels for both drinking and motive power and embryonic hydroelectric power from steam. He was able to bring these interests to commercial fruition with involvement in the removal of water from local mines, the redistribution of water through conduits, and to supply clean water to Newcastle's growing population.

His big engineering breakthrough, however, came about via a fishing trip to the River Dee. While fishing, Armstrong noted that a nearby water-wheel was only powered by a small proportion of the wide, fast-flowing river. How much power could be achieved, he wondered, if the whole flow of the river could be tapped? Using the knowledge of mechanics he had accumulated, he developed a piston powered by the full force and weight of a channelled flow of water. This development of 'hydraulics' might be described as being a lucky event, but the reality is that Armstrong had trained himself to be serendipitous, through his inquisitive mind and his widespread interests. It was this tinkering that enabled him to develop hydraulic power even though he was not an engineer but a lawyer by train-ing, and to go where no other engineer had been – and there were many great engineers at the time, including Brunel, Stephenson, Watt, Whitworth and Telford. His passion and interest in how things worked through play, experimentation and creative vision gained him a significantly high profile and enlarged his professional networks to include Faraday, Wheatstone, Brunel and Stevenson, and led him to scientific recognition in 1846 as a fellow of the Royal Society.

It also led to commercial success. He persuaded Newcastle town coun-cil to divert some piped water from a new reservoir scheme to run to the docks, where he used his cylinder and piston design to build and power the world's first modern hydraulic crane. It proved to be quicker, cheaper and easier to operate than traditional cargo unloading methods. It was a brilliant adjunct to motive steam power, which up to that point had been making all of the headlines. It was timely, too, as the Industrial Revolution was producing bigger, heavier and more frequent loads that were being transported around the globe on bigger ships and all of this needed better handling equipment. Orders for three more of his hydraulic dockside cranes followed immediately.

Armstrong's legal and business experiences gave him the confidence to start his own business, and he was supported in this by his extremely capable wife, Margaret. He left his employment at the legal practice to establish W.G. Armstrong & Company in 1847 with a capitalisation of £19,500 and patents valued at £3,000. He bought just over 7 acres of land next to the River Tyne at Elswick in Newcastle and began to supply cranes to other docks as well as train companies and bridge builders. Within the year, the capital investment was increased by an additional £43,000. Within five years, Armstrong was producing seventy-five cranes a year and would subsequently produce an average of 100 every year for the next fifty years. He produced other hydraulic equipment too, such as powered gates needed to close increasingly larger docks around increasingly bigger ships. He also continued to innovate around hydraulic power, producing a weighted 'accumulator' (a pressurised storage reservoir) that could provide power of up to 600psi (41 bar, or over forty times standard pressure at ground level) and could be used to provide hydraulic power even when the water supply was less than ideal, making hydraulic power an option for any site around the world. Similar accumulator systems are used today for backing up hydraulic power systems in cars and aircraft.

One of the founding principles of the company was to restrict dividends and to reinvest profits in the business, which allowed the Elswick works to continue to grow – the same principle that has today enabled Amazon to grow into a global behemoth. Armstrong's works were described by Winston Churchill's father, Lord Randolph Churchill, as 'one of the wonders of the world' and the company was visited by the Royal family, overseas royalty, sultans and diplomats, and military from around the world, including Ulysses S. Grant. Walter White, librarian to the Royal Society, described what they would have seen, and what he saw in his visit of 1858, as: 'brawny smiths forging chains link by link, and small mountains of finished chains lying ready for transport not far from the ruthless machine by which their strength had been tested. I saw an iron bridge being built for India, and small iron steamers for the negotiation of Indian rivers; and huge engines for sundry purposes.'

This revolutionary work on hydraulic cranes alone would have been achievement enough, but Armstrong went on to produce another far-reaching innovation that revolutionised the arms industry. Armstrong's first interests in armaments were provoked by the failures of existing British artillery in the Crimean War of 1853 to 1856. British artillery at that time was comprised of cast iron or bronze cannon, largely unchanged over the course of half a century since the Napoleonic wars. The inadequacies of these cannon were being exposed in the cold, muddy and hilly terrain of the Crimean peninsula, where 150 soldiers and eight officers took three hours to manhandle two 2-ton guns into position. Spurred on by the unfolding chaos of Crimea, Armstrong brought his fascination and knowledge of wrought iron to the design of artillery. Supported by his friend, James Rendel, and with advice from Brunel and the great engineer James Nasmyth, he proceeded to develop a wrought iron cannon made with a steel core surrounded by fused steel rings, which was a much lighter and more manoeuvrable field gun and which was stronger and capable therefore of taking a bigger or more efficient charge. By twisting the steel core, he enabled an enlargement of the 'rifling' used in small arms, producing artillery that could project spinning, canister-shaped missiles (shells) rather than spherical cannon balls and thereby realising greater range and accuracy. He also designed concussion fuses to allow these projectiles to explode on impact and additional breech loading to allow much faster reload rates. The speed and accuracy of the artillery produced were astonishingly better than had ever been seen before. In military testing of an 18-pounder Armstrong gun against the army's best weapon, a 32-pounder, the Armstrong gun was one-third of the weight and used one-third of the charging powder, yet fired 900 yards (822m) further. It was also significantly more accurate, scoring twenty-two hits at 300 yards and ten hits at 2,000 yards, with the army gun failing to hit the target at all.

The military nature of arms meant that commercialisation of artillery was not as simple as the crane business. As both the technical expert the army needed and the supplier the army needed, he was in a conflicted position where enemies could accuse him of exploitation, and there were many enemies among the traditional arms manufacturers. The Whitworth Company was particularly antagonistic, helping to disparage breech loading and persuading the government to return to muzzle-loading guns, which stifled sales of Armstrong guns. In 1859 orders for Armstrong guns were cancelled and in 1862 the government further prevented Armstrong from exporting guns abroad, leaving the company in a difficult trading position. Armstrong, however, weathered the storm. One of the deciding factors was the development by the company of a slower-burning charge, which provided a more powerful force but required a longer gun barrel, returning the emphasis to breech-loading rather than muzzle-loading guns. The company began once again to make sales both home and abroad. It also diversified into machine guns and naval guns – typically weighing in at 100 tons. It also recovered the drive to re-enter the burgeoning train business and between 1860 and 1864 built fifty locomotives, including the Baikal train ferry, which was shipped in 7,200 pieces and rebuilt in Russia.

In 1864 the crane and armament businesses were merged, and in 1882 merged again with local shipbuilders to form the industrial powerhouse of Sir W.G. Armstrong & Company with capital of £1.58 million. Blast furnaces and giant steam hammers were added, allowing the company to produce, on a large scale, cranes, armaments, bridges, steam engines, pumps, locomotive turntables and steam locomotives. The company provided the mechanism for Newcastle's famous swing bridge, which was built in 1876 and is still going strong today 150 years later, and then provided a similar opening mechanism in 1894 for London's Tower Bridge (which failed only once during its long working lifetime). Entry into shipbuilding allowed it to bring its spirit of innovation and knowledge of iron and engineering to the design of ships. Consequently, it would at times be Britain's biggest shipbuilder, producing ships for countries including Spain, China, Japan, Argentina and the US. It pioneered and built iron-clad armoured ships, inventing the cruiser-class ship and building HMS *Victoria*, the world's first steam- and dynamo-powered battleship. In fact, because of its unique capabilities, it was the only company in the world capable of building and arming a battleship. It also designed and built the *Yermak*, the first ice-breaker ship, and the *Glückauf*, the world's first ocean-going tanker, carrying 3,500 tons of oil, and it built over 100 tankers over the next twenty years.

In 1897, Armstrong merged with its great engineering rival Whitworth to form Sir W.G. Armstrong, Whitworth and Co. Ltd. Whitworth had itself been one of the great engineering companies that had helped to revolutionise the approach to accuracy and repeatability that epitomised

Victorian engineering and enabled mass production. It was, though, beginning to struggle commercially and Armstrong made his move to prevent the emerging company of Vickers taking over Whitworth and becoming a bigger rival. That was also the year that (Sir) W.G. Armstrong retired. For over fifty years, Armstrong had steered the company through great leadership and innovation to be a world powerhouse in engineering. It was a hugely successful global engineering company producing hydraulic cranes and equipment, trains and armaments that were sold around the world. The company base at Elswick in Newcastle now stretched for three-quarters of a mile along the River Tyne and employed over 25,000 people. Armstrong died just three years later, in 1900, with profits for the company in that year standing at £664,000 (around £77 million at today's values).

The company continued to prosper after Armstrong's retirement under the control of his associate, Andrew Noble, initially benefitting from the First World War when 78,000 people were employed by the company. How many of the company's beneficiaries and employees at the turn of the twentieth century would have found it believable that the Armstrong name would soon disappear? Problems, however, became apparent once the war was over. One thing was the range and variety of equipment the company produced: aeroplanes, airships, water planes, engines for airships and accessories, guns, mountings, ammunition and all war materials, forgings, castings, nickel, chrome, vanadium and tungsten and high-speed steel, stampings, hydraulic and electric cranes, hoists, bridges, dock gates, sluices, capstans, warships, submarines, passenger and cargo ships, ice-breakers, train ferry steamers, oil tankers, propeller shafts, shells, fuses, primers, explosives, armour plate, touring cars, luxury cars, motor transport vehicles, motor tractors, turbine rotors, drills, lathes and machine tools. The list is impressive, but such diversity is difficult to manage effectively and efficiently. It might not have been so bad if the company was well organised, and led, but it wasn't. After 1900 the company lacked the leadership to continue to evolve in the way that the charismatic and knowledgeable Armstrong had achieved. Although (Sir) Andrew Noble was capable, he combined both chairman and chief executive roles in a way that is unusual today and was seen to become dictatorial and aggressive. There was rivalry and dislike between him and the other company stalwart, George Rendel, and Noble appointed two of his own four sons as directors while Rendel's own talented son departed the company. William Cruddas, the finance director, said to Rendel's brother Stuart, 'Elswick is in a bad way, there is no mistake about it. The sums that have been recently lost by incompetence I believe you have some idea of'[1] and this was said before the chaos of the First World War. After Noble stepped down, the company was then taken over by John Meade Falkner, better known as an author of fiction books.

The other problem the company was facing was a big downturn in trade. After the conclusion of the war, the decline in war orders was augmented by a global depression. Orders for armaments crashed and neither government nor industry could afford big capital equipment orders. The Newcastle yard, which specialised in large ships, was hit particularly hard. The 78,000 people it employed, which had sounded impressive, incurred a wage bill of £1 million per week and became a millstone around the company's neck. It should have laid off staff, but one in four of Newcastle's citizens earned their living at the Armstrong plant, and it struggled to pare down and release the workers as it should have done.

The company instead reorganised, with divisions led by active directors looking towards a number of mergers in order to diversify, and it sought to muscle in on the iron locomotive, hydroelectric, turbine and paper sectors. In 1919, Armstrong-Whitworth took over the Siddeley-Deasy vehicle business to help its transition into cars, which it spun off as Armstrong Siddeley Motors. Armstrong Siddeley produced luxury vehicles and aero engines. The company also had an eye on the emerging flight industry and in 1912 it established a subsidiary called Armstrong Whitworth Aircraft (AWA). AWA produced a number of planes, including the RAF's post-war Siskin fighter, as well as the R series of airships. Although diversification seemed sensible, it wasn't successful. It brought together areas of expertise in emerging sectors, but these spin-outs were too far removed from Armstrong's core business. They also produced nothing as innovative as the hydraulic and rifled armaments that set the company on its way and tended to be high-value products. In the depression years, was the high-end car market of Armstrong Siddeley the right way to go, when companies like Ford and Morris were succeeding in producing the cheaper, mass-produced cars that were more affordable to more people? Without a civil aircraft business or a war, could the fledgling armed services like the RAF alone support so many aircraft companies, such as Armstrong Whitworth Aircraft, all producing so many designs?

The financial damage caused by the downturn of orders following the cessation of First World War hostilities, and by the subsequent depression and reduced orders for large engineering projects worldwide, just took too much out of the company, which had such huge outgoings to maintain. Many of the new developments the company had engineered subsequently proved to be expensive failures, and the paper milling venture was a particular financial disaster, which was divested at much cost. The losses thus continued, and were £625,767 in the first month of 1926 alone. In 1927, the company merged with another of the great Victorian engineering concerns, Vickers, to form Vickers-Armstrongs Ltd, which focused on defence and engineering. Note that Armstrong Whitworth Aircraft (AWA) was not included in the merger. AWA and Armstrong Siddeley Aircraft Co. both later merged with the Sopwith Aviation Co. Ltd, causing some confusion over aircraft company identification around the name Armstrong.

Further Armstrong divestments followed as the company tried to shore up its losses. In 1929 the car maker Armstrong Siddeley's shares were sold back to J.D. Siddeley. Ownership of Armstrong Whitworth Aircraft was also sold off to J.D. Siddeley at the same time. The Vickers holding company then bought out Vickers-Armstrongs in 1935. In 1937 the company's iron-making business was sold off, and locomotive building was abandoned. From 1942 to 1943 the remaining Armstrong businesses were wound up.

It is worth noting that Friedrich Krupp AG ('Krupp'), Armstrong's German equivalent, would survive the First World War and exist in its own right up until 1999, when it merged with Thyssen AG to become ThyssenKrupp. This was despite losing half of its capacity and equipment as reparations, being banned from arms manufacturing and running at a loss for many years. Some of the factors that helped Krupp survive would include laying off 70,000 workers, supporting the community – but beating down strikes and wage rises, becoming part of the European-wide Raw Steel Association cartel of 1924, and covertly continuing military sales. The ironic payment by the British Vickers company in 1926 for using Krupp fuse designs in the First World War presumably also helped, as did the failure to effectively prosecute company heads for war crimes committed in the war, and in the later Second World War, particularly around slave labour.

There is no argument that Armstrong had been a big and powerful company. It was a world leader in its industries, and it has been said that the British Empire was built on its output, a company that defined Britain as the workshop of the world. It wasn't a perfect company, of course. Although it employed thousands of people and it created a series of educational and scientific institutions that have served Newcastle and the North to this day, including the restoration of Bamburgh Castle, it had its share of industrial disputes with its workers. It is also often cited as being the world's first global defence manufacturer, but many people find the Armstrong name hard to palate because of this and its associated imperial and military connections, citing the slaughter rent by the company's guns on the men of the American Civil War or in the bloodied fields of the First World War. Without Armstrong, however, Europe may have yielded to First World War German imperial aggression and later, without Armstrong's legacy, the world may have yielded to Adolph Hitler's right-wing dictator ideology.

It would, though, be wrong as well to say that the Armstrong name then simply disappeared as its divested subsidiaries still continued after the core company's demise. Armstrong Siddeley continued to trade independently and produced cars up to 1960 as part of a group merged with Hawker and Bristol. The whole concern, however, was absorbed into Rolls-Royce in 1966, who six years later sold off the once-revered Armstrong Siddeley name rights to the Armstrong Siddeley Owners' Club.

The Armstrong Whitworth Aircraft (AWA) business, also under Siddeley's ownership, continued to produce planes but was then itself bought out by Hawker Aircraft – along with other British aircraft companies including Avro, Folland, de Havilland, and Gloster. The aircraft designer A.V. Roe was the first Englishman to fly in an English-designed and powered plane, and created the Avro 504, the most-produced plane of the First World War, before selling his interests in his Avro company to Sopwith. Avro would later produce the famous Lancaster bomber, while A.V. Roe and his new Saunders-Roe company would produce flying boats and the world's first hovercraft in 1959. In time its helicopter business would be taken on by Westland, and its marine businesses would merge into Vickers-Armstrongs, before merging back into Westland but with the hovercraft business being allowed to fade away.

The resultant merger of these plane interests was the Hawker Siddeley Aircraft Company, one of just two main aircraft producers' names that survived from the many smaller British aircraft concerns that had evolved through the twentieth century. As a member of the FTSE 100 share index, it was a major performer in the British economy and a major player in the aircraft industry, showing in its portfolio of output: the Hawker Hurricane, Hawk Trainer, Sea Hawk, Nimrod, Buccaneer, Trident and the Harrier Jump Jet. On 29 April 1977, however, as a result of the government's Aircraft and Shipbuilding Industries Act 1977, Hawker Siddeley Aircraft was merged with the British Aircraft Corporation and Scottish Aviation to form British Aerospace (later renamed BAe and later again BAE Systems). BAe sold its corporate jets rights to Raytheon, who sold them on later to investment companies. Other parts of the company were rationalised and sold to BTR in 1992 for £1.5 billion. The Hawker name survives now only as a small producer of mining switchgear.

At the same time, BAE Systems had taken over the Vickers-Armstrongs rump, so other parts of the old Armstrong Company still existed in spirit. BAE Systems continued to maintain a defence works at the old Armstrong Elswick and Scotswood Road sites in Newcastle, producing armoured cars, but this last connection with the original Armstrong works was finally closed down in 2012. Among the other Armstrong legacies, it is worth noting that Charles Algernon Parsons, who would invent the steam turbine, was an apprentice in the early days at the Armstrong Company. His company, C.A. Parsons, established in 1889, mutated into Reyrolle Parsons and then to NEI Parsons. This became another major northern employer, building the power equipment for many British power stations before coming under ownership of Rolls-Royce. It still operates today, albeit in much-reduced format, as part of the German multinational company Siemens.

5

Vickers Ltd

The Vickers Company was another of the great powerhouses of British engineering through much of the nineteenth and twentieth centuries.

Vickers logo. (© BAE SYSTEMS, courtesy BAE Systems plc)

In 1829, Robert Stephenson advanced the slowly evolving locomotive industry by developing a sophisticated and successful engine design. His Rocket locomotive won the Rainhill Trials on the pioneering Liverpool–Manchester development track and demonstrated in an instant to a stunned nation where the future of transport lay. The costs of development were, however, massive and prohibitive to both government and financiers, which meant that progress was initially slow. When interest rates fell, though, ordinary people recognised that good returns could be made in this emerging industry and started investing heavily during the 1830s and '40s as part of a 'Railway Mania' boom.

In actual fact, as many as a third of the routes agreed by the government were not built, and many investors suffered as a result. A Sheffield-based miller called Edward Vickers was not one of the losers. He invested wisely, and his returns allowed him to assume control of his father-in-law George Naylor's Sheffield-based foundry, which had been founded in 1828. He consolidated the foundry with his brother William's steel rolling operation and his neighbour Jonathan Marshall's steel business, forming Naylor Vickers and Company. Metal was an obvious focus for a Sheffield entrepreneur. The city had a proud history of metalworking, having been a centre of cutlery production since the Middle Ages. The cutler Thomas Boulsover developed a method of fusing copper and silver that became known as Sheffield plate, creating items that looked silver but had a copper core and cost a fraction of the price of solid silver. Sheffield iron workers had recently been producing blister steel – iron that had been baked with charcoal to absorb carbon and produce the steel, which was far stronger than iron. It had also been the birthplace of the crucible steel process.

In the 1840s, Sheffield's Benjamin Huntsman would, like Abraham Darby before him, use coke to good effect by melting iron at very high temperatures in small clay crucibles. The additions of blister steel and flux compounds enabled Huntsman to obtain small quantities of the very high-quality, high-tensile-strength steel of uniform crystal structure that he needed for clock making. The high-quality steel would prove to be useful as 'tool steel' for cutting other metals. Sheffield would take to this 'crucible steel' method, and over a period of 100 years, steel production in the town rose from 200 tonnes per year to 80,000 tonnes per year, around half the total produced in Europe.

Naylor Vickers and Company became part of the Sheffield steel-making fraternity, producing steel castings and specialising in church bells. Edward Vickers' sons, Tom and Albert, joined the company and added technical and business know-how while moving the business in 1863 to the banks of Sheffield's River Don. The company name changed to Vickers, Sons & Company and for some years prospered as demand for iron grew in line with Britain's industrialisation. They supplied iron and steel for bridges and rail work and started to expand into marine shafts and propellers and forge work. They also exported to the US, where home-produced iron that was particularly in demand for the expanding railroads was in short supply. By 1847 the company profit was £22,900, over £2 million in today's values and 50 per cent more than the company was valued at when set up ten years earlier.

It was, however, a move to branch out into armaments that saw the company begin to emerge as an industrial superpower. In 1888 they produced armour plate for the first time and followed this in 1890 with their first artillery weapon. This move was just in time for the Naval Defence Act of 1889, which saw the British government allocate significantly more money towards military spending. This was at the time of the Ashanti, Afghanistan, Zulu and Mahdi conflicts, coming on the heels of Crimea and with the Boxer and Boer fighting ahead. The navy was also transitioning from the wooden ships that had fought at Trafalgar to the monster 'iron clads' covered in 24in-thick iron. The company, therefore, also moved into shipbuilding itself with the purchase of a naval yard at Barrow-in-Furness in a deal brokered by the wealthy banker Nathan Rothschild. Rothschild also held significant shares in the Maxim-Nordenfelt gun company, which then came to Vickers as part of the deal. The Nordenfelt background would bring with it submarine expertise, and the Maxim element would bring machine gun technology. The Vickers company then made and sold their version of the machine gun, which came to be known as the Vickers gun. The Germans made their own version of this called the Maxim, and it would be these guns that would later deal wholesale slaughter across battlegrounds including the fields of Flanders in the First World War.

The technical expert Tom Vickers stepped down in 1909, and it was under the business-like chairmanship of his brother, Albert, that the company grew yet further. Military and non-military ship orders followed and Vickers secured the order for the navy's first submarine, *Holland 1*. The company became a specialist in submarine design and construction, producing twenty-nine craft up to 1906. It continued to expand, changing its name to Vickers Ltd and securing half ownership of the John Brown and Company shipyard on the River Clyde along with the Whitehead torpedo company – inventors of the first successful torpedo using gyro and depth-seeking technology. The range and size of the company meant it could now compete with the Armstrong Company, which had secured their own position in metalworking, armaments and shipping. Together, Armstrong and Vickers were part of the great British shipbuilding era, collectively producing 61 per cent of all new vessels in the world in 1911, including giants such as *Titanic, Britannic* and *Olympic.*

Vickers also sought to diversify, and in 1911 invested in a car spin-off from the Wolseley Sheep Shearing Machine Company Limited, which would become known as the Wolseley Tool and Motor Car Company (Wolseley). Under the name Vickers Ltd (Aviation Department), it also began to develop aviation interests, including taking a site at Brooklands in Surrey, which would become the embryo of British aviation and where they produced notable planes such as the Vimy. After the First World War, John Alcock and Arthur Brown would complete the first non-stop crossing of the Atlantic Ocean in a Vimy. The plane would be the Royal Air Force's principal bomber through the 1920s and was in service up to 1933.

During the First World War itself, Vickers provided significant support to the British war effort. In the first eight weeks of the war, 1,972 Vickers machine guns were ordered alongside 360 large guns. It produced munitions, fuses, ships, submarines, engines, aircraft, airships and tanks. Like Armstrong, the company would be later criticised for its military connections, although without its contribution it is hard to see how Europe could have defeated German imperial ambitions. As with Armstrong, it also emerged from the war in a different state and in a different world, and it looked for work to offset the decline in military demands. It started in 1919 under the new chairmanship of Douglas Vickers by assuming rail interests and electrical interests, taking over British Westinghouse and Metropolitan Railway to form the Metropolitan Vickers Electrical Company (Metrovick). Metrovic later took on the railway interests of shipbuilder Cammell Laird to form the Metro-Cammell Train Company. Vickers Aviation also grew and it took over the famous seaplane company of Supermarine and in so doing assumed the responsibility for the development of the Spitfire. It would also employ the famous designer Barnes Wallace, who during the 1920s pioneered geodetic construction principles on the R100 series of airships.

Like Armstrong, however, Vickers also struggled to find its way in this new post-war world. The airship industry never really, well, took off. Its Wolseley car division had overexpanded and struggled against the volume of competition and companies such as Morris Motors, who had been able to undercut costs through mass production. Large-scale products such as ships, trains and planes were hit by the depression of the 1920s and 'peace toys' – optical instruments, magnets, springs, tractors and vehicle chassis – did not cover the scope of business the company needed. Over the next few years, the company reorganised and began to divest its non-core interests. The Wolseley car business was then sold to William Morris in 1927. The sale of Metropolitan Vickers and its electrical interests followed. Despite these actions and the hope of better times, the company continued to write down assets on a yearly basis until it became apparent that the futures of both Armstrong and Vickers companies would be more secure if they merged, as they did in 1927 to become Vickers-Armstrongs Ltd, run by Sir Herbert Lawrence.

The resulting Vickers-Armstrongs business was a big company. In 1935, even before rearmament for the Second World War began, it was one of the largest manufacturing employers in Britain, behind only Unilever and ICI. As the country moved into gear for the second world war of the century, Vickers-Armstrongs then geared up to respond to the Nazi threat, where it produced 33,000 guns in readiness for war. It had been the only company in the UK to have continued to work with tanks after the First World War and moved its expertise to the Elswick works to produce the tanks the British army now needed. These included 8,000 Valentines that played an important role in the North African desert campaign, which provided Britain with its first major wartime success and encouraged the US to join the war. The company's shipyards produced aircraft carriers, four battleships, three cruisers and fifty-three submarines as well as a number of supply vessels. Working from its Brooklands site alone, its air division produced over its lifetime over 16,000 aircraft and overall it produced 20,000 Spitfires and 11,500 Wellington bombers. Barnes Wallace redeployed the geodetic structure principles he had used in airships in the design of the Wellington bomber instead of the traditional hoop and runner design. This enabled a lighter and stronger construction that removed vulnerable stress points. Planes could continue flying even after being hit because the load would be spread over the entire frame of the aircraft and the Wellington could take a lot of punishment, saving many lives. Wallace also designed the bouncing bomb and the huge Tallboy and Grand Slam bombs, which were finally able to destroy deep Nazi military sites, including those for the V1 and V2 missiles that momentarily threatened a Nazi comeback.

The transition for Vickers-Armstrongs after the war was better thought out and more smoothly implemented than it had been after the first. At Brooklands, Vickers-Armstrongs Aviation was developing a number of aircraft, including the Valiant and Vampire bombers and the Vanguard and VC10 commercial airliners. The Vampire was Britain's second jet aircraft and the first powered by a single engine. Only slightly bigger than a Spitfire, it could climb to 50,000ft and exceed 500mph in level flight, making it the world's fastest plane at the time. The VC10 was also a well-designed plane that set the time for the fastest crossing of the Atlantic – a record it held for forty-one years.

The Metro-Cammell rail business would eventually produce trains for the Hong Kong Mass Transit Railway and the Channel Tunnel, along with London Underground rolling stock, British Rail Pullmans and locos for many African and Asian markets.

On paper things still looked busy, and yet there were deep problems underneath and the company still struggled. The decline in post-war military still hit hard. Barnes Wallace's pioneering work on laminar flow and swept-wing planes was cut following the Sandys Defence White Paper in 1957 in favour of the BAC TSR-2 and Concorde (which would both prove to be expensive failures). Wallace's work was passed to the US in an attempt to gain funding support, but this proved unsuccessful – and the Americans would themselves deploy Wallace's ideas in their F-111 plane. It was not just that military orders declined but also that the type of hardware Vickers was producing was beginning to look outdated by the end of the war, when jets, radar, missiles, rockets and electronics were appearing. The US government, for example, started work on the heat-seeking Sidewinder missile in 1946, while the US Hughes Corporation AN/APS-20 radar installed in 1949 in Douglas AD-3W Skyraiders gave the US military 'over-the-horizon' radar capability. (The technology at the heart of these, coincidentally, came from the development of the cavity magnetron, which was shipped to the US in 1940 and described as 'the most valuable cargo ever breought to our shores'.)[1]

However, these areas were not Vickers specialities and neither they nor the British government had the wartime resources to develop such research strength. Nor could they operate well in their traditional areas, as one of the big post-war problems for the country was getting the iron and steel needed to get industry moving again. Iron and steel had been under government control during the war and remained so post-war following the 1946 Iron and Steel Act in a bid to control the flow and price of the material. Vickers' steel-making division – which had produced the high-temperature blades and components for Frank Whittle's first jet engine – hence became effectively, then fully, nationalised as part of the British Steel Corporation. This removed the company from its original roots as an iron and steel business and although there would be denationalisation and renationalisation in the future, the area of steel in Britain would now be forever mired in controversy and failure.

British shipbuilders still struggled to get the materials needed to build ships after the war and also found it difficult to get the licences needed to build these ships under a wartime hangover of government control that was slow to lapse. Shipping companies were now able to register ships abroad and were increasingly able to buy cheaper ones overseas as well. The 1965 Geddes Committee reported that British-built ships were slow to be constructed across a disorganised industry with inefficient methods and poor employee relations. The government supported the failing Fairfield Shipyard, then realised that it could not support the even larger failing Cammell Laird, Upper Clyde and Harland and Wolff yards and needed to act, resulting in the Aircraft and Shipbuilding Act. Vickers' shipbuilding interests, which had emerged from the Vickers-Armstrongs conglomeration, were nationalised in 1977 to become British Shipbuilders. Five years later, with half the shipyards closed, the Act was repealed and yards were reprivatised. British Shipbuilders emerged as VSEL and later passed through GEC to BAE Systems Submarines. Swan Hunter took over the Armstrong High Walker yards on the Tyne, but were also nationalised as British Shipbuilders in 1977, then privatised again as Swan Hunter in 1986 and finally closed down in the late 1980s.

The aircraft business also struggled with stiff competition from the numerous British and American aircraft companies emerging from the war, all fighting for reduced military orders and commercial contracts in a world that had not yet developed a civil aircraft industry. Despite being a good design, the VC10 sold poorly with a mess of airline companies and the government dithering about supporting the plane as a British product or not. As a consequence, Vickers' aircraft interests were merged with Bristol, Hunting Aircraft and English Electric (makers of the great and last all-British jet fighter, the Lightning, a plane that could famously take off into the near vertical and proceed to break the speed of sound in the upright climb) to form the British Aircraft Corporation (BAC). Vickers chairman Lord Robens opposed the Act, but it had been a Labour Party manifesto pledge and the government was committed to its implementation. The Vickers name that had been associated with so many famous aircraft was dropped in 1965. In 1977, BAC was nationalised under the Aircraft and Shipbuilding Act to form British Aerospace, which would become BAE Systems.

The Metro-Cammell rail business was sold to GEC Alstom in May 1989 before being closed in 2005. Vickers' other engineering interests, such as packaging, steel-making and materials testing, were also to be sold off. The famous Vickers Hardness Machinery that set the 'Vickers Hardness' test as an industry-wide standard for a material's ability to withstand plastic deformation would continue as part of UK Calibrations Limited based in Kidderminster. The remainder of Vickers Plc was acquired by Rolls-Royce, who subsequently sold the defence arm to Alvis Plc (known as Alvis Vickers). This remained until 2004, when the Alvis Vickers name was changed to Vinters and was acquired by BAE Systems. With this, the Vickers business name finally disappeared completely, having been in operation since 1828.

6

Birmingham Small Arms

Birmingham Small Arms (BSA) was originally an arms company, one that helped to develop the concept of precision engineering and interchangeable parts more widely in Britain. For many people, it is perhaps better known as a much-loved giant of a motorcycle company.

The armament industry was a thriving British business in the Middle Ages. The production of large-scale ordnance such as cannon had thrived in the wooded and iron-rich Weald areas of the South Downs, making Sussex Britain's industrial heartland for many years, but it had since moved to the Midlands, where coal and coke were providing the higher temperatures needed to produce better-quality iron. These Midlands-based producers tended, however, to be small and disparate, and further away from the seat of power in London. King William III, a Dutch import to the British monarchy (reigned 1689 to 1702), complained that he found weapon sourcing in Britain to be nearly impossible compared to the vibrant arms trade he knew on the European mainland. Warwickshire MP Sir Richard Newdigate responded to this complaint by co-ordinating with five principal Birmingham gunsmiths to undertake a trial order in 1689 for 200 Snaphance muzzle-loading muskets monthly at 17s each. The arrangement worked well and more orders followed in the subsequent decades, at home but later also to overseas merchants. Military orders increased further throughout the nineteenth century in line with the number of conflicts, which included the Napoleonic, Nepalese, Ashanti, Burmese, Chinese, Sikh, Crimean,

New Zealand, Indian, Bhutan, Zulu and Boer wars. Many of the guns were outsourced from the Baker design, the first rifled gun replacing the smooth-bored Brown Bess musket, and seen in the hands of Sharpe's riflemen in the associated TV series. By the time of the Battle of Waterloo in 1815, the Birmingham collective employed 7,000 workers who were turning out 500,000 weapons a year. For the Crimean War (1853 to 1856), they made 150,000 'Brummagem' guns in an eighteen-month period, which was twice as many as the government obtained from all its other military sources.

'Brummagem' (like 'Brummie') is a colloquial name for Birmingham, which in some cases had and still has a derogatory association with being shoddy. The government, perhaps worried by its reliance on a specific Birmingham supply chain and recognising the growing need for more and more arms, began to look wider for suppliers to fulfil its orders and increasingly began turning to a factory at nearby Redditch instead. The Redditch Company had started in 1851 making sewing needles, but diversified into cycle parts. When it struggled, it was taken on by Albert Eadie and Robert Smith and renamed as the Eadie Manufacturing Company Limited. The new Eadie Company began supplying precision gun parts to the government's own ordnance factory, the Royal Small Arms Factory at Enfield, and the Eadie Company henceforth began operating under an assumed name of Royal Enfield. Significantly, this company was utilising the milling machinery and interchangeable parts processes that Eli Whitney had popularised in the US for arms manufacture. By turning to mass production they were able to supply 2,000 guns per week and, importantly, these were at a low, known and calculable cost.

The Birmingham manufacturing collective recognised the need to change in the face of the threat posed by Royal Enfield. In 1861, sixteen of them responded by concentrating all of their previously outsourced artisan worker/producers into one group known as the Birmingham Small Arms Company Ltd, better known as BSA. The new company was formed with start-up capital of £24,500 (somewhere between £2 million and £22 million in current figures depending on the value calculation method). They bought a 25-acre site at Small Heath in south-east Birmingham, near where today's Birmingham City football club is sited, and built a giant red-brick factory. The site was well located, connected to the Grand Union Canal, the Great Western Railway and with a private route – Armoury Road – that linked it to roads to Coventry, Warwick and Stratford.

The company started slowly, though, with a cumbersome committee-led administration, but by 1863 a board of directors had been appointed to run operations more efficiently, headed by the chairman, J. Goodman. Its first order for 20,000 Turkish rifles was received in the same year. By 1868 BSA was the largest private arms company in Europe, providing weapons for the Austria–Prussian and Franco–Prussian wars, and British contracts were finally secured the same year. In 1873 Prussia ordered 40 million cartridge cases from the company, and to supply this size of order, it liquidated and then re-established itself with an additional new munitions plant at Adderley Park.

However, releasing state-of-the-art weapons overseas was contentious because the country was on a near-war footing with Russia and Turkey and this caused the government to implement a knee-jerk ban on the sale of stock overseas with a motion to scrap all future overseas arms sales. In 1878 the government placed a moratorium on arms orders and sold off its stockpile of older weapons cheaply overseas. BSA was hit hard and went into half-time working for four months before closing completely for the rest of the year. The factory reopened in 1879 with a few rifle orders, and continued to grow patiently as conflicts arose once again, including the Afghan, Zulu and Boer wars.

The downturn that followed this latest round of campaigning, however, meant it was clear that the fragile and cyclical state of arms orders was not enough to guarantee ongoing business survival and BSA started to seek new work. It found a solution among the bike manufacturers that surrounded it in the same Midlands region. The precision machining and mass production techniques used to make robust and high-calibre military ware served the nascent bike industry well and BSA started making the components that independent bike companies found hard to produce themselves. They provided the high-quality castings, forgings and press works at previously unseen levels of tolerancing and engineering. In 1880 they also released their own bike, a bought-in design called the Otto Dicycle, which they made only in limited number. However, from this they gained the confidence to produce more. They did this from further imported designs but also off their own drawing boards, from which they developed the world's first rear-driven safety bicycle.

Production of this nascent bike business ceased in 1888 when the government placed an order for 1,200 Lee Metford rifles each week – the first British magazine-loaded rifle. This order became the company's priority but once fulfilled, they returned to bikes and again started with components. They designed and specialised in hub gears, which were licensed to become Sturmey-Archer gears (the production of which only ended in 1955). By now the bike market and industry were exploding and by 1895, £4,500 worth of orders were being filled each week. The Adderley Park site was re-equipped for this purpose and included the 'novelty' of both women workers and the operation of night shifts. Towards the end of the century, however, it became increasingly evident that the country might yet again become involved in more fighting, this time in South Africa. In 1897 BSA sold the Adderley Park munitions business to the Nobel Dynamite Trust (which in due course became a forerunner of ICI) so that it could concentrate solely on small arms and ordered in advance the steel needed to make 20,000 rifles. It was a prescient move. The Boer War began in 1899 and there was an upsurge in arms orders of 2,500 rifles per week, which only BSA was ready to supply instantly. As the war progressed, production rose to 10,000 rifles per week – requiring 15 million machining operations to be completed every week.

In 1900, the chairman, J. Goodman, who had been in post since 1863, died at the age of 83. Shortly after, in 1902, the Boer War wound down and when the fighting was over the British government sat back once again with a laissez-faire approach to the support of its arms businesses. Many engineering companies consequently folded in this early twentieth-century period, also pressed increasingly now by a newly emergent German industry. BSA survived by falling back once again on bicycles, which it determined would from now on comprise its main business focus. By 1908 it was again making not just components but its own BSA bikes under the lead of Dudley Docker. Docker was a relatively unknown entrepreneur of the period, but he was an extremely influential British businessman. He built a varnishing and paint business, which worked with the growing locomotive business, arranged the amalgamation of train carriage companies to form the Metropolitan Amalgamated Railway Carriage and Wagon Company (one of Britain's largest firms at the time, employing 14,000 people), became a director at Avery Weighing, Midland Bank, and numerous railways companies and helped to found the Federation of British Industry. For the record, he also played first-class cricket for England and was a keen sponsor of Ernest Shackleton's South Pole expeditions.

Under the later and energetic lead of Sir Hallewell Rogers, BSA also started to look at motorised bicycles. The first motorbike was invented in Germany in 1894 by Hildebrand and Wolfmüller, and Britain's Colonel H. Holden had (possibly) followed Daimler with the world's second motorcar and the country's first motorbike. The 1865 Red Flag Act had limited motor vehicles to a maximum speed of 4mph, which required somebody to walk in front of the vehicle with a red flag, but when the 1896 Emancipation Act repealed the flag requirement and raised the limit to 12mph, bike companies began to see opportunities for these powered forms of transport and began to experiment with motorised versions of their cycles.

BSA did not rush into the fray. For five years it experimented in putting the new combustion engine into its bike frames to make sure it produced high-calibre motorbikes and its first was finally released in 1910. These and subsequent bikes benefitted from this research and the company's precision engineering excellence, and were quiet and vibration-free compared to the standards of the day. BSA's interchangeable and mass production approach also made parts cheap and the entire production sold out in 1911, 1912 and 1913. It ventured into the car business by initially working with the pioneering and local Lanchester Motor Company, but then BSA bought the UK Daimler company in 1904 (a firm born in 1896 under licence from the German Daimler company) and establishing Britain's first true motorcar company.

The First World War saw BSA turn once again to arms. It produced under licence all of the famous Lewis guns used by the British military during the war, including those used in aircraft, as well as the interrupter gearing that allowed a fighter plane's guns to be fired through the propeller. The Lewis gun alone required 2,600 gauge checks to ensure its manufacturing accuracy, while Maxim gun parts required tolerances down to 2.5μm. BSA also built the Daimler engines used by many of the fighter planes. It also developed the concept of the caterpillar track that was later adopted in the development of tanks, which saw limited use near the end of the conflict. By the end of the war in 1918 the company had a factory triple the size of the original built fifty-seven years earlier and a workforce of 13,000.

The director's passion was said to be about precision engineering and making the company the best, not necessarily around the maximisation of profits. The firm had not raised its prices to profiteer from the war and the directors themselves had spurned pay rises despite the increasing size and scope of the company that they managed. After the war, BSA adopted a policy of benevolent employment, keeping workers in place even when orders reduced, and working with them. It was conjectured that this might have been out of fear, having seen the results of worker power in the Russian revolution of the same period, but there was a compassionate side to the company directors, who included future Prime Minister Neville Chamberlain. This benevolence led to families working at the company for generations, as well as a positive and healthy attitude to listening to both workers and customers. There were 3,043 industrial disputes during the General Strike throughout Britain in 1926 but none of these were at BSA.

The scope of the business was now huge, extending to munitions, rifles, engineering parts and metallurgical and tooling expertise following the company's acquisition of Sheffield's oldest steel firm. Cars contributed to the group profits as well, although they were never fully integrated or particularly successful and always appeared as a sideline interest. The company also failed miserably with aircraft. In 1920 it bought out the world's largest aircraft company at the time, Airco, but failed to undertake due diligence in checking the company's accounts, which were dire. BSA had to cut their dividend payouts for the next four years as they tried to recoup the losses. It was, however, motorbikes that were at the heart of the business and how it would become best-known. This was in spite of the fact that the bike market was not an easy one as there was fierce competition from numerous companies who were turning to new business interests following the end of the war. There were, for example, around 284 motorbikes on sale in 1920 and many came from companies that were themselves famous. Triumph was created in 1888 and sold its first bike in 1902; Norton was born in 1898 and released its first bike in 1902); and AJS and Calthorpe were both born in 1909. Others included Veloce, Clyno, Royal Enfield, Brough, Vincent, and

Douglas. There were also competitor parts companies including JAP, who supplied engines to 137 different machines.[1]

Many of these companies were developed from bicycle companies and many were centred in and around the Midlands area: Selly Oak, Redditch, Wolverhampton, Nottingham and Coventry. These companies together created a powerful British motorbike industry. It was an industry flowing with innovation. The Triumph Speed Twin 500 weighed less than the common single-cylinder design of the time but had more power and torque and was the basis for Triumph's success. Phil Irving designed the V-engines that powered Vincent bikes (and later Brabham cars), which were strong enough to become the first structural engines – forming a loaded component of the frame rather than simply sitting in the frame. Alex Scott developed telescopic forks, kick starters, water cooling and foot-operated, two-speed drives that became bike standards. Rex McCandless designed the swing arm, which not only saved weight but added strength and smoothness to the ride. Other innovations included horizontal engines, anti-dive suspension forks, DOT adjustable suspension and safety helmets, the latter developed by surgeon Hugh Cairns following the death of T.E. Lawrence on a Brough machine.

Despite this intense and innovative competition, BSA thrived and stood out through the quality of its build and its own innovative design work. In 1919 it produced its first v-twin model, which was 20 per cent cheaper than some of its competitors. In 1923 it produced a side-valve, single-cylinder sports model, light and simple and ideally suited to the depressed state of the era. In 1924 it produced the round tank 249cc B2 model, which was a sensation for its speed and price of under £40. In 1927 two riders completed a high-publicity world tour with two 8hp models and sidecars covering 24,000 miles in nineteen months. In 1928 it produced its first two-stroke bike, the 174cc model A. In 1929 and 1930 it introduced 'sloper' bikes, so-called because the engine was mounted with a forward incline that produced a lower centre of gravity. Kliktronic gear changes and Lucas magneto starters followed. These bikes added to a range of twelve motorbikes and three 3-wheeler bikes that it offered, but more followed. The 1931 Blue Star had overhead valves and a four-speed gearbox and 1933 models included fully water-cooled engines. A range of eighteen Empire Star bikes was offered from 1935 and immediately became show-stoppers. By 1938 one in four motorbikes in the UK and overseas was a BSA, and the company was selling twice as many as its nearest competitor.

In the interwar period, BSA had mothballed some factory space in case it was ever called on to return to arms in the national interest. At the outset of the war, it was therefore the only company turning out rifles for the military. It also produced BESA tank machine guns and 600 .303 Browning machine guns per week, many of which armed Spitfires and Hurricanes, rising to 3,800 per week by 1942. One of its innovations involved using chrome plate instead of the more usual nickel to add resistance to wear on gun parts. This would become common practice in industry, including, for example, its use by Rolls-Royce on the Spitfire's Merlin engine valve parts. BSA's Daimler division also produced over 6,000 of the famous Daimler Dingo Scout armoured car, which outperformed prototypes from Morris and Alvis and was considered to be one of the best fighting vehicles Britain produced in the war. Production was achieved despite the fragmented 'shadow factory' system, which sought to spread manufacturing across a number of outlying and smaller factory units so that they were less susceptible to aerial bombing. Following Luftwaffe bombing of Small Heath in 1940, production was spread to sixty-seven outlying manufacturing plants employing 28,000 people operating 25,000 machine tools. The war also saw the company continue to produce motorbikes, including 126,000 M20 machines that came off the production line at a rate of one every five minutes, as well as lightweight folding models for paratroopers. This was done under the effective leadership of CEO James Leek, who also acquired Sunbeam bikes and motorbikes in 1943 and Ariel Motors Ltd from Jack Sangster in 1944, now making BSA the world's largest motorbike manufacturer.

The difficult post-war years and their restrictions on metal, petrol and the home sale of goods meant that motorbikes were more prevalent in Britain than cars and the company returned to bike production, where it continued to innovate. Hydraulic damped forks were introduced from 1945, cams were harmonically designed to reduce noise, and valve offsets would rotate each valve slightly through each engine cycle to reduce wear. BSA's key offering was a small bike known as the 125 Bantam, which latched on to the austerity market. The Bantam (D1) was an easy-to-ride bike and easy to service, which was essential because 1940s and '50s petrol was of low quality with a low octane of around 77, so engines ran on low compression and needed regular de-coking. Bikers liked it, commuters liked it, learners liked it, the Post Office liked it and it would remain in production from 1948 to 1971. The simple carburettors it used are still made today by Burlen fuel systems.

In 1951 BSA bought out the struggling Triumph motorbike company from Jack Sangster. Sangster was a colourful motorbike entrepreneur who had already grown and sold Ariel bikes to BSA. He also employed and developed some of Britain's most famous motorbiking design fraternity, including Val Page, Bert Hopwood and Eric Turner, and he had picked up the struggling Triumph in the 1930s for £50,000. He now sold his Triumph Engineering Co. Ltd to BSA for £2.5 million. In the early part of the 1950s, Britain accounted for 70 per cent of world trade in bikes and bike parts.[2]

In 1953 BSA separated out its cycle and motorcycle businesses into two separate entities. Its cycle business had been declining since the end of rationing in 1954 and this was sold to the Raleigh Cycle company in 1956. The Daimler car business was then sold to Jaguar in 1960, and in 1961 it finally ended the capacity it always kept on standby for arms production. It was now solely a motorbike company, where it was doing well, with 80 per cent of sales exported coming off the back of a stream of ever-improving bikes; the D2 was a D1 uplifted to 150cc, and the D3 offered improved power then added a newly invented swing arm in 1956. In 1955 the Dandy and Beesa scooters were marketed. The D10 had a good 10bhp, the D14/4 had a 4-speed gearbox, the D5 was uprated to 175cc, and there was the better-looking D7 and an uprated B175. Lighter bikes included the C15 250cc Sunbeam and Tiger scooters. Older models such as the Sunbeam twins and sidecars were stopped. Profits rose from £1.5 million to £2.5 million in 1957 and were a record £3.5 million in 1960. Within ten years, however, the company would be virtually bankrupt – terminated by overseas companies that included a small mechanics repair team and an organ specialist.

Despite the success of small bikes like the Bantam and Beesa, the pre-war Triumph Speed Twin 500 had laid the foundation for power to be important to British bike designers. The invention of the swing arm had also reinvig-orated British design, including, for example, the Manx Norton from 1951 onwards. Engineers enthusiastically swapped engines between frames in the search for winning combinations, leading to a host of café racer bikes. In 1968 BSA released the BSA Rocket 3, which also focused on speed and power, which it had in abundance, but sales were not as good as expected and suffered from the release of the Honda CB750. The Rocket looked great, had a higher top speed, better handling and tougher build quality than the Honda, but the CB750 had disc brakes and electric starting and was more reliable with a horizontally split case that did not leak oil like the BSA. The Rocket 3 became known as a biker's bike with adverts dominated by glamorous girls, while the Honda became known as a bike that was easy to own and ride, giving it a much bigger market to aim at and earning it the soubriquet of the first superbike. For five years after 1968, global sales of superbikes grew 40 per cent and this effectively masked the state of BSA's poor production. The big range of bikes at BSA made its production messy and inefficient, and it could not compete on price with the cheaper-made bikes. The BSA still sold well in the UK, but in countries like the US it did poorly in comparison.

In the British home market, imports started with a wave of Italian mopeds, increasing in sales from 2,000 to 38,000 in one year. In 1962, Britain signed a trade deal with Japan, and within two years imports rose from 7,000 to 100,000.[3] Honda, a company that had only started in 1937 and emerged from the war with just twelve employees, then produced the Super Cub in 1958, which opened up new markets. Small, lightweight bikes of 50 to 124cc were made using polyester resin and were particularly suited to Asian markets, young markets or commuters. They were a far cry from the power-focused British bikes. BSA scooters and smaller bikes tended to be more solidly built and of 175cc or more. Honda also planned its production to be ten times the company's production rate in a new factory based on VW's efficient production-line methods. BSA, by contrast, was still stuck in its antiquated buildings that stifled modernisation and development, and this was an endemic problem for British industry. When BAE Systems closed down the sprawling Victorian Elswick plant in Newcastle, it said the heating bills alone cost it £1 million per year. Honda's low-cost Cub would go on to be the best-selling vehicle of all time, selling by 2017 over 100 million units and providing the financial impetus for Honda to become a global engineering giant.

In 1969, Yamaha also entered the XS650 into the market, having taken over Japan's second-biggest bike company Showa, which had itself taken over Hosk. Hosk had developed a two-stroke 500cc engine in 1955, which Yamaha adopted for the bike. These Yamaha engines were built on German pulse jet engine technology developed during the war in the V1 and V2 missile programmes, and taken to Japan by the defection of East German motorbike rider Ernst Degner. The German engines used the expansion of gases down the exhaust to add thrust to that developed by the pistons in the cylinders, giving enormous extra power and the familiar popping sound of the Doodlebug bomb. In a motorbike, the sound of these two-stroke engines was incredibly noisy and tinny, while they burnt oil at a fast rate and needed extra gears to keep the revs up because of their limited power band. However, the power-to-weight ratio was incredible and far superior to the British two- and three-cylinder engines (even today, they outperform four-cylinder engines, and are only kept outside of racing domination by restrictive rules). Japanese bikes hence quickly cornered bigger markets, earning positive publicity by winning the competitions that had previously been the British domain.

Barry Ryerson, who worked at BSA, made the point in his biography of the company that it was not just the arrival of Japanese competition that killed BSA. The company could have survived a Japanese onslaught if it had been better run, but it could not survive both of these factors.[4] Ryerson was particularly scathing of the company's senior management, and this view was supported at the time by an evaluation of the company by the accounting and auditing company Cooper Bros & Co. Ltd (Coopers, a firm founded in 1854 and which today forms a part of PricewaterhouseCoopers, PwC.) Coopers were commissioned by Lord Shawcross, who took over as chairman in 1971, and identified two key management failings. Firstly, it was felt that the board of directors were pursuing actions that were centred on making money and they were failing to understand that motorbikes were the business of the company. Their priorities were instead focused on the business practices of mergers, growth and policy. The second point was there was a disastrous communication culture that failed to connect the directors with the staff, managers, designers and employees, and even customers. This was all a far cry from the founding principles of engineering excellence and benevolence. What had happened?

During and after the war, BSA was chaired by Sir Bernard Docker – the son of Dudley Docker, who became the director of the business in 1906. James Leek was the chief executive officer (CEO), and together they gave the company the strong business and technical leadership that all engineering companies need. In 1956 the effective and successful James Leek retired as CEO, while Docker was starting to look out of touch. Although he had chaired the company throughout the war and profitably afterwards, he was seen as being exuberantly rich and overly influenced by his (gold-plated) Daimler-driving wife. When Docker tried foolishly, and unsuccessfully, to appoint his wife's brother-in-law to the role of general manager, the board of directors used this, and Docker's lack of provision of effective information to the board, as key failings and he was removed shortly after.

Docker was replaced as chairman by Jack Sangster, and Eric Turner ('E.T.') became CEO. Sangster had headed and grown both Triumph and Ariel motorbike companies and looked to be a good choice on paper. Turner also looked to be a good choice. He was a motorbike man through and through, and he understood the threat from Japan ahead of anyone else. Sangster, however, was only appointed initially on a temporary basis and Ryerson suggested this, coupled with a complacency to rely on the comfort of his previous achievements, meant he never engaged sufficiently or committedly enough at BSA. He reorganised the company into business units, which Coopers would later criticise as encouraging the communications failure. Turner was also noted as being a tyrannical manager: 'If E.T. produced a drawing which, in practice, wouldn't do the job it was intended for, nobody could tell him so.'[5] One example of the problems this caused was the failure of the Sunbeam/Tigress scooters, which should and could have been world-beaters to rival the Honda Cub but which were abandoned because of overheating issues with the Turner-designed engine. He was also a man with Triumph and Ariel experience who failed to recognise the different culture at BSA. For example, the Umberslade Hall research centre was set up as a separate entity to the factory and brought in non-motorbike engineering experts. However, it became expensive to run and effectively contributed nothing.

In 1961, Turner took over as chairman from Sangster, but he struggled to get the investment the company needed to improve and even began to look away from motorbikes towards other products. He also appointed a new CEO in the form of Edward Turner (no relation), who was not from a motorbike background, and in selecting him, a number of excellent and experienced motorbike men were overlooked, including Bert Hopwood and Doug Hele. Edward Turner's reign as CEO ended in 1963 and he was succeeded by Harry Sturgeon. Again though, Turner had chosen an outsider, and Sturgeon's investments were questioned, as were his commitment and abilities beyond salesmanship. Sturgeon died of cancer within three years and was replaced in 1967 by yet another outsider in Lionel Jofeh, of whom it was said, 'What he knew about making motorcycles one could write on the back of a postage stamp.'[6]

Having conquered the small–medium bike market, Japanese power bikes like the XS650 began to put the squeeze on all British companies in their primary market. Triumph and Norton marques struggled on, but the poor communication, poor decision-making, poor investment and sidelining of internal design and management expertise meant that the BSA group and its BSA brand were in particular trouble. John Hatch, who represented investment bankers Lazards and who sat on the board, labelled the Small Heath plant as 'out of date and unsuitable for motorbike production', noting that a building there referred to as 'new' in fact dated back to 1913. Under Jofeh's reign, production became delayed, missing the 1970 US season entirely. By 1971 the BSA Group's yearly losses were £8 million, with £3 million to the BSA motorbike division alone, and the company's competition department was closed. In 1972 there were a further £3 million of losses and borrowings rocketed to £22 million. Chairman Eric Turner and CEO Lionel Jofeh both left, and Lord Shawcross took over. These changes were a far cry from the reign of (Sir) Hallewell Rogers and (Sir) Edward Manville, who had worked successfully together as Chair and CEO from 1910 to 1931, or the (Sir) Bernard Docker and James Leek combination of the 1940s and '50s. During their leadership BSA had been a pioneer of precision engineering and, at times throughout its history, the owner of twenty-six companies and four overseas subsidiaries. It had been the largest manufacturer of cars and bikes in the country, the largest manufacturer of motorbikes in the world, and the largest small arms and heating pump manufacturer in Europe.

BSA engineers produced a potentially viable recovery plan that saw a rationalised product range, and it was considered that the company might have taken over the Norton Villiers bike group as they were still outselling its products by nine to one. Financiers Barclays Bank were, however, sceptical about the plan, presumably by the contrary reports of two consulting agencies (PA recommending growth and Coopers Brothers recommending rationalisation). They instead encouraged the company to seek government support, which was available as 'Selective Assistance', either as 'section 7' (regional) or 'section 8' (of national importance), or under the government's new Industry Bill (1972). Irrespectively, financial speculators saw the writing on the wall and started to bet against BSA. As they did so, BSA's share price dropped, and along with it, confidence and its ability to finance components dried up. BSA and its Triumph subsidiary were instead then sold to Norton Villiers. Norton Villiers was owned by Manganese Bronze Holdings (MBH) group, and they would buy out other famous British bike companies, including AJS, Matchless and Royal Enfield, to form Norton Villiers Triumph (NVT) in 1973.

The merger, however, effectively put an end to BSA. The BSA Rocket 3 was dropped by NVT in favour of the Triumph Trident badged version of the same bike. The merger deal had been sweetened by £4.9 million of government support, which was just enough to avoid parliamentary scrutiny, but crucially was not enough to turn the declining industry around. Once again, this was further supported by the government, whose mantra failed to grasp that putting money into inefficient, lame duck companies does not lead to one big efficient company. Small Heath production ceased soon after and it then moved to Coventry. Plans to build Triumph engines at Small Heath were abandoned in 1974 and in 1975 the buildings on Armoury Road were sold off, with the factory offices demolished in 1976. Norton Villiers Triumph then itself collapsed in 1978.

At the time of the NVT collapse, Spanish company Gamo bought the BSA gun brand and BSA air rifles, which are still made in Birmingham. The historical remnants of BSA holdings also have interesting stories. The Airco company it disastrously bought was combined with Daimler into

Daimler Airway, which became the major constituent of a business that would morph into British Airways. Both the BSA bikes and BSA's Daimler car divisions sold to Raleigh and Jaguar would do well for long periods, although the Daimler brand is now effectively parked. In 1960, after buying up many bike and component companies, Tube Investments (TI) bought Raleigh (owner of BSA-branded bikes), creating a bike giant that supplied 75 per cent of the British market. Raleigh sold its US bike rights in 1982 to Huffy Corporation, which was able to sell Raleigh-named bikes around the world. Many of these would be made in Japan. In 1987, German-owned Derby Cycles recombined Raleigh by buying the US concerns and the British concern from TI. In 1989 production of mass-produced Raleigh bikes ended in the UK, and it then focused only on high-end and professional bikes. However, all production in Britain ended by 2003. In 2011 there was a management buyout led by Alan Finden-Crofts, but this company would then be sold in 2012 to the Dutch Accell Group. BSA bikes are made and sold by TI Cycles of India. TI itself would at times own Simplex, Reynolds Tube, British Aluminium, Russell Hobbs, John Crane, Creda, and Dowty. It became defunct in 2000 following its merger with Smiths Industries to form the Smiths Group.

The BSA company motorbike name itself was purchased as a management buyout by the NVT management. The BSA motorbike concern made some military bikes with Yamaha engines, usually for overseas countries, but it mostly made spares. The company merged in 1991 with the bought-out remnants of Norton to form a new BSA group, which supplied a range of genuine spares for enthusiasts. This concern bought out MZ (GB) Ltd, but was itself taken over in 1994 by the Regal Group and moved to Southampton as BSA Regal Group. Some specialist hand-built machines were built, but sales were below expectations. BSA Regal was demerged in 2017, forming a building services group and an engineering holdings company making precision engineering parts, tube equipment and cutting tools. The BSA remnant motorcycle business was bought out by the Indian Mahindra group with some plans to revive the brand. MZ, which formed a spares business with BSA, was sold, and the Norton spares part of the business was sold to a new spare parts company called Norton Motors Group based in Andover. The actual Norton Motorcycles brand would be kept alive in the US for fifteen years but was then bought by British businessman Stuart Garner, who had tried to stage a revival with new production based in Donington, but not without controversy over the intention behind the revival following its failure and claims of fraud in 2020.[7] Indian motorbike company TVS has since acquired Norton and invested £100m in the company, including a new manufacturing facility in Birmingham's Solihull.

7

The General Electric Company

The General Electric Company, known as GEC (and not to be confused with the General Electric Company in the US, which is usually known as GE but is sometimes also referred to as GEC) was a major electrical conglomerate designing, making and selling consumer and defence equipment, electronics, transport, power, communications and electrical engineering. It provided unprecedented service to the British economy over a 100-year period, rising to be one of the country's biggest companies and placed third in the FTSE 100.

Electricity has been known about for thousands of years, but it would be renaissance scientists like Gilbert, Boyle, Galvani, Volta and Franklin who moved the phenomena out of the vaults of curiosity and into the limelight of scientific exploration. Michael Faraday's discovery of the electric motor in 1821 was followed by electric circuits (Georg Ohm, 1827) and electromagnetic waves (James Clerk Maxwell, 1861). In due course, a whole series of practical applications of electricity followed, including the telephone (Alexander Graham Bell, 1876), the phonograph (Thomas Edison, 1877), the lightbulb (Joseph Swan, 1879) and the radio (Marconi, 1885).

A German–Jewish immigrant to the UK named Gustav Binswanger recognised from the beginning the potential of electricity and started in the 1880s as a London electrical wholesaler called Binswanger & Company. Binswanger changed his name to Gustav Byng, and along with fellow immigrant Hugo Hirst, they changed the company name to the General Electric Apparatus Company, effectively starting GEC in 1886. The company searched Europe for the latest electrical products, helped to standardise equipment, published the world's first electrical catalogue and in 1888 started to manufacture its own electrical products, including bells, switches, telephones and ceiling roses from an existing factory in Salford.

Most electrical products were limited to the rich individuals who could actually afford them, or the Leiden cells or water wheels that provided their necessary power. The invention of the steam turbine (Charles Algernon Parsons, 1884), the transformer (Otto Blathy, Miska Deri and Karoly Zipernowksy, 1885) and alternating current (Nikola Tesla, 1888), however, started to make electrical power more widely and cheaply available. As Edison said in 1879, 'We will make electricity so cheap that only the wealthy can afford to burn candles.' Factories rapidly ditched their slow, bulky and expensive animal, steam engine and waterwheel power-generating equipment in favour of electrical power generated from central sources, and as electrical power became more widespread, so followed the growth in electrical products in a process often now referred to as the Second Industrial Revolution. GEC was formally incorporated as the General Electric Company in 1889 and was ideally placed to exploit this expansion. In 1900 it became a public limited company (plc) and in 1902 opened its first purpose-built factory at the Witton works in Birmingham.

Following the death of Gustav Byng, Hirst (later Baron Hirst) oversaw a rapid growth in company fortunes, lit both physically and metaphorically in 1909 by investment in tungsten filament lamp production. Its Osram bulbs saw the company begin to trade around the world. The company expanded further through the development of electrical products such as lamps and searchlights for use in the First World War. This pattern of growth through innovation was repeated throughout the next eighty years and was supported by sound business development, including the acquisitions of heavy engineers Fraser & Chalmers and meter makers Chamberlain & Hookham. Mergers included valve manufacture through the Marconi-Osram Valve Company in association with Marconi, while spin outs included the Express Lift Company. Its product range would hence embrace everything from the making of electricity, the distribution of electricity and the use of electricity, including lighting, communication, transport, meters, lifts (elevators) and radio valves. 'Everything Electrical', as the company publicity would say. Its innovations, supported by extensive research facilities at Wembley, included the radar wave-producing cavity magnetron, the Chain Home and GEE radar systems used to defend Britain from the Nazi onslaught in the Battle of Britain, supported by pioneering British electronics firms Pye, EMI and A.C. Cossor. Throughout most of this period the company was relentless in its growth.

GEC faltered as many companies did after the end of the Second World War as demand for products and equipment fell, needing heavy investment while experiencing a period of disorganisation. Cossor, for example, would operate from 1859 until taken over by Philips and Raytheon in the late 1950s and early 1960s. Pye would run from 1896 as a spin out from Cambridge University's Cavendish Laboratory that would specialise in TV production but would struggle with reducing factory costs against Sony and Hitachi imports and was taken over by Philips in 1976. EMI was a major conglomerate with outputs that included stereo sound, microwave radar and CT scanners. After troubled sell-offs, the rump music business was sold off to Terra Firma Capital Partners in 2007. EMI's electronics partner, Thorn, was one of the world's largest lighting companies, known for famous trade names such as Kenwood, Radio Rentals, Mazda light bulbs, Rumbelows, Ferguson, and Tricity. It would be bought out in 1998 by the Nomura group but also then pass to the Terra Firma private equity firm. GEC, however, weathered the storm and continued pioneering developments, including the National Grid, and later microwave ovens and nuclear power generation.

In 1963 the company became fully rejuvenated under the lead of (Lord) Arnold Weinstock, who assumed control after a merger in 1961 with Radio & Allied Industries Ltd. Radio & Allied was itself formed five years earlier from the merger of two companies making radio sets and radio-based equipment, Sobell Group and McMichael Radio. Weinstock streamlined GEC back into profitability, divesting the Witton works and producing high-voltage electrical equipment, motors and rectifiers while continuing the process of mergers. Under Weinstock, GEC took over Associated Electrical Industries (AEI), which itself had already adsorbed Metropolitan-Vickers. Also brought into the GEC fold via the acquisition of AEI were British Thomson-Houston, Siemens Brothers, lighting company Edison

Swan, domestic appliance specialist Hotpoint and smelting specialist Birlec. The pedigree of these companies was outstanding. Metropolitan-Vickers might not be as well known today as Hotpoint or Edison Swan but formerly as British Westinghouse, it had built the world's first transistor computer and the first British axial flow jet engine, and operated one of the biggest heavy engineering plants in the world at Trafford Park in Manchester with reputedly the longest corridor in the world. British Thomson-Houston had roots back to 1892 and provided electrical power for motive equipment including trams, buses, and lightbulbs under the Mazda trade name and in 1937 provided the facilities for the world's first jet engine conceived by Frank Whittle at its Rugby works. Siemens was a British company formed by one of two German Siemens brothers. Also, with roots going back to 1863, it specialised in dynamos, signalling equipment, arc lamps and under-sea communication cables (the first to lay directly across the Atlantic).

This conglomerate was made even larger in 1968 by absorbing English Electric. Like AEI, English Electric also came with a collection of pedi-gree companies in its portfolio. These included the company started up in Darlington by Robert Stephenson in 1823 to build railway engines following the first locomotives he built in 1814 (and six years before his famous Rocket locomotive) and the Marconi Company set up in 1897 to exploit Guglielmo Marconi's developments in radio communication. The Vulcan foundry train manufacturer, Willans & Robinson steam engine & power generators, and Dick, Kerr & Co. locomotive manu-facturer were also in the fold. Further acquisitions included weighing machine specialists W. & T. Avery (who had taken over the steam engine company of Boulton and Watt in 1895), hi-tech electronic company Cincinnati Electronics, and a move into medical imaging with Mitel, Picker Corporation and Cambridge Instruments. This subsidiary, known as GEC Medical, produced the world's first magnetic resonance imag-ing (MRI) unit in 1982. In 1985 GEC took over Yarrow Shipbuilders. In 1988 it formed defence and communications company GEC-Plessey Telecommunications (GPT), which it later took over completely along with Plessey's avionics and naval interest with a joint venture it had formed in 1989 with Siemens (GEC Siemens). Also in 1989, GEC merged with French company Alstom to form a joint venture around power generation and transport, and which then bought the rail vehicle company Metro-Cammell. GEC also acquired the electrical defence company Ferranti, and Vickers Shipbuilding and Engineering (VSEL).

Given the scale and pedigree of its growth, it is unsurprising that by the 1990s GEC was Britain's largest employer, with a staff base of around 250,000 people. That would today be twice the size of the current British army, ten times the size of the BBC and twice the size of Royal Mail. It was reported to be valued at £10 billion with yearly profits of £1 billion and a reputed £1 to £3 billion stored in liquid assets. Its position seemed unassailable. Yet, in less than half a decade, the entire GEC colossus would come crumbling down and disappear, taking with it the vast array of British-owned electrical expertise and history dating back to the start of the Industrial Revolution.

(Lord) Weinstock would take some of the blame. He was viewed by many as focusing on acquisitions and penny pinching rather than investment and expertise. Wages were low, buildings were shabby, supplier payments were usually late, research facilities such as the Rugby and Lincoln Laboratories were closed down, while only twenty-nine of the 171 AEI plants taken over were left unscathed. Increasingly the company also turned to military contracts rather than entrepreneurial ventures. The company consequently built up a cash mountain but failed to innovate and produce the consumer products that overseas electronic companies such as Intel, Motorola and Texas Instruments were starting to churn out in the US, particularly around semiconductors. What it did produce, such as radar and TV sets, were poor quality and overpriced.

Weinstock retired in 1996, and leadership of the company was taken on by George Simpson. Simpson was an experienced businessman with a good track record at companies that included the Rover Group and Lucas Industries. He was, however, a fixer rather than a builder, and an outsider appointed to run the company with an aggressive agenda to increase the company returns with a plan to divest the company of its traditional low-margin interests and to move forward into higher-value sectors. For GEC, this meant moving away from engineering and into more technology-oriented interests – as they had already started with the earlier purchase of Ferranti. It was a strategy supported by the experienced chairman Sir Roger Hurn and finance director John Mayo, and presumably egged on by city financiers keen to see GEC release the cash mountain that Weinstock had so dearly wrought and from which they would secure their own percentage.[1] The company hence started to divest. In 1996 Express Lifts were sold to Otis Elevators. GEC test arm Marconi Instruments was sold off. In 1999, its defence arm, Marconi Electronic Systems, was sold off to British Aerospace (which became BAE Systems). This included the US defence and electronics business Tracor, which GEC had just bought. Cash reserves and proceeds from business sales were invested into mostly US technology companies to build the new direction, and the remainder of GEC was renamed Marconi Plc to emphasise the change in nature of the company.

Simpson would say in the company's 1998–99 accounts: '1989/99 was a significant year for GEC. I believe future historians will see it as the turning point in the modern development of our company.' In some ways he was right, but not in the positive sense he meant because his strategy was a spectacular failure and caused one of Britain's worst corporate collapses.[2] In a later television documentary, Simpson argued that to diversify into higher-value goods and to invest into hi-tech was what many others were doing at the time and that he did nothing wrong, and nothing that was not expected or normal practice at the time. However, because everyone else was doing the same thing at the time, the prices of the businesses the company was seeking to buy had begun to rise. The value of equity markets listed on the technology-orientated NASDAQ index rose from 1,000 to 5,000 between 1995 and 2000,[3] and GEC, therefore, paid over the odds for the companies it was buying. It then became apparent that while new technologies were exciting and promised much, it was in fact difficult to find a business model that actually made a return. Internet businesses today find it hard to do the same, but in the early days of technology this realisation was only slowly starting to become apparent. When high-profile technology companies Dell and Cisco began large-scale selling of their stocks, investors started to realise more clearly what the technology market was actually like and where the market was going and started to panic sell. This dotcom bubble would replicate the frenzy of the 1720s South Sea Bubble and the Railways Mania of the 1840s that had gone before. The majority of publicly traded dotcom companies folded, taking GEC's future income streams with them and their investments – and their investments were massive. GEC shares, once trading at £12.50, were reduced to £0.04.[4]

In 2003 the rump GEC, trading now as Marconi Plc, was restructured as the Marconi Corporation Plc, with shareholders receiving 1 Marconi Corporation share for every 559 shares held in Marconi Plc. The company was a key supplier of internet signalling equipment, including Asynchronous Transfer Mode, Gigabit Ethernet and Internet Protocol Devices, but its share values dropped again when it failed to become involved in a UK network upgrade programme. It succumbed, along with its subsidiary Marconi Communication, to a takeover by Swedish company Ericsson in 2005. The last remaining remnant of the once-mighty GEC conglomerate was renamed Telent, with a staff base of around 2,000 and revenue from telecommunication equipment of around £400 million. Telent was bought out and delisted by the Pension Corporation in 2007 and continues to operate as a private business with services that include supporting delivery of the country's ultrafast fibre broadband network, similar in a way perhaps to the way its predecessors had helped deliver the national grid.

It is difficult to write briefly about all of GEC's legacies within a short case study given the breadth of its size and complexity, but a few other examples could be highlighted. Hotpoint (or the Hotpoint Electric Heating Company) had operated on its own, as part of its US owners, as part of AEI and part of GEC. When GEC took ownership in 1967, it was the UK market leader for electrical white good appliances. In 1989 GEC formed a new division called General Domestic Appliances (GDA), which would later include Redring, Xpelair and Creda brands and which formed a partnership with the GE of the US. Italian company Indesit would complete a takeover of this venture by 2008, with three of the four Hotpoint sites in the UK, which once employed 7,000 people, closing. Marconi Medical Systems was the outcome of several name changes and mergers from companies that included Picker Corporation, Cambridge Instruments, Watson & Sons Ltd, and A.E. Dean & Co. Within this group, the first Magnetic Resonance Imaging (MRI) scanner was produced in 1982. The company was bought out by Philips Electronics in 2001. In the final example, BAE Systems, which had bought out GEC's defence arm, would benefit from increased US military spending, enabling it to become the largest foreign company in the US defence market.

8

Morris Motors Ltd

Morris Motors was once the largest car company in the world outside the US. Over half the cars on British roads were once made by Morris and during the period 1920 to 1932, the company sold more cars in the UK than Ford, Vauxhall and its main UK rival Austin combined. Today's biggest car company Toyota has, by comparison, around just an 11 per cent share of the UK, and world, car market.

If you search online or in a library for the man 'William Morris' you will find a lot about the William Morris who was the driving inspiration behind the Arts & Crafts movement. This art-based William Morris is lauded for his socialist and influential design thinking, and yet his achievements pale in comparison to those of his namesake industrialist, the William Morris who would go on to become Lord Nuffield. It seems surprising that less is written about the industrialist Morris, a man who transformed the British car industry, helped to build the Spitfires that defeated Nazi Germany in the Battle of Britain and left behind a stunning legacy of educational and health benefits to the nation.

William Morris the industrialist and the man behind Morris Motors was born William Richard Morris and was known to his colleagues as 'WR'. He was born in 1877 into a relatively poor background, but from an early age he was a keen cyclist at a time when bicycle development was beginning to snowball. Pedals had been added to bikes in around 1862, just fifteen years before Morris's birth. Rubber tyres came in 1867, metal replaced wood in 1868 and spoked wheels were introduced in 1869. Around 1876,

Harry Lawson designed the 'safety bike' that, unlike the Penny Farthing, allowed a rider's feet to be near to the ground. In 1885, John Kemp Starley produced the commercially successful Rover safety bike with equal-sized wheels, front-wheel steering and a chain-driven rear wheel, upon which bikes took the form that we would recognise today. Lawson would later develop motorised versions of Starley's design, setting forward the Rover motorbike and then the Rover car company.

These developments made bicycles increasingly more viable as forms of transport and demand grew, and yet they were still considered dangerous – too fast and particularly prone to break on rough tracks. However, this combination of exciting new technology, growing consumer interest and reckless danger made cycling ideal for young men like Morris, and he became a proficient cyclist of near-professional, national standard. He also enjoyed nothing better than tinkering with the mechanics, and it was inevitable that Morris's career would start with bikes. At the age of 16, after a brief period of working in a bike company, he realised how much money he was making for his employer and, after being refused a pay rise, he set up his own bike repair business in the shed at his parents' home in Oxford, using as capital four borrowed gold sovereigns. Trade was successful enough for him to move out of the shed and set up a shop in Oxford High Street, where he also began to assemble bikes under his own Morris brand. It was this early experience that taught him to work hard, keep prices low and to advertise well in order to make sales.

He then sought to merge his interest in bikes with another exciting emerging technology – the internal combustion engine. Developments in the internal combustion engine had been progressing for at least the past 100 years through a mixture of experiments, engineering practical features and scientific theory. However, progress really took off in 1876 following the patenting by Nikolaus Otto, Gottlieb Daimler and Wilhelm Maybach of an engine that combined and enhanced much of this earlier work and became the mainstay of engine design through to today; the four-stroke compression charge in in-line cylinders. In 1884 Edward Butler invented the spark plug, coil ignition and the jet carburettor, making the engine more reliable and easy to operate. This was the high technology of its day, blending transport, engineering, materials and chemistry – similar perhaps in domains to today's development of driverless electric cars but more like internet-based businesses in terms of accessibility to budding entrepreneurs and engineers like Morris.

Morris began producing his own motorised bike in 1901 and in 1902 he moved the business to Longwall Street in Oxford, where he established Morris Garages, the initials of which would later form the famous 'MG' car marque. After some commercial ups and downs, including breaking up with some business colleagues and partners, Morris eventually began to make good. He made and sold bikes and motorbikes as well as looking towards the emerging car industry. He began selling cars as an agent for companies such as Humber, Singer, Standard and Wolseley, and provided a taxi service using a Wolseley car. Wolseley (not to be confused with the more modern engineering supply company that has until recently operated under the same name) had started in the UK as the Wolseley Sheep Shearing Machine Company in 1889 and formed a car business in 1901 through a collaboration with Vickers and a talented Wolseley foreman by the name of Herbert Austin. It would for some time be Britain's biggest car company, producing 3,000 in 1913 and increasing to 12,000 in 1921. In 1918, the Ishikawajima Ship Building and Engineering Company would produce Wolseley cars under licence in Japan (and this company would eventually become Isuzu Motors).

It was, though, only a matter of time before Morris added an engine and two more wheels to his bikes to produce his own car, as Karl Benz had first done in 1886. Many car companies such as Singer, Rootes and Triumph would start as 'revolutionary' bike companies. Even the pioneers of flight, the Wright brothers, had started life as bicycle engineers, where experience of bicycle balance helped them understand the need for balanced control through wing warping to achieve sustained powered flight. Morris started car production in 1912 with the Bullnose Morris using bought-in components assembled in a disused building at Cowley near Oxford. Car production stopped from 1914 to 1918 as the factory supported the war effort during the First World War and began again the following year as Morris Motors Ltd.

It was a period of intense competition. In 1919 consumers had a choice of 270 models of car to choose from, and in 1922 they could choose from one of 183 car companies. Morris cars were, however, not designed to show off the ingenuity of the engineers driving forwards the new technologies but were developed from the perspective of the consumer in what we might now call an example of human-centred design (HCD). Consequently, they were easy to drive and easy to repair. They were also well built and cheap. Some of the great engineering companies often combined a technical genius with a talented businessman: Boulton and Watt, Rolls and Royce, or Wozniak and Jobs, for example. Morris may not have been a genius in either engineering or business, but he was extremely good in both domains, which was a powerful combination. He was a dedicated and selfless entrepreneur within the British car industry. He was never gregarious, and not even a natural speaker, but he worked long hours to make his mark under high stress and was solely devoted to cars. He was also a natural leader who could recognise outstanding talent and could make tough decisions when necessary.

One of Morris's insights was to introduce into Britain a modern approach to mass production. This had been developing in the country ever since the Lombe Brothers had built the first fully mechanised factory in the world, the Lombe Silk Mill in Derby, in 1704,[1] and Richard Arkwright's factory system had pioneered the principles of power and specialist machinery at his Derbyshire cloth factories during the 1770s and '80s. At the turn of the century, the Birmingham Soho Foundry of steam engine pioneers Boulton and Watt also introduced specialised tasks for staff and interchangeable parts – a system also seen in the production of guns by Eli Whitney in the US in 1801, and ship pulleys by Marc Isambard Brunel in 1803 in the UK. The Soho works also pioneered modern personnel and accounting practices. A hundred years later, the factory manager, William Hipkins, would die in the sinking of the *Titanic*. The building survives today as part of the Avery Weigh-Tronix and Avery Berkel weighing scales business. It is, however, Henry Ford who is usually credited with wholesale introduction of modern mass production. He designed and released the simple Model T car in 1908, which could be produced very cheaply by employees specialising in particular parts of production, using standardised interchangeable components that from 1913 were assembled on a moving production line. This system would also launch the industry of management consultancy, notably through the work of F.W. Taylor and his 1911 book *The Principles of Scientific Management*. Charlie Chaplin would produce a cutting statement of the effect of this method of working in his film *Modern Times*, but the approach revolutionised industry and Ford achieved astonishingly low costs, which enabled swathes of US consumers to buy their first car. Morris adopted the same production principles with similar degrees of success.

During the 1920s, Morris Motors accordingly continued to expand, and production facilities were extended to additional plants at Abingdon, Birmingham and Swindon. His business acumen also allowed him to recognise the need to vertically integrate suppliers into the production process, and he would do this astutely through taking advantage of business opportunities whenever they arose. He acquired Hollick and Pratt body makers, who had suffered through business failings and works fires. The Osberton radiator company were then acquired, as well as E.G. Wrigley & Co., an engineering components business that failed following the collapse of a large business deal. In 1923, he purchased the UK-based Hotchkiss business, a company well-known for the supply of weapons and munitions in the US Civil and First World Wars but had since become experts in engines and transmission equipment. He bought the engine company F.G. Woollard and by applying his production principles, he was able to increase production from 300 units a week to 2,000 within two years with minimal change in resources.

Morris also acquired the S.U. Carburettor Company, which was named after the 'Skinner Union' of the two Skinner brothers, who in 1904 had invented a variable venturi carburettor. 'Venturi' means restricted tube and this could be controlled by a carefully tapered needle piston, which could be profiled for different applications. A butterfly valve automatically adjusted the position of the needle according to the airflow in the engine, and therefore maintained a constant pressure in the venturi irrespective of engine revolutions. This gave cars a smooth and efficient method of delivering pre-mixed fuel and air into an engine. However, the Skinner brothers struggled to make their mark in business and sold the company to Morris. He picked up a bargain and secured ownership of carburettors that made his cars smooth and reliable, and which would also be used by Rolls-Royce, Bentley, Rover, Riley, Jaguar, Triumph, Volvo and Saab, as well as in the Mini and Maestro cars and the Spitfire's Merlin and Griffon engines. Notoriously, the constant pressure within the carburettor was affected by a rapidly diving Spitfire, which actually flooded the carburettor rather than starving it as commonly believed. The pilot would have to invert the Spitfire before diving, unlike its fuel-injected Messerschmitt and Focke-Wulf rivals, which then obtained a distinct flying advantage. This problem was temporarily overcome with the addition of a drilled coin, which restricted the rapid movement of fuel into the carburettor float tank – a solution referred to as 'Miss Shilling's orifice' after the designer Beatrice Shilling.

Morris also started the Pressed Steel Co. joint venture producing innovative pressed steel car bodies. A machine press using hydraulic, pneumatic or mechanical power can produce a car body part more quickly and accurately than a press hammer or cutting and forming techniques that a traditional coachbuilder might use. This company went on to supply body parts for most UK car companies, including Hillman and Rolls-Royce, as well as items for railway cars, aeroplanes and refrigerators. The one supplier Morris could not secure and integrate into his business, however, was a steel manufacturer. Morris was to complain regularly about the power the steel barons had over his industry and his lack of supply.

However, by vertically integrating the quality suppliers and components he did have into the manufacturing business, and replicating Ford's mass production principles, Morris was able to produce his high-quality cars at low cost. He dropped prices at a time when everyone else was doing otherwise. Hence, despite the intense competition, he was able to expand from producing 400 cars in 1919 to 56,000 by 1925, with models including the Morris Cowley and Morris Oxford. Morris also produced trucks and commercial vehicles, and specialist (MG) sports versions at the Abingdon factory. Morris overtook Wolseley and then Ford in 1924 to become Britain's biggest car manufacturer, with over half of the cars on its roads made by the company. General Motors offered to buy Morris Motors for £11 million, a considerable sum that valued the company at more than twice that estimated by Morris himself. Morris considered the offer for just a few seconds before responding, 'The Morris organisation is not for sale.' General Motors instead acquired Vauxhall Motors, another of the pioneering British car companies with engineering roots dating back to 1857.

In 1927, Morris Motors acquired Wolseley, which had grown to become Britain's biggest car company during the first decade of the twentieth century but was suffering from overexpansion and overpricing at the hands of Morris's low-cost approach. It had also lost its main engineering expert, Herbert Austin, who had left to start his own Austin motor business. Morris bought Wolseley out of receivership for £730,000, adding Wolseley's six-cylinder car range to his own, while thwarting the ambitions of rivals Austin and General Motors. Morris adapted the newly designed Wolseley 8hp overhead camshaft engine to form the basis of the Morris Minor released in 1928 and the MG Midget in 1929. The Minor, designed by Leonard Lord, would be a foray into the small car market, leading to the production of over 86,000 cars in a range of models from 1929 to 1934. These small cars were timely, given the economic depression of the time and helped the company to remain competitive.

During the 1930s, the number of British car companies contracted threefold from its 1922 peak to around fifty-eight, but these combined made Britain Europe's leading car producer. Of these, Morris was the dominant player with over a quarter of British production and 2 million of its cars on British roads alone. It was the largest car company in the world outside the US. During this same period, the Morris Car Company changed its name to Morris Motors Ltd and became publicly listed. It had eight directors, although it was distinctly under Morris's ownership, chairmanship and management direction. Morris was ennobled as Viscount, the fourth rank in the British peerage system, entitling him to be referred to as Viscount or Lord related to a relevant area. For Morris, this would be the village of Nuffield in Oxford, so his formal title became Lord Nuffield. The Morris business empire would also be renamed the Nuffield Organisation. Further expansion was achieved largely through reinvesting profits, although some shares in the public business also had to be issued to pay for acquisitions – including the Riley motor company – and to enable the new Morris holding company to incorporate many of its other acquisitions and subsidiaries.

In 1939, the Nuffield Organisation employed around 30,000 people and produced a neat new car, the Morris Cowley, but as war approached it turned more towards military production with items that included Bofors guns, jerry cans and 50,000 tea chest-sized mine sinkers, which helped to protect the British coastline. Around 10,000 Morris C8 artillery tractors were built, popularly known as the Quads, which were used in the Korean and Malayan conflicts. Morris developed and built Crusader tanks used in the successful British campaigns in North Africa. It repaired 75,000 RAF aircraft and produced the American-designed Liberty L12 engines for use in both tanks and aircraft. It also produced over 3,000 Tiger Moth aircraft and turned over funding and factory expertise to help towards the building of a massive factory at Castle Bromwich for the production of Spitfires. Initially this was done under the auspices of Morris Motors itself, but given the difficulties the company encountered with building works and rapidly changing aircraft specifications (far faster in the war than the more normally sedate car industry), the factory was turned over to Supermarine and Vickers staff after Morris was famously, and rarely, bested by Lord Beaverbrook, Minister of Aircraft Production. (After a heated telephone discussion around production, Morris suggested to Beaverbrook that he might like to take control of the Spitfire factory. The comment was made sarcastically, but much to Morris's surprise, Beaverbrook is reported to have responded with, 'That's very generous of you, Nuffield. I accept!' He then hung up, instantly calling Vickers and ordering them to take control of the factory and bring in managers from Supermarine.)

After the war, the allocation of steel was in short supply and was prioritised for companies that were exporting at least 75 per cent of their products. This overseas incentivisation, coupled with the reduced capacity of European car manufacturers, enabled British manufacturers to provide 52 per cent of the world's exported vehicles. This same restriction would also lead to the pioneering development of aluminium-based vehicles, including the highly successful Land Rover. The 1950 Cowley plant was capable of producing a total of 150,000 Morris and Wolseley cars a year, which included a new Issigonis-styled Morris Minor that was said to 'define Englishness' and would sell 1.3 million cars altogether.

In 1952 Morris surprised many people by merging Morris Motors Ltd with his long-time rival Austin. Together, as the British Motor Corporation

(BMC), they would employ nearly 40,000 people and produce cars under the marques of Morris, Wolseley, Riley and MG as well as Morris Commercial motor vehicles, agricultural tractors, marine and industrial engines. Morris never revealed why he merged his companies. He had no children to succeed him, but more likely he recognised that the company needed a resurgence after the war. He had culled the long-standing company directors and hired new men but had still seen other companies beginning to produce cheaper and better cars, and more of them. He had always battled against cheaper imports. The Americans had at that time cheaper coal, cheaper steel, and cheaper labour. While he replicated Ford's mass production, Morris's piecemeal approach to acquisitions meant that production facilities were spread out and were never as efficient as the purpose-built factories in the US, and those that would start to appear in other countries around the world. Nor could Morris replicate the scale of the US market and hence achieve the low-cost production of the Americans. While he achieved UK sales of tens of thousands before the First World War, Ford had achieved sales of 472,000 by 1914.[2] British car companies could never make the same amount of profit. The Americans, and even the Europeans, did not face the restrictions on metals after the war that the British car companies endured. The decline of the empire market also began to take its toll, while fluctuating values of the pound and political manoeuvring over tariffs and post-war material supplies exacerbated Morris's abilities to defend home sales while foraging abroad. Austin's designer and managing director, Leonard Lord, even argued that the British overseas sales success in previous years had only been achieved at a financial loss. It seems likely, therefore, that Morris thought the combined UK concerns of Morris and Austin would be better able to take on the world. The two companies had actually collaborated during the war, and Morris admired Austin and had often seen in their cars some innovation that he had then copied. It was Austin that had produced the Baby Austin Seven, which Morris later followed with the Morris Minor. Austin was also producing 50 per cent more cars than Morris at its Longbridge plant.

William Morris chaired the joint company for its first year before retiring at the age of 75, but with and without him, the merger was not a success. The two companies were quite different; there were no synergies in parts, engines or production, disparate cultures and resources that were never integrated. The potential synergies were not realised, and in fact the opposite happened: Austin incorporated some of the inefficiency of Morris – rather than vice versa. It would later be argued that Morris had held the reins of power for too long and that the post-war company had been slow to find a new direction. The strategy had simply been more expansions, which suited the 1920s and '30s but not the new post-war landscape. Company minutes showed that Morris's managing director, Miles Thomas, did have a cogent plan for reconstruction and reorganisation but that this was thwarted by Morris, and Thomas would leave the company soon after to head up British Overseas Airways Corporation (BOAC, which would later become British Airways).

US car imports were still growing and by the mid-1950s had the leading market share of vehicles on British roads. German car production was also growing, building on the VW Beetle, which the British had declined to take on from Germany after the war. VW then made 1,785 Beetles in 1945, rising to 1 million in 1955. By 1956 VW overtook Britain to become Europe's largest car manufacturer. (Some 21 million Beetles would be produced, making it the most successful car of all time.) BMC instead released in 1959 the more modern Mini (like both the Minor and the Triumph Spitfire, all styled by Sir Alex Issigonis), which would achieve record sales and iconic status. However, there is much argument and evidence to suggest that the Mini was actually a commercial disaster. Technical innovations it introduced became dead ends for future development, and assembly was often by hand rather than through automated machinery. Parts were shipped in from various disparate factories, making mass-produced flow production difficult, which had been a problem that Morris had struggled with for all its cars. Accounting failures also seemed to hide these failings, meaning that for years the Mini actually lost money on every car produced. Let me just state that again: the Mini most likely lost money on every single car manufactured – nearly 500,000 of them. It wasn't that the car was simply loss-making – there are many examples of cars that do that – it was that the company wasn't at first sure about the profitability, then failed to make it profitable when the financial problems were recognised.[3]

Faced with ever-pressing demands, the merged Morris and Austin companies, as the British Motor Corporation (BMC), merged again with Jaguar to form British Motor Holdings (BMH). In 1966 the Pressed Steel Company joint venture in which Morris had a large share also merged with Jaguar and BMC to form part of BMH. The pressed steel business was merged with BMC's press subsidiary Fisher and Ludlow and became the world's largest independent car body and car tool manufacturer, based mainly at Swindon and supplying parts to British companies as well as Volvo, Alfa Romeo and Hindustan Motors. BMH, though, struggled to maintain market share and by 1966–67 was reported to be making an annual loss of £3.4 million. Sales of old favourites such as the Morris Minor began to flag as people chose instead more modern and increasingly foreign-produced cars.

Under government pressure, with a view to achieving economies of scale and drawing on the experience of Leyland Company, which was by contrast performing well with Standard, Triumph, Rover, Alvis and Leyland truck brands, nearly every British car company was merged in 1968 to become British Leyland Motor Corporation (BLMC). BLMC then held great marques in Rover, Jaguar, Mini and Land Rover, and maintained 40 per cent of the UK car market while exporting 40 per cent of its output to Europe. BLMC was, though, never a great success. It was beset by organisational problems, rivalries between these various car marques both within the company and on the road, industrial relations problems, and problems with poor quality, all at a time when German, Japanese and American car companies were beginning to move in exactly the other way. BLMC was partially nationalised in 1975 to try to avoid the spectre of Britain having no car industry at all. The company was renamed British Leyland, then BL, at which point the Nuffield Organisation and its famous marques disappeared. The last MGB, which had been produced at the Abingdon plant for fifty-six years, rolled off the production line in 1980. The Morris brand was permanently parked, alongside that of Austin and Wolseley.

BL produced a range of mostly unspectacular and unloved cars, including the Maxi, Toledo, Marina, Princess, Allegro and TR7, which fared poorly against the likes of the Ford Escort, Ford Cortina, Toyota Corolla and Renault 6. The trickle of foreign cars on British roads turned into a torrent. As Morris had predicted, and fought hard against, every import cost the UK jobs and between 1975 and 1982 almost half the workforce in Coventry was axed by the top fifteen companies. Of this, BL shed over 19,000 or 70 per cent. The government attempted to prop up Chrysler, then BL, amid cries that government meddling in the cancellation of projects, directing where facilities could be built and controlling growth through Industrial Development Certificates had made matters worse. Amid the fallout, support companies went bust, including the large Alfred Herbert Machine Tool Company and Dunlop Rubber, inventor of the pneumatic tyre, one of Britain's biggest companies and one of the first multinationals, which had been in business since 1889.

BL sought to divest non-core businesses, form strategic alliances and changed its name to its strongest brand, Rover, but in 1988 it was sold by the government to British Aerospace. They tried to run the business from 1988 to 1994 but then sold the Rover Group to BMW, which was also unable to stem the losses. In 2000, BMW sold Rover to the Phoenix private equity consortium in a highly contentious sale. Workers thought the plans for the newly developed new Mini would stay with Rover, but BMW retained the rights and with it the writing was on the wall for Rover and British-owned mainstream car production. The four key players in the Phoenix consortium then netted high profits before the firm collapsed in 2005 and was sold as MG Rover Group to the Chinese Nanjing Automobile Group. Ownership of the Wolseley, MG, Austin, and Morris marques subsequently fell under the control of SAIC Motor Corporation Limited. The S.U. Carburettor name and rights were acquired by Burlen Fuel Systems Limited of Salisbury, which continues to manufacture carburettors, pumps and components for the classic car market.

While William Morris reaped the financial benefits, he knew that the sacrifices he had made came at the expense of an easier life, family (he had no children) and health. He spent the majority of the remainder of his life as he had set out, tinkering quietly in his shed, until he died in 1963 at the age of 85. He would almost certainly have been horrified to see his efforts for the British-owned car industry fade away to become a shadow of its former self. From this point onwards, only specialist low-volume companies such as McLaren and Morgan would carry the flag for actual British-owned car companies. However, Morris's legacy undoubtedly includes car production, which the country can still be proud of, with major plants such as those at Sunderland and Derby drawing on British experience and expertise. The 1956 Morris Oxford design was still produced in India as the Hindustan Ambassador up to 2014. Jaguar and Land Rover are successful as part of the Indian Tata group, which to date still use parts of the Castle Bromwich factory set up by Morris to build Spitfires. Mini is still owned by BMW. The Pressed Steel business passed to BMW when they acquired the Rover Group in 1994, and under Swindon Pressings Limited now produces most of the body panels and sub-assemblies for the Mini cars produced by BMW at the Cowley site.

Morris's legacy is, however, not just cars. His approach to low-cost production would eventually be copied by other British companies in other industrial sectors. Perhaps most surprising of all, though, is the possibility that his biggest legacy may not actually be in cars and industry at all, but instead be in education and health. Despite his wealth, Morris was not profligate or flashy, and he disbursed much of his wealth in charitable acts. It was said that he made £30 million and that he gave away £30 million – billions at today's values. He did this not just at the end of his life but throughout it and without strings, unlike the ultra-rich today, who either seem to seek to spend their wealth on islands and football teams, or with conditions in acts of guarded philanthrocapitalism. Morris's philanthropy included numerous unrecorded individual financial gifts, such as supporting the Sea Cadet Corps, the Red Cross, older people's institutions and children's organisations. In health-related areas, he purchased a cyclotron for medical research, designed, built and distributed 1,700 iron lungs for free, gave money for buildings at Guy's and other hospitals, and donated millions of pounds to establish medical schools, educational colleges and theatres at universities, including at Oxford and Southampton. Rheumatism, cellular biology, transplantation immunity and cortisone were just some areas widely researched with Morris funding. A £3,000 donation by Morris to Howard Florey allowed enough of Fleming's penicillin to be made and developed for practical uses, and saved thousands of lives from the Second World War onwards. His Nuffield Trust provided the pilot for the National Health Service (NHS), which the trust continued to support. He also gave widely to education. Nuffield College in

Oxford University, for example, is a world-leading centre of postgraduate social study – the first to admit men and women – founded with a gift of £900,000 (around £60 million in 2018 values). In fact, Morris made several donations to Oxford that helped to maintain its world-leading academic status. He also donated £10 million as an endowment to establish the Nuffield Foundation in 1943 to improve research that would support social and educational policy for the benefit of people.

9

De Havilland Aircraft Co. Ltd

The de Havilland Aircraft Company was one of the most prolific and innovative of aviation companies, or indeed of any type of company. Throughout a long period, it developed groundbreaking planes and played a major role in developing the airline industry.

De Havilland logo. (© BAE SYSTEMS, courtesy BAE Systems plc)

In 1804 the Englishman George Cayley produced an outstanding body of work that described for the first time the principles of flight, including descriptions of lift, drag and aerofoils. Cayley even invented the kind of lightweight-tension, spoked wheels that would henceforth be used extensively in aviation and bike industries. His subsequent glider flights are considered by some to be the first true controlled flight by man, albeit piloted by an apparently unwilling Cayley employee. This was 100 years before the Wright brothers' flights and many people, therefore, consider Cayley to be the 'father of aviation'. However, the Wright brothers would in 1903 justifiably claim the accolade of being the first in the world to achieve controlled, powered flight, having worked out the principles of 'wing warping', which allowed the pilot to vary the flight dynamics and thereby control the aircraft. However, their Wright Flyer would initially be launched through a catapult and rail system, and the Brazilian Alberto Santos-Dumont would lay a claim to be the first to perform true controlled flight when four years later he both took off and changed course in his plane.

Once the principles of flight had been proven, a host of adventurous entrepreneurs, notably in the US, Italy, Britain and France, ventured into the fledgling aviation business. In Britain, A.V. Roe became the first Englishman to fly in an English plane in 1909, from Walthamstow marshes. Many of the British pioneers proceeded to provide planes for the Royal Flying Corps in the First World War, including Sopwith, Avro, Gloster, Airco, Bristol, Vickers, Supermarine, Shorts, Folland and Boulton Paul. Many of these companies achieved fame and often long and distinguished industrial service, and are deserving of the spotlight on their own, but it is de Havilland that perhaps stands out as being the most remarkable of Britain's many aviation companies.

Captain Sir Geoffrey de Havilland (OM, CBE, OBE, AFC, RDI, FRAeS) was born in 1882 and studied at Nuneaton Grammar School. Like many of the great early aviators such as Albert Ball, James McCudden and Howard Pixton, he was highly adept at both flying and engineering, giving him a combination that touched on aviation genius. He studied at the Crystal Palace School of Engineering before gaining his engineering experience, first at the power plant business of Willans & Robinson in Rugby, then at the Wolseley Tool and Motor Car Company and finally at the Iris Motor (Bus) Company. However, his interests were always in the promise of the flight industry and in 1908 he borrowed £500 (around double a yearly salary) and designed and built his first aero engine. He subsequently started his own plane company, supported by his wife and brother-in-law, Frank Hearle. It was a bold move, as there were many people who simply did not believe that flying would develop as an industry. Not many people could fly, for one, and other bodies such as the government were looking at airships rather than planes. De Havilland was also working to a small budget and would also be up against the big British engineering companies in Armstrong and Vickers, who would certainly be moving into the flight domain … if it took off. Designing aircraft was also exhausting physical work based in cold unheated barns. Not only that, de Havilland was not only one of the many that could not actually fly, but he had not even seen a plane in the air and would not do so until April 1909! It was in 1910 that he flew his first plan – perhaps unsurprisingly, it crashed. The next time, however, he took off in a revised design and it became one of the first half a dozen British planes that actually flew. De Havilland was appointed assistant designer and test pilot at the Army Balloon Factory at Farnborough (later the Royal Aircraft Factory, RAF) in December 1910 and the War Office then bought the aircraft. His design would become the F.E.1, which was improved further as the F.E.2. The F.E. designation used by the RAF denoted that the plane had the engine at the rear, pushing the plane through the air as those designed by pioneer Henri Farman had done. F.E. therefore stood for 'Farman Experimental', although it is also sometimes referred to as a 'Fighter Experimental'.

During the opening year of the war in 1914, de Havilland served as both a pilot in the Royal Flying Corps and as a designer working directly for the RAF. He later worked as a designer at the Airco company, which worked for the RAF. His flight record identifies him as being one of the world's leading pilots at the time, although following a flying injury, he started to concentrate his effort on being a designer and test pilot than a fighter pilot. He would still go to the front line in France to work with pilots to make sure his designs were well suited to their needs in another early example of human-centred design (HCD). He consequently produced nine designs throughout the war, including fighters, bombers and trainers such as the B.E.2, B.S.1, DH.1 and DH.2, all of which were usually innovative and ahead of their time.

The B.E.2 biplane, for example, was designed with an engine at the front of the aircraft, which pulled the plane through the air in what was known as a 'tractor configuration', in contrast to the F.E. types. The RAF acknowledged that Louis Blériot had been the first to produce established tractor designs, so the 'B.E.' designation stood for 'Blériot Experimental'. The B.E.2 pioneered controllability through ailerons rather than wing warping, employed a fixed tailplane with movable rudder and had balanced, dihedral wings. The design set new standards in testing, not just in aircraft but across the industry as a whole. The plane was, for example, hung upside down with weighted wings to simulate real-time wing loadings, and through testing, the company discovered the flight dynamics phenomena of elevator flutter. Around 3,500 B.E.2s were built, and the plane achieved a British altitude record in 1912 by flying at over 10,000ft, and that was with a passenger. To set this into context. this was just nine years after the Wright brothers' first flight and at a time when other early flying machines built by pioneers such as Samuel Cody and Maurice and Henri Farman were still very much prevalent but only flying at heights of hundreds of feet.

De Havilland's design work also included the B.S.1(later the S.E.2), which like the B.E.2, was ahead of its time with a revolutionary streamlined, monocoque fuselage that presented the world with the first purpose-built, fast, single-seater fighter, capable of around 90mph. The RAF identified these fighter planes as 'scouts', designating them with a 'Blériot Scout' or B.S. prefix. De Havilland's D.H.1 was the first to have the DH designation, which was used in all company designs from then on. The DH.1 climbed at a fast 700ft per minute and is considered to be the first aerobatic fighter. The manoeuvrability of the DH.2 that followed allowed British pilots to aim the plane at the enemy in order to target and fire, rather than waving a gun in the buffeting slipstream. This practice, and plane, therefore helped to end the dominance that German types had been beginning to establish known as the 'Fokker scourge'.

The DH.4 bomber could fly at around 143mph and at 22,000ft, and they were built by companies that included furniture manufacturer Waring and Gillow (which dates back to the 1730s and is still existence today as part of Allied Carpets). Some 3,227 of these were built in Britain during the war, and they continued to be made after it, being sold to air forces around the world. An additional 4,846 DH.4s were built during the war under licence in the US. After the war, the US army contracted a number of American firms, including the Boeing Aircraft Corporation, to produce a variant of the plane. Their DH-4B variant became known in the US as the 'Boeing' and provided the platform for much US air development up to 1929. In 1918, another de Havilland design, the DH.9 bomber, set yet another altitude record by reaching over 30,000ft, and this type would also achieve overseas sales.

At the end of the war, a total of 9,000 out of the 55,000 planes produced in Britain during the conflict had been designed by de Havilland and the Airco Company that de Havilland worked for. Airco could claim to be the world's largest air industry company, but for all of their successes and the promise of future air travel, they struggled for business as the poor post-war global economy made mass air travel slower to materialise than expected. Airco was instead sold to Birmingham Small Arms (BSA) in 1920 but closed almost immediately when BSA discovered how financially unsound the company actually was. Airco's former owner, George Thomas, nevertheless financially supported de Havilland in setting up his own firm, the de Havilland Aircraft Company, using some of Airco's assets that included the design team, de Havilland's future brother-in-law, Frank Hearle, forty-five production staff, two airframes and a wealthy client in Alan Butler, who became company chairman and financier and helped to secure £50,000 start-up capital. Geoffrey de Havilland was neither chairman nor chief executive of the company, preferring to devote his time to aircraft design rather than management. This core group would work closely as a talented and effective team over the years, producing a vast number of aircraft, first at Stag Lane in Enfield and later at sites including Hatfield in Hertfordshire.

Within eight years, the company grew to a size that enabled it to go public, which it achieved not just by designing planes but by building the airline industry as a whole. It led, for example, in the development of aviation services such as hiring air taxis, pilot training, crop dusting, filming and photography. It was, however, primarily a design and build service, and despite its track record in military aviation, its core emphasis was in the production of civil and commercial planes. The original DH.4s and DH.9s with enlarged and enclosed fuselages provided embryonic passenger services, including ferrying British government ministers to and from European meetings such as the Treaty of Versailles. A DH.14 operated the world's first scheduled international air passenger service when it flew from London to Paris on 25 August 1919. The DH.18 was thus the first plane to be specifically designed as a dedicated passenger aircraft and was highly successful, offering both comfort and low operating costs.

Seventy-three types numbered from DH.22 through to DH.95 then came from the drawing boards between the two world wars. The DH.34

was particularly successful, adding speed to the comfort and low costs already being realised. Although it was still a biplane, the large size of this developing passenger plane, which could accommodate ten people, marked it out as significantly different from the 'kites' of the First World War. DH.50s also found service, particularly with the Australian Flying Doctor and Qantas airlines. The company's biggest success, though, was with the smaller Moth series that appeared from 1925 onwards. This was a pioneering series of simple, robust, lightweight biplanes, including the Gypsy Moth (DH.60G) and the Tiger Moth (DH.82) powered by the company's own lightweight Gypsy engines, with engine design and production being another bold business investment. These planes were easy to fly and provided the basis for the new flying clubs appearing around the country and which served as an introduction to flying for many budding pilots, including those who would enter the Royal Air Force (RAF) in later years. The Tiger Moth became known as the 'plane that trained the Empire', selling in twenty-five countries around the world. The Moths also set many aviation records, with Amy Johnson's record-breaking solo flight from England to Australia in a Gypsy Moth in 1930. The DH.83 Fox Moth was a successful four-person passenger plane, and the larger and more economic DH.84 Dragon was a real step towards a viable commercial airliner and provided the Irish airline Aer Lingus with its first passenger aeroplane. The experience gained from the sheer number of its developments was invaluable to the de Havilland Company, not only in aerodynamics but in engine and propeller design, which the company operated as associated business units. The DH.88, for example, beat the rest of the world by winning the inaugural England to Australia MacRobertson Trophy Air Race using innovative thin wings, split trailing edge flaps and variable-pitch propellers, while the DH.89 entered service as a designated, high-speed mail plane and airliner. The DH.91 Albatross and DH.95 Flamingo airliners were at the point of release to the market when the Second World War largely put an end to civilian air travel.

For the war, de Havilland proposed a twin-engine fighter-bomber, but this was rejected by the RAF. Its priorities were for a fast, single-seater plane using a single engine and a high-load capacity bomber powered by four engines. There was no need, the RAF thought, for a twin-engine plane that would have neither the speed of the single-engine fighter nor the load-carrying capacity of the four-engine bomber, and which would instead take away valuable resources such as the Rolls-Royce Merlin engines. However, De Havilland thought otherwise and using their own finances produced within just eleven months the twin-engine Mosquito. Its shape, it was later said, was based on the streamlined form of the pike fish, which helped to make it quick. It was the fastest operational plane in the world for the next two and a half years, yet it also had a high load-carrying capacity.[1] It could carry 1,000lb (454kg) of bombs for 1,500 miles (2,400km), a good proportion of the load of a heavy bomber but travelling at the speed of a fighter at 400mph. It was also able to carry 10,000lb of bombs, and was said to be able to carry the same load to Berlin as a Flying Fortress but quicker and using less fuel. It hence proved to be one of the war's most versatile planes, with seemingly unlimited uses. It operated as a fighter, night fighter, bomber and U-boat interceptor, and for reconnaissance and target finding (pathfinding), and in all roles it seemed unstoppable by the German Luftwaffe. It was made from wood and fabric resources in woodworking factories, so its production did not hinder the construction of Spitfires and Lancasters. German air force leader Hermann Göring is famously said to have commented:

In 1940 I could at least fly as far as Glasgow in most of my aircraft, but not now! It makes me furious when I see the Mosquito. I turn green and yellow with envy. The British, who can afford aluminium better than we can, knock together a beautiful wooden aircraft that every piano factory over there is building, and they give it a speed which they have now increased yet again. What do you make of that? There is nothing the British do not have. They have the geniuses and we have the nincompoops.

For these reasons, the 'flying piano' plane is believed by many to actually be better than both the Spitfire and the Lancaster but perhaps less famous because its wooden construction made it less capable of surviving over time. Over 7,000 Mosquitos were built, but there are currently only three flying examples left, which is a shame as the type truly deserves a place in the Battle of Britain Memorial Flight.

A more streamlined, single-seater development of the Mosquito followed just after the war named the Hornet. It utilised the 'laminar' or smoothed planar flow of air over the wings to reduce turbulence and drag. Incidentally, that was a concept first noted by eighteenth-century British engineer John Smeaton, who saw that windmill 'sweeps' were more efficient when cambered. De Havilland also pioneered the use of Redux, a metal-to-metal and metal-to-wood glue developed by Aero Research Ltd at Duxford (hence REsearch at DUXford). This enabled the construction of lighter and stiffer components, giving the Hornet even more remarkable characteristics than the already remarkable Mosquito and making it the highest-ever performing propeller-driven aircraft.[2] Eric 'Winkle' Brown, widely recognised as the world's greatest ever test pilot, said of the Hornet: 'From the outset, the (Sea) Hornet was a winner ... manoeuvres in the vertical plane can only be described as rocket-like.'[3]

The company's propellers were also pivotal to its success in the Second World War. De Havilland trialled a French-made variable-pitch propeller on its DH.88 in 1934. This innovation enables the blades to be fine-tuned to give the grunt needed to take off, then provide the economy or speed needed in level flight. Otherwise, the engine would be needed to strain more on take-off, as if setting off uphill in top gear in a car or bike. Having secured a licence and subsequent expertise in these types of propeller, the company produced over 146,000 during the war, while repairing and returning to service over 40,000 more. More effective than variable-pitch propellers, however, were constant-speed propellers. On a bicycle, this would be akin to being allowed to pedal at a constant cadence and leg power, allowing maximum effort while the bike itself sorted out the necessary gearing. At the height of the Battle of Britain, the company designed, built and installed 1,000 constant-speed propellers for all front-line RAF fighter planes, giving the Spitfire, for example, 7,000ft more ceiling, a faster rate of climb, reduced take-off length and maximum power at any required time. Subsequent to this conversion and during the period 8 to 15 August 1940, German planes were shot down at an average of eighty-one per day, four times the British losses. It was said by the RAF that 'without the conversion job the figures might have been reversed'.[4]

After the war, the company produced a number of planes, including 3,500 at a new plant in Chester that had operated as a 'shadow' factory in the war.

Types included the Dove and the Heron transports and the Chipmunk trainer. The engineering excellence of the propeller division was used to develop a range of equipment such as flow meters and alternators, which were used not just for aircraft but across a wide range of industries and introduced strain gauge testing to the UK. The division also innovated around both aluminium and hollow steel large propellers for increasingly larger and more powerful planes. To produce a thin-walled, complex metal form 2.5m long and capable of converting 1,000hp into thrust is some undertaking. The company, however, recognised that the future of fighter and large civil aircraft lay not with propellers but with jet engines.

The story of the jet engine starts with Sir Frank Whittle, another of the practising and practical engineers who appeared throughout British history. He trained as a Royal Air Force aircraft mechanic and developed a keen skill in both mathematics and model plane making. He was put forward for flight officer training, during which he wrote a dissertation indicating the finite nature of aircraft speeds using current technology. His paper mooted the idea of adding a compressor to a gas turbine and using the exhaust to add thrust. Whittle presented the idea to the RAF in 1929 but it was rejected as impractical – a view shared by most experts in turbine and engine research. With the support of fellow officers, however, he patented the idea himself and presented it to British Thomson-Houston (BTH) based in Rugby (the company that later merged with Metropolitan Vickers to become Associated Electrical Industries, which was itself later incorporated into GEC). However, BTH baulked at the costs of developing the idea. At this point the RAF sent Whittle on a two-year engineering course, and it was during this time that he met people with the support and connections that made it possible to take the idea further. Power Jets Ltd was established in 1936 and built a prototype engine at the BTH works. Only after Whittle's prototype fired up in 1937 did the government and RAF start to take notice and supply some long-overdue project funding. Faced with rearmament and other pressing needs, however, the project never got the full amount of funding it needed, and Britain's jet technology advantage slipped away. It has been argued that had the jet engine been developed by Britain in the 1930s, then the Second World War would have been over in days, not years. The development delay and the failure to maintain the original patents at Power Jets had allowed German engineers at Junkers and Heinkel to also start working on jet engines and with more government support than in Britain. It was hence Germany who was first to launch a jet-powered fighter into the air with the Me 262, although it was not quite the complete article and prone to failure. In 1941, however, the first British jet engine, the Power Jets W.1, was installed in the E.28/39 test plane built by Gloster, some thirteen years after Whittle first proposed the idea. Rolls-Royce assumed control of jet engine production in 1942, and the Gloster Meteor was launched shortly after in 1943 and proved to be the more successful combat fighter of the war, using Whittle and Rolls-Royce-developed engines.

De Havilland were not far behind these developments. Off their own bat once again, and based on the work of engineer Frank Halford, the company produced a compact, powerful and simplified Whittle-type jet engine in 1942 that would come to be known as the Goblin. The Goblin became only the second British jet engine to fly and actually beat the first – Power Jets – to pass a type test and receive a type certificate issued for an aircraft propulsion turbine. The Goblin remained largely the same in principle for the next thirteen years, powering, for example, SAAB and Fiat designs. De Havilland evolved a number of different Goblin marques and in time it evolved into the Ghost and the Gyron, one of the first supersonic engines. In the US, Lockheed bought and learned from the Goblin, while it formed the basis for de Havilland's own development of jet planes and the first of these was the DH.100 Vampire. This was the second RAF jet fighter after the Meteor and the first single-jet-powered fighter, defying the logic of the time that dictated only twin engines would be powerful enough. It was the first jet to cross the Atlantic Ocean, the first to reach 500mph (alongside the Goblin-powered US Lockheed Shooting Star) and reached a record altitude at 59,114ft. It served the RAF in various marques up to 1966, by which time 3,268 planes had been built, and even today a few preserved examples thrill crowds at air shows as they scream across the skies.

The DH.108 developed at the same time was the first British swept-wing, tailless jet and was built as an experimental subsonic type but is believed to have become the first British plane to go supersonic by breaking the sound barrier in 1948. The US X-1 had been the first to break the speed of sound in 1947, but it had been purpose-built and dropped from a piggyback flight in order to achieve it, whereas the DH.108 had taken off and climbed under its own power. In the process of extensive flight testing to achieve its high speeds, it had become evident that air, which was known to be incompressible at low speed, started to behave differently towards supersonic speeds, forming a different density and acting more like a liquid than a gas. This compressed air could be moving over the plane's surfaces at supersonic speeds even if the plane itself was not, resulting in shock waves, buffeting, instability and poor control. The DH.108 hence pioneered the understanding of the 'compressibility' of air as planes moved from subsonic to transonic flight, which had previously been unknown. This understanding was then employed in the next de Havilland development, the DH.106 Comet, the world's first jet passenger aircraft. The Comet was a remarkable plane, flying at twice the speed of previous passenger designs. It had twin engines mounted side by side and closer to the fuselage than is nowadays normal, but it looked and performed in all other ways like the passenger planes of today. From 1952 onwards, it saw service with the embryonic British Overseas Airways Corporation and other airlines, and the basic design would last through to 2011 in the RAF's Nimrod maritime patrol development.

In addition to jets and jet engines, de Havilland's Propeller Division was now pioneering rocketry and would probably have been better named as de Havilland Propulsion. Rocket engines were developed as a concept to support take-off for Comet airliners, but were not used when the jet engines proved powerful enough on their own. However, the combination of solid fuel rockets and jet turbines, coupled with radar and infrared control, formed the basis of Britain's first ground-to-air missile. Firestreak was developed in 1957 as one of the RAF's first heat-seeking air-to-air missiles, used on the de Havilland Sea Vixen and Gloster Javelin and in use up to 1988 as part of the armoury for the English Electric Lightning fighter. The Blue Streak was also developed in 1957 as a liquid-fuelled, medium-range ballistic missile that was intended to deliver nuclear warheads instead of dropping them from conventional bombers.

Despite all of these innovative developments, history, experience, advanced know-how and successes, de Havilland's days were now numbered. Britain was struggling with post-war austerity, Europe was shattered, and Britain's Commonwealth partners were retrenching, so that one of the issues the company was facing was the limited post-war air market, a market in which many British plane companies were competing. As the British government reduced its demand for aircraft, so the interest from other overseas governments waned in accordance. Opportunities in any of the company's markets in civil aircraft, trainers or military planes were therefore restricted. This limited market was also a highly confusing place. As plane technology advanced, military and embryonic passenger companies were uncertain about what services to run and what planes to specify. The government, via the Ministry of Defence or the RAF, would produce a range of constantly changing orders, while the Defence White Paper of 1957, for example, steered the focus of spending towards missiles and away from planes. As a result, the innovative Saunders-Roe SR.177 rocket-jet was cancelled after twelve years of work and investment. Henry Folland had built one of the most successful fighter planes of all time, the First World War's SE.5, described as the Great War's Spitfire. Despite producing numerous designs, however, his company would not receive another order until some forty years later in the Gnat trainer of 1955. The Miles Aircraft Company would produce 100 designs, but only the Magister and Master would be produced in any significant numbers and the firm would go bust in 1947. For de Havilland, in between the two world wars they had produced seventy-five aircraft designs designated DH.22 through to DH.97. Of these, thirty-eight were not built, while many of those that were produced were in low numbers. After the Second World War, twenty-two planes were designed, designated DH.104 to DH.127, but eleven of these were not built. The investment in resources in these projects was enormous. De Havilland would produce some great post-war military planes in the Vampire, Venom and Sea Vixen, but it was up against other great planes such as the Hawker Hunter and the Gloster Javelin and production numbers, and therefore income, for all of these planes were limited.

Alongside the issue of competition and declining markets was the problem of limited post-war resources needed to develop planes at a time when the costs of development were increasing. The days of wood and doped canvas with wire controls were long gone and emerging in their place were all-metal planes with expensive joining methods, sophisticated electronics and complex engines requiring extensive development and testing. These took longer and longer times to design, build and test. The company needed between £8 and £10 million investment to develop a competitive Mk5 version of its Comet, needing perhaps 15,000 working drawings, but British Overseas Airways Corporation (BOAC) would only commit to twenty planes rather than the thirty this required, and the project died.

It was a similar story with jet engines. Perhaps better-funded R & D might have helped the Goblin engine to be developed further or more quicklym but this was difficult in austerity Britain, or perhaps the company was just too overstretched to look at both engines and planes. German pioneers, including Helmut Schelp, Anselm Franz and Hans Pabst von Ohain, all joined or led US jet development. They helped to tame the complex technology and produce better engines than the Goblin, including the Pratt & Whitney J42, then J57 and General Electric I-40. Of the major economies, only the US had survived in a decent shape and with the necessary market and funding capacity to develop its air industry. The Americans had half the number of companies in their home market bidding for twice the amount of business than the Europeans, and the US government also co-ordinated its civil and military spending in a way that maximised potential. It also had the post-war finances to provide aid overseas, which would often need to be returned to the US as orders for US goods, including planes. De Havilland's fourth version of its Comet was a good plane, but it was competing against Boeing's 707 and Douglas DC-8, both of which were faster and more economical to operate, and orders for the Comet dried up completely.

Blue Streak was a similar mighty but doomed effort from the propeller division of de Havilland. Although it was supported by the Royal Aircraft Establishment at Farnborough and the Rocket Propulsion Establishment at Westcott, it was competing against the might of US research funding via NASA's Jet Propulsion Laboratory in California, which had inherited the wartime research of German rocket pioneer Wernher von Braun and his engineers. Despite the effort, Blue Streak was cancelled because of cost. Despite the concept of protective silos (which the US would adopt), it was considered vulnerable to pre-emptive strikes, and there were difficulties in finding suitable sites. Instead, Britain would purchase missiles from the US, which was felt to be progressing such rockets faster and more cost-effectively and the Trident of today is highly contentious because of reasons that include its cost. Blue Streak did not enter military service because of cost but were instead used for the Black Prince satellite launcher, although this too proved to be cost-prohibitive. Commonwealth support was sought, but rejected. US companies Thiokol and GE picked up with rocket and turbojets where de Havilland left off.

If cracks were starting to appear in the de Havilland business model, sadly they were also starting to appear in the planes, too. The tailless DH.108 plane may have helped to uncover the secrets of compressibility, but it was an expensive venture in many ways. The plane only revealed the secrets of compressibility by becoming unstable at the slightest whim. Even a change of wind speed or direction could tip it into an unrecoverable flight position in what we might now call a good example of chaos theory. The great test pilot Eric Brown described the plane as the most dangerous he ever flew, while veteran war hero John Cunningham said flying the plane was the only time he got scared. The three prototypes all crashed and claimed the lives of three de Havilland test pilots. The DH.108 was inspired by the German Me 163 Komet, but one wonders if the company simply backed the wrong horse in investing heavily in this plane. The US drew instead on the German Me P.1101 swept-wing plane, leading to an understanding of variable sweep seen on the X-5 experimental jet.

A design flaw in a leading-edge wing structure would also down a prototype Sea Vixen at the 1952 Farnborough Air Show, killing experienced pilot John Derry, his co-pilot and twenty-five spectators. It was, however, failures in the Comet that had become critical to the company's future. De Havilland had got the design of the world's first passenger jet 99.9 per cent right, but a plane needs to be 100 per cent right. The Comet suffered three tragic and high-profile crashes in two years, with thirty-three lives lost in 1953, thirty-five and then a further twenty-one in 1954. It has become well attested that the early versions of the plane had 'square' windows, which caused problems. Windows in buildings are, of course, normally square, and it is easy to see how traditional understanding of this would follow into an airplane – but square corners are points of weakness where cracks appear and stretch in a process called propagation. In the case of the

Comet, this meant ultimately the windows dropping out, depressurising the plane, which then crashed, although, in fact, it was not a problem just involving the windows. De Havilland had tested rigorously against this happening. The forward fuselage section was tested for failure by pressurising at up to 2.75 pounds per square inch (psi) (19.0kPa), overpressure and depressurising for over 16,000 cycles representing 40,000 hours of service. Windows were tested under a pressure of 12psi (83kPa) (4.75psi or 32.8kPa above expected pressures). This suggested that the design should not have failed, but they had only tested sections of the design. What nobody fully understood at the time was that testing a part of a plane was not the same as testing the whole thing. The Royal Aircraft Establishment subsequently built a test rig for an entire Comet fuselage, which revealed unexpected stress behaviour patterns. It also showed up construction flaws where rivets had been used instead of glue, which exacerbated stress weaknesses. They also identified a new failure mode phenomena where repeated cycles of forces being applied and released can cause metals to fail at lower than expected values in what is now called metal fatigue. The effect can be seen in an old-fashioned light bulb where the tungsten filament will be subjected to repeated backwards and forwards cycling of alternating electric current until it begins to become weaker, stretching and thinning until it becomes too weak to support itself and blows. The cyclic forces in a plane might appear through take-off and landing, through everyday flying strains or through thermal heating or cooling. In the Comet, failures occurred after 3,057 flight cycles with roughly three to nine times less than the metal's theoretical limit. These higher-than-expected stress concentrations appeared in the skin of the aircraft, not just around the window corners but particularly in service hatches in the roof and side.

Under these failures, the image of an advanced, competent and professional company was losing its validity, and de Havilland started to lose some of its credibility. For a long time the brand essence of the company had been captured in the sentiment 'ahhh, de Havilland', but now it was looking more like 'agghh, de Havilland'. The further tragedy for Geoffrey de Havilland would be exacerbated by the fact that one of the test pilots lost in a DH.108 crash was his eldest son, Geoffrey Junior. Geoffrey Junior had flown with his father on the same day he flew his first plane in 1909 – when the young de Havilland had been just eight months old. Geoffrey's young-est son, John, had also been killed three years earlier in 1943 following a mid-air crash between two Mosquitos, while his wife, Louise, was said to have suffered a nervous breakdown following these deaths and died shortly after in 1949. It was now, during this time when conditions for the company were starting to get difficult, that the de Havilland team that had worked so closely for so long was also starting to disband. Science expert Charles Walker retired in 1954, while engine specialist Frank Halford died unex-pectedly in his sleep in 1955, taking with him forty-five years of experience. His right-hand man John Brodie died four years later in 1959. Production specialist Harry Povey retired in 1956, having started as works manager in 1917. Frank Hearle left in the same year. Business leaders Wilfred E. Nixon and Aubrey Burke also departed. All of these people had worked well and closely together under the charismatic and personable qualities of Geoffrey de Havilland.

The end for the de Havilland company came in 1960. To try and over-come some of the issues relating to development costs, the company had pooled some resources with Hunting, Avro and Fairey under the revised name of Airco in order to bid to develop a plane to replace the Viscounts operated by British European Airways (BEA). BEA chose de Havilland's DH.121 plane over a rival group formed between Hawker Siddeley and Bristol, but subsequent specification changes by BEA caused de Havilland economic difficulties. It was then taken over along with its 15,000 employees by the Hawker Siddeley group, at which point Sir Geoffrey de Havilland retired.

De Havilland's DH.121 design was then released by Hawker Siddeley in 1962 as the Trident, the first three-engined jet airliner and the first to be capable of making a blind weather landing while carrying passengers. However, the design was modified to be smaller to fit the needs of its main client, British European Airways, which made it expensive for the com-pany, delayed in its offering and less attractive to other airlines. They turned instead to the Boeing 727 with a similar three jet layout. Hawker Siddeley released the medium-range corporate jet DH.125 in the same year, but it was the last type to be given the de Havilland brand name and it then disap-peared from the British aircraft industry in 1963. Canadian and Australian subsidiaries worked on for a period as De Havilland enterprises but came to be owned by Bombardier and Boeing respectively.

In 1977, following the Aircraft and Shipbuilding Industries Act, Hawker Siddeley, Scottish Aviation and BAC were amalgamated. BAC was itself formed in 1960 from an amalgamation of English Electric Aviation, Vickers-Armstrongs, the Bristol Aeroplane Company and Hunting. BAC produced planes such as the VC10 (still to this day the fastest subsonic passenger jet to cross the Atlantic) and the 1-11. It also produced the Concorde, drawing heavily on de Havilland's wing design expertise to create a passenger plane capable of flying supersonic at over 1,300mph. For those too young to have seen Concorde, and thus lucky not to have lived near its flight path, the only way to experience the feeling of seeing that most majestic of planes might be to imagine a swan landing amid ubiquitous and utilitarian pigeons. It seems likely that BAC also drew on de Havilland rocketry expertise in the development of Rapier, Sea Skua and Sea Wolf guided weapons and subsequent control subsystems for Intelsat satellites. The newly nationalised company was known at the time as British Aerospace but would become known as BAe. Many designs started by de Havilland came into production as part of the new consortium, including the BAe 146 and the BAe 125 business jets. Some 1,600 125s were built between 1962 and 2013.

British Aerospace was denationalised as a public limited company in 1981 and diversified into a number of other industries through acquisitions such as Royal Ordnance, Heckler & Koch, Rover Group cars, Arlington Securities property and Hutchison Telecommunications. It formed a number of alliances that saw it become involved in anti-aircraft missiles and fighter plane dynamics. The company would produce Tornado fighters, Hawk trainers, Rapier missiles, aircraft carriers, submarines and the Typhoon as part of the European-wide Eurofighter consortium, all drawing on the in-house knowledge of transonic flight, compressibility, vibration and metal fatigue. A merger with the German DASA group, however, was cancelled at the last moment in favour of purchasing GEC's Marconi Electronic Systems defence business, with the amalgamated company known from then on as BAE Systems. DASA instead merged with the French Aerospatiale Matra and later Spanish CASA to form the

European Aeronautic Defence and Space Company (EADS) in 2000, and now owns an 80 per cent share of Airbus.

British Aerospace struggled in the 1990s as property and airline industries went into recession, while government defence spending went under review. Rover car sales dropped by around a fifth and in 1991 the company's share price dipped below 100p for the first time. It issued a profits warning and then bungled a rights issue intended to raise more cash.[5] It restructured in 1992 and laid off 47 per cent of its workforce, with two-thirds of these coming from its newly evolved BAe 146 (later known as the Avro RJ series) production. It also wrote off £1 billion in assets, which was the largest in UK corporate history. A fire sale followed, seeing Rover Group sold to BMW and its business jets portfolio sold to US company Raytheon. Arlington Securities, space systems and communications subsidiaries were also sold off. In 2006, BAe withdrew and sold its Airbus shares, and although UK production facilities continued to make wings, its ownership was transferred to the Airbus group. At this point, all UK involvement in civil airliner production ceased.

Geoffrey de Havilland had been in the flight business for over fifty years. In fact, his cousin, the actress Olivia de Havilland, made headlines in 2018 with a defamation court case so that the two de Havillands would be headline news spanning an entire century. In that time, Croydon Airport would come and go as Britain's premier airport, Brooklands would come and go as the epicentre of British aircraft development, and de Havilland's Hatfield site would shine brightly before fading and becoming a part of the University of Hertfordshire campus. But how it had shined. The de Havilland company had produced the fastest-ever propeller-driven plane, the first successful jet engine, the first civil jet airliner and designed the first non-specialist plane thought to have broken the sound barrier. The company produced 46,000 aircraft and its propeller and warplane designs were crucial in the defeat of Nazism.

Unlike some of the other British companies that failed, de Havilland had not overstretched itself with doomed mergers and acquisitions policies, or sought to diversify into unrelated markets, or appeared to have made any catastrophic business decisions. Circumstances seemed, however, to conspire against the company. It could have been very different. They could still have prospered with the Albatross and Flamingo planes, which were very much ahead of their times, and might have evolved into a British Boeing had the Second World War not intervened. Had the Gnome engine been better resourced and developed more quickly a De Havilland engine company may still have been operating today alongside Rolls-Royce. If the Blue Streak project had come good then it may have morphed into a true aerospace company. If BOAC had ordered thirty instead of twenty Comet 5s then maybe the company would still be here operating as British Airbus. It was, however, hard after the war for one company alone to achieve the level of development the industry now required, and the company lacked the scale of investment it needed.

Things might still have been different for the company too if the Comet 1 had worked from the outset or, it has been suggested, if subsequent Comet designs had been given a different name in order to shake off the stigma attached to the Comet 1. The delays in finding the design fault caused by the unknown phenomena of fatigue allowed better planes from overseas competitors to catch up and surpass the Comet. What helped other countries catch up was the decision de Havilland made to release to the world the results of the Comet crash investigation findings. The understanding of fatigue was made known to the world on humanitarian grounds rather than economic ones. This followed on from the earlier decision of the British government to cancel the Miles M.52 turbojet aircraft and then to pass the secrets of the variable tail to the US, allowing the Americans to become the first to break the sound barrier with the Bell X-1. Miles would go bankrupt shortly after, then limp on in various subsidiary forms. It is also widely reported that de Havilland revealed its DH.121 design to Boeing looking for collaboration, in conversations that were short and went nowhere. The DH.121 would emerge later as the Trident, but Boeing would shortly after produce the 727-100, which was very similar to the Trident. Trident production would, however, only amount to 117 planes while the 727 would sell 1,800 and allow Boeing to follow up with the 737, which would go on to become the best-selling airliner of all time with over 10,000 sold – more than six times that of its more famous 747 jumbo jet colleague.[6]

There were many legacies deriving from de Havilland, not least for British Aerospace and Airbus. Dan-Air, for example, purchased second-hand many of the existing Comet 4s and their low-cost operations helped to develop the package holiday industry. The RAF operated the Comet-derived Nimrod patrol aircraft, which was in service until 2011. Rolls-Royce inherited de Havilland's engine technology and test equipment from its propeller division. The Blue Streak formed the first stage of the Europa rocket with a consortium of European partners known as ELDO (European Launcher Development Organisation). Failures, however, in the French elements of the rocket led to cancellation of the project in 1973, with Blue Streak dying as well. The ELDO Europa consortium would tie up with the European Space Research Organisation to form the European Space Agency. Britain contributed about one-third of the investment that France and Germany would each both make.

10

Imperial Chemical Industries

Imperial Chemical Industries, better known as ICI, would, from its conception, be a firm fixture within the top British companies in the Financial Times Share indices and would for many years be the largest manufacturing company in Britain and Britain's biggest exporter.

Prior to 1926, Britain had chemical expertise in a number of small companies that specialised in fertilisers, large-scale and specialised chemicals for industrial and agricultural sectors, polymers and specialist materials, paints and explosives. These companies included the Brunner Mond Company, which started in 1873 and specialised in soda ash, soap, fat and TNT. In 1888, Ludwig Mond, surprised that nickel valves he manufactured were being attacked by carbon dioxide in the manufacturing process, discovered that nickel and carbon monoxide reacted to form nickel powder. It stood against chemical convention by showing that a metal could behave as a gas, and led to a cheap method for producing nickel – a key component of the newly emerging 'stainless' steel. The United Alkali Company was formed in 1890 from the merger of forty-eight small chemical companies based largely across the northern part of Britain. The consolidated company also specialised in soda ash production for the glass, textile, soap and paper industries. British Dyestuffs Corporation Ltd formed in 1919 from the merger of British Dyes Ltd and Levinstein Ltd, producing, as the name suggests, a range of dyes. Nobel Explosives began life in 1870 when Scottish industrialists found the £24,000 needed to set up a factory to exploit the invention of dynamite by Swedish innovator Alfred Nobel. The company would amalgamate with Kynoch, Nobel Industries and Eley Brothers to produce gelignite, guncotton and cordite, and employ 13,000 people.

Even though these companies were large and represented an increasingly consolidated group of British chemical companies, the fragmented nature of the industry still made it difficult to compete against even larger overseas concerns, which included the American DuPont and German IG Farben. British dye companies, for example, had grown since the discovery of the synthetic dye mauveine by the scientist William Perkins in 1856 but were surpassed from 1875 onwards by the German dye industry. The German companies formed dye cartels with both economic and resource advantages over the small, independent British producers, invested more in research and development and provided better technical support to clients at a point where most British companies simply mailed out information circulars. In 1926 therefore, these four leading British chemical companies merged to form one large company known as Imperial Chemical Industries (ICI) with a deal struck aboard the *Aquitania* during a transatlantic voyage. The Brunner Mond Soda Ash business, for example, would become ICI's Soda Ash Products (Group), and grow through mergers and acquisitions, and several name changes, to become one of the company's most successful divisions and a global leader. The Nobel Explosives company would continue as ICI Nobel and its roundel emblem of a blue circle containing wavy white lines provided ICI with its iconic logo.

ICI would hence, from its start, be a large concern with 33,000 employees operating from plants spread out across the country at locations including Stockton-on-Tees, Cleveland, Blackley, Runcorn and Winnington. In its first year of operation it produced a turnover of £27 million and pre-tax profits of £4.5 million, which was impressive given the prevalent global depression. It mainly made chemicals, explosives, fertilisers, insecticides, dyestuffs, non-ferrous metals and paints, but it would have some side industries, including Sunbeam motorcycles, which it inherited at its formation. It was therefore ideally placed to research and exploit the increasing scientific development in the understanding of chemistry, and particularly the emerging science of polymers. The company even has a claim to have coined the term 'plastic' for polymers, and it certainly helped to pave the foundations for the development of the plastics industry. In 1933 it discovered a way of synthesising polythene, a polymer made of long chains of ethene molecules now used in items from food wrapping and film to moulded plastic items and squeezable bottles. It also developed Polymethyl methacrylate (PMMA), which is better known as acrylic or by ICI's own brand name of Perspex in the 1930s. Acrylic was used in car and aircraft windscreens and would develop widespread uses, including furniture and signs. During the Second World War, surgeons removing shattered aircraft windscreens from the faces of pilots found that the acrylic splinters had not reacted with the eyes, which would lead subsequently to the development of contact lenses.

Over the next decades, the company continued to generate ground-breaking and innovative products including polyester fibre, Phthalocyanine, alkyd-based paints (better known by the ICI/DuPont named of Dulux), colour photographic film (with Ilford), polyethylene, polyethylene terephthalate (Terylene), Crimplene, diphenylmethane diisocyanate (MDI, an ingredient used in the manufacture of polyurethane foam used, for example, in refrigerator insulation), the high-performance polymer PEEK, the anti-malarial drug Paludrine, halothane anaesthetic agent, the herbicide qualities of Paraquat, Fluothane (a replacement for chloroform and ether that became the most commonly used anaesthetic in the Western world), the beta-blockers Inderal and Tenormin (which would be a bestseller in the world), Tamoxifen (a drug used in the treatment of breast cancer) and Quorn (produced with RHM). It is easy to skip over these developments but any of them are deserving of having their own story told. Most people will recognise acrylic, Paludrine and Dulux paint but how many understand the complex technologies behind them. Dulux paint, for example, well known from its advertisements with an Dulux Old English Sheepdog, are alkyd based. Alkyds are polyesters that are modified through fatty acids that tend to form flexible coatings – ideal for paint. The fatty acids can be produced from low-cost, sustainable sources, making the paint mix less dependent on oil, and can be modified to dry quickly or to have varied flow properties known as thixotropy.

In the 1940s, ICI obtained a licence to manufacture nylon fibre, which it exploited through the establishment of a joint venture called British Nylon Spinners with Courtaulds. In the late 1960s and '70s, it undertook a further series of mergers and acquisitions, which was standard business practice at the time. It failed in its bid to take over Courtaulds but instead acquired the British Nylon Spinners joint venture that the two companies shared. It also expanded its fabric interests by taking over Viyella. This was originally a twill weave of merino wool and cotton that was developed in 1893 and credited as being 'unshrinkable' and the first branded fabric in the world. Over the years, the Viyella name had developed into a business entity that covered a range of fabrics and by the 1960s operated forty factories across the north of the UK. ICI Fibres then became the third largest fibre group in the world.

ICI's purchase of the US Glidden company also made it one of the largest paint companies in the world. It also took over Atlas Chemical Industries, Beatrice Chemical Division and Glidden Coatings & Resins and proceeded to develop further polymers. One of these was the Polyether ether ketone known as PEEK, another ingenious but easily overlooked innovation. PEEK is a colourless, organic, semi-crystalline thermoplastic polymer with a tensile strength of around 100 N/mm^2, making it typically 100 times stronger than the polypropylene which might be used in a standard kettle and around half as strong as aluminium or a third as strong as basic steel. It has a much lower density aluminium or steel, making it ideal as a replacement for metal where strong but lightweight parts are required, such as in aerospace. It is also highly mouldable, configurable by varying its production temperatures and pressures, strongly resistant to acids, alkalis, oil, alcohol and hydrocarbons and highly resistant to temperatures. It can operate happily at 250°C, which is unusual for a polymer (plastic) material. It also has a strong resistance to the shedding of particles under pressure ('off gassing'), which makes it suitable for applications in medical imaging or the manufacture of modern technology products such as plasma screens or mobile phones that require ultra-high vacuum conditions to avoid contamination.

In 1984, ICI became the first British company to achieve £1 billion in annual pre-tax profits, a figure it repeated several times during the next decade, reaching £1.5 billion in 1989. Even up to the late twenty-first century, it remained a worldwide force, employing more than 130,000 people and boasting at its peak a market capitalisation of £11 billion. For eighty years then, ICI had been a highly respected, world-leading company at the forefront of British industry and even playing a role in the early investigation of nuclear weapons. By the start of the 1990s, however, the company fortunes were starting to look less unassailable. The first cracks appeared when ICI was subject to a takeover bid by Lord Hanson. James Hanson and his company Hanson Trust had become experts at spotting and making offers on underperforming businesses, which were then turned around or asset stripped as necessary. His large portfolio of companies included corporate stalwarts such as Ever Ready batteries and Imperial, and his bid for ICI triggered an intensive battle. He considered that ICI was just too big, and that its values of duty to the country betrayed its economic requirement to evolve. More competitors were starting to take a toll on sales, and some of these were benefitting from an emerging European community.

Although the bid was unsuccessful, ICI initiated a standard business response to a takeover by divesting non-core businesses. It also accorded with the changing strategic view that companies should focus on their core business. That core was to be led by a belief in the need to rely less on low-value bulk chemicals and to obtain more growth and bigger profit margins from higher-value products further up the supply chain – particularly paints and speciality chemicals. The soda ash business was therefore divested in 1986, agricultural and merchandising were sold off in 1991, nylon interests were sold to DuPont in 1992, and in 1993 the management of the PEEK polymer division would buy the division out from ICI and set up as Victrex. Also in 1993, pharmaceuticals and biological products were transferred to an independent business called Zeneca and Syngenta.

Acquisitions for the newer high-value targets followed these divestments. Under the lead of former Unilever director Charles Miller Smith, who took over ICI in 1994, a rare CEO appointment from outside ICI, the company started to buy out a number of businesses, some of which were former Unilever concerns: National Starch & Chemical, Quest International, Unichema, Crosfield, Rutz & Huber. It then proceeded to divest itself fully of its traditional chemical businesses in order to reshape and recoup its acquisition debts. Bulk chemical interests were sold off, including polyester interests to DuPont. Crosfield catalysts and silica products were sold off at a loss to the US company W.R. Grace. Viyella material was ended and its production mill in Barrowford, Lancashire, was demolished in 1999. Diisocyanate, advanced materials, speciality chemicals and titanium oxide businesses were sold off. The last bulk of ICI's industrial chemical business sell-offs was to Ineos in 2000, while ICI Nobel – which had diversified less successfully into nylon and nitric acid in the 1960s and was later known as Nobel Enterprises – was sold to Inabata in 2002.

From now on, though, the company started to struggle. Question marks would be made against the decision to move the company away from its traditional competencies. Perhaps it had simply moved too late, or too fast. Over a five- to ten-year period, it had conducted more than fifty separate deals and was unwieldy with new sectors that were difficult to integrate. Perhaps it simply paid the price for overvaluing its acquisitions, which cost the company around £6 billion, including the £4.9 billion purchase of Unilever's speciality chemicals. The performance of its Quest and National Starch business, acquired in the Unilever deal, for example, was extremely poor. The company was left with £4 billion of debt and particularly high levels of debt to equity (the levels of borrowing to the value of the business referred to as gearing or leverage).

In 2001 it had to cut its dividend by 50 per cent. The following year it raised £800 million in a rights issue and had to cut the dividend again after rating agencies threatened to downgrade its rating to junk status. In 2003 it was forced to issue a profits warning that wiped 40 per cent off the value of its shares, putting its position in the FTSE 100 at risk. With high debts and underperforming business units, the company attempted to cost cut and restructure.[1] The flavour, fragrance and oil- and fat-based (oleochemical) businesses were sold off in 2006 for £1.2 billion, leaving it centred on the paint, starch and adhesives division. This was, though, a shadow of the former ICI, and despite potential pension liabilities of £9 billion, ICI was quickly subject to a takeover bid and was eventually bought by Dutch firm AkzoNobel for £8 billion, who only maintained the Dulux paint brand.

Although the ICI name disappeared in 2008, many of the technologies that ICI developed along with the factories and in many cases the employees are thriving in Britain under different ownership. The divested soda ash division was merged and acquired more growth, until it was bought by Tata Chemicals in 2006 and rebranded as Tata Chemicals Europe in 2011. Victrex is now a business specialising in supply and application of high-performance polymers based around supplying PEEK to industry. Some 7,000 million tons of PEEK-type polymers are produced in the UK per annum, supplying parts for over 15,000 aircraft, 200 million cars, 1 billion smartphones and over 9 million medical implants. Nobel Enterprises was sold to Inabata in 2002 and then to the Chemring group in 2005 to become Chemring Energetics UK Ltd, employing 300 people on the Ardeer site in Ayrshire. The Viyella business name and assets underwent a series of name changes centring on the Coats brand name, undergoing a series of owners, including the Austin Reed retailer. The Nobel Industries roots of ICI, specialists in metallurgy including titanium and uranium processing, ammunition and explosives, would be known in the 1950s as ICI Metals and merged with Yorkshire Imperial Metals. Their name changed in 1962 to Imperial Metal Industries, or IMI. IMI became fully independent in 1978 and proceeded to divest smelting and founding operations, vending and business analysis sections to become a specialist fluid control engineering company now based near Birmingham and employing around 10,000 people.

Ineos had been an initial management buyout of BP's chemical division and the devolved company grew through further acquisitions of BPs ethylene oxide and glycol businesses and from the purchase of commodity chemical interests from BASF as well as ICI. It bought the remainders of ICI's industrial chemical business sell-offs in 2000 for £300 million, and acquired one of Britain's oldest refineries at Grangemouth (and birthplace in 1851 of shale oil refining), along with the North Sea's most important oil and gas pipeline system, providing an integrated business producing fuels and chemicals used for plastic manufacture. By 2017, the company could show profits of around £4 billion on revenues of £40 billion with 17,000 employees, making it Britain's largest privately owned company. Ineos owner Sir James Ratcliffe claimed part of his success was due to the inability of companies like ICI to correctly value their businesses, which were under pressure or 'unloved'.[2]

The agribusiness Syngenta was formed from the merger of Zeneca's agro-chemicals with the agribusiness of Novartis and subject more recently to acquisition by the Chinese state-owned ChemChina business. The company is a world leader in crop-spraying chemicals (and still the largest producer of Paraquat) and employs around 2,000 staff in the UK, around 800 of which are based in the former ICI facility in Berkshire. The Zeneca business itself, spun off from ICI, merged with Astra in 1999 to form AstraZeneca, which was in the top eleven of world drug-producing companies, employing over 4,000 staff in sites in the UK and Sweden. Some 38,000 British jobs are now dependent on AstraZeneca, including 11,500 within the company producing around £440 million of manufacturing output. Its R & D facilities are still in the laboratory complex in Cheshire set up by ICI and receiving around £750 million of research funding (accounting for 5 per cent of research and development spending by UK-based companies). Some of this research work has been pivotal in tackling the Covid-19 pandemic that paralysed the world in 2020.

A 100-ton floating crane by Armstrong, Mitchell and Company built in 1886 using the hydraulic system that made Armstrong's fortune and enabled British industry to haul its industrial trade with ease. (© BAE SYSTEMS, courtesy BAE Systems plc)

Battleships were ironclad warships that symbolised military power in the late nineteenth century, and led to an arms race, particularly between Britain and Germany. This is an example of an early battleship from the Armstrong Elswick works, which stretched for a mile along the banks of the River Tyne. It is seen here manoeuvring past the Newcastle Swing Bridge, which is itself powered by Armstrong hydraulics. (© BAE SYSTEMS, courtesy BAE Systems plc)

Vickers was formed in Sheffield in 1828 and expanded to become a great British industrial company. Seen here is the Barrow Ironworks in 1890, which the company acquired following its takeover of the Barrow Shipbuilding Company in 1897. This moved the company from making ship components into ships themselves, as well as machine guns. Aspects of Vickers have survived in parts of other companies through takeovers, but the Vickers name disappeared completely in 2004, while the last original Vickers factory closed in 2013. (© BAE SYSTEMS, courtesy BAE Systems plc)

Three Vickers VC10 airliners in production at the factory site in Brooklands, Surrey, birthplace of British motor racing and aviation. Cramped and dispersed production has regularly hampered industrial production, which continues today to be less efficient than equivalent overseas competitors. (© BAE SYSTEMS, courtesy BAE Systems plc)

Vickers built Britain's first submarine, *Holland 1*, at the Barrow-in-Furness works in 1901. Britain's first nuclear-powered submarine, built by Vickers Armstrongs, was launched in 1960. The reactor design resulted from the 1958 US–UK Mutual Defence Agreement, similar to the 2021 AUKUS agreement enabling Australian submarines with nuclear power technology. (© BAE SYSTEMS, courtesy BAE Systems plc)

The light aircraft carrier HMS *Invincible* was built by Vickers Shipbuilding Ltd at Barrow-in-Furness and launched in 1977. The company subsequently morphed through a series of name and ownership changes until becoming a part of BAE. In 2017 BAE Systems launched two Queen Elizabeth-class carriers, as part of a joint venture that included the British company Babcock International and French multinational Thales Group. (© BAE SYSTEMS, courtesy BAE Systems plc)

De Havilland's DH.108 was developed in 1945, but would still turn heads if it was seen in the sky today. The design revealed much about the principles of transonic flight, enabling future aircraft to break the speed of sound, but this came at some cost to the company's reputation and fortunes. (© BAE SYSTEMS, courtesy BAE Systems plc)

The Comet was the world's first jet-engined passenger aircraft, first flying in 1949. This example is registered F-BGNX and seen in 1953. The Comet revealed much to the world about fatigue failures and testing methods, but again at the reputational expense of de Havilland and British aviation generally. (© BAE SYSTEMS, courtesy BAE Systems plc)

The long-range Blue Streak ballistic missile, seen here on its test stand at de Havilland's Hatfield test site. The push for rocketry and space development was, however, a step too far for the company and post-war Britain. (© BAE SYSTEMS, courtesy BAE Systems plc)

View from the Shard of the now urbanised former London Docklands, which originally spread into the distance down the Thames and included Surrey Commercial Docks to the south side and West and East India, Victoria and Royal Albert Docks to the north. Canary Wharf has grown out of the Isle of Dogs site of Millwall, Limehouse and Poplar Docks as a commercial services sector that helps the economy but does not replace the scale of trade that preceded it. (© Author)

The River Wandle rises near Croydon and runs through south London to disgorge into the Thames at Wandsworth. The fast-flowing river provided power for milling grain noted in Norman times, and the copious amounts of water were ideal for the action of dyeing and bleaching cloth. During the Middle Ages and beyond, the river had around 100 mills along 10 miles of banks and was described as 'the hardest-working river in the world', with a cotton industry thriving long before the Lancashire industry was established. Fabrics for Liberty of London were made here, and socialist thinker William Morris established his factory here, striving to provide crafted beauty to all in the face of mass-produced artefacts. By the end of the twentieth century, after 1,000 years of industry, the mills and even Britain's longest-running continuous production brewery, Young and Co. in Wandsworth, were gone.

11

International Computers Ltd

International Computers Ltd (ICL), was never one of the great British companies, nor even a name that may be known by many people today. However, it emerged from a raft of outstanding British innovation in computing and was the flagship of British enterprise.

Counting is simply not an intrinsic, regular phenomenon for animals, including humans, and the first evidence of human counting only dates back to 50,000 years ago. This is a mere drop in the ocean compared to our evolution, and even the records of our earliest tools appeared over 2 million years ago. To help with this most unnatural of processes, people developed a range of helpful tools, from notches and tally sticks through to the abstract concept of numbers themselves by the Mesopotamians 5,000 years ago. Subsequent abacuses and medieval counting machines have helped to give numbers and calculation a rich history of innovation, but it is the development of the computer that has transformed counting so massively in our world today.

A computer is a device that can act upon information and produce results and outputs according to a variable set of instructions, and many people consider that the first modern example of this was the mechanical, analytical engine designed by the Englishman Charles Babbage.[1] Although only partially complete, Babbage's machines built from 1822 onwards included separate data and programme memories, instruction-based operations, conditional actions and separate input and output functions much as a computer today has. The English mathematician Ada Lovelace developed an algorithm for Babbage's design to calculate Bernoulli numbers (a sequence of rational numbers in number theory) for which she would receive credit as the first computer programmer.

Elsewhere and later, Joseph-Marie Jacquard developed a system for programming the weave pattern into a loom using punched cards, which laid the foundations for inputting information into early computers. In the UK, the (later named) Powers-Samas company adopted the punched card principle to input data into a mechanically operated machine. In 1880, the American Herman Hollerith used the punched card approach for inputting US census data into an electromechanical tabulating machine, which is from where the Industrial Business Machines (IBM) company would evolve. In 1902, The Tabulator Ltd Company obtained the licence rights to sell Hollerith's machines in Britain. It had, though, agreed to a very bad agreement that required it to pay a 25 per cent royalty to Hollerith even for its own technical developments, which from 1920 right up as far as 1948 restricted the company's profitability when it started to manufacture its own devices as the British Tabulating Machine Company.

Other advances in electronics at the turn of the century were, well, electric. The General Post Office, for example, started to use electronics in its telecom exchanges as an alternative to electromechanical signal processing, while an increasing number of mechanical counting and data processing devices started turning to electronics instead of punched cards. The British Bell Punch Company founded in 1878 to make ticketing machines, later produced the ANITA, the world's first all-electronic desktop calculator, and one of the first pocket calculators, and it became the largest calculator supplier in Britain.

Running alongside the development of electronic calculating devices was a growing development in analytical computers. These use constantly changing elements as inputs and outputs rather than the discrete on-off signalling of digital or electronic computers. Typically this might be used for tide prediction, wind measurement or even bomb sight aiming, and their development culminated in the ENIAC machine built at the University of Pennsylvania in 1946. While these were useful and clever, it was evident to most people that discrete and digital computing would be the way ahead and it was, therefore, only time before developers would merge the usefulness of the analogue computer with the advancing world of electronic calculators.

The principles of this confluence were described by the British scientist Alan Turing in 1936 in a seminal paper on computer theory. Turing also enacted his ideas, firstly in the development of the code-breaking, programmable Bombe machine and then the Colossus computer at Bletchley Park, supported by engineers from the British Tabulating Machine Company, the Post Office and the National Cash Register Company (NCR). He then worked with NCR to produce the N530, then with the National Physical Laboratory to produce the ACE stored programme machine, and finally with Manchester Computers at the University of Manchester. From 1947 onwards the Manchester team developed a number of computer innovations: SSEM (or 'baby'), which was the world's first 'Turing complete' computer and included a stored memory function (something the US ENIAC machine did not have), the first transistorised computer, and the world's fastest computer in 1962. The Manchester Mark 1 was produced by the British electronics company Ferranti as the world's first commercially available, general-purpose computer. A whole series of machines were subsequently developed between the Manchester and Ferranti partners, including the MUSE and ATLAS, which were the world's biggest and first supercomputers. Elsewhere, British scientist Maurice Wilkes, working at Cambridge University, produced the world's second computer with a stored memory function known as EDSAC, and he also developed the microprogramming of firmware that would simplify central processing unit (CPU) development.

Despite these developments, these early machines were big in size, small in power, prone to fail and expensive to produce, which is why in 1943 the president of IBM, Thomas Watson, is famously reputed to have said, 'I think there is a world market for maybe five computers.' Even in 1951, Cambridge computing Professor Douglas Hartree advised Ferranti salesman Vivian Bowden that, 'We have a digital computer here at Cambridge; there is one at Manchester and one at the NPL. I suppose there ought to be one more in Scotland, but that's about it.' Yet in 1951 the innovative British catering company J. Lyons & Company (Lyons) took the risk of installing and operating one. They established the world's first business computer, which was a development of the Cambridge University EDSAC prototype and known as the Lyons Electronic Office (LEO). Lyons in time used LEO to run the stock systems and to do payroll calculations for other companies, including Ford Cars. The Meteorological Office then bought its own LEO machine. Lyons and the Meteorological office helped to clearly establish the potential for computers in business, and the stage was now set for the transformation of the world through computers.

British organisations were poised to play a pioneering step in the commercialisation of this new world. Ferranti and Manchester University installed Britain's first computer for the Ministry of Supply. A long-established instrumentation company called Elliott Brothers, with a track record in telegraphy, had started researching immediately after the Second World War and produced the Elliott 542 computer in 1950. It installed Britain's second computer, the Elliott 401, in 1953. In 1952, Ministry of Defence scientist Geoffrey Dummer conceived and presented the idea for the integrated circuit. In 1955, the National Physical Laboratory (NPL) produced the world's first fully transistorised computer, working closely with the English Electric Company. The engineering firm Metropolitan-Vickers adopted the transistor design to produce six of its own fully transistorised Metrovick 950 computers. The British Tabulating Machine Company (BTM) produced 100 or so of its HEC machines during the 1950s.

IBM was, however, beginning to dominate the market, having produced the first mass-produced computer, the 650, followed by the first fully integrated, vacuum tubeless computer, the 1401, underpinned in due course by the System/360 architecture. This led to consolidations within the British industry. BTM merged with its rival Powers-Samas in 1959 to become International Computers and Tabulators (ICT), which added the computer division of Ferranti four years later and absorbed the computer division of Elliott Brothers to start to export a range of ICT-branded computers around the world. Meanwhile, the LEO team at Lyons were spun off from the catering business to build computers for other companies but merged and then were subsumed into English Electric as English Electric Computers. The British Post Office placed with English Electric Computers Europe's largest-ever computer order for LEO computers at its sites around the country. English Electric Computers, however, then merged the division again with Marconi to form English Electric Leo Marconi. Under the direction of Harold Wilson's new Ministry of Technology and the government's Industrial Expansion Act (1968,) the two leading combinations of English Electric and ICT were merged in 1968 to form International Computers Ltd (ICL), with the aim once again to consolidate a fragmented industry so that it was big enough to take on the world. ICL was second only in size to IBM.

ICL, therefore, brought together all of the main British computing expertise into one business that was part-owned by Plessey, English Electric, ICT and the government. ICL's starting position was with computers such as the English Electric System 4 and the ICT 1900 series, which were large, mainframe computers similar to the LEO machines. Some of these were compatible with the IBM standards, which enabled compatibility across peripherals, hardware and software, although some were not. A delay in ICL's creation coincided with an economic downturn, which meant a reduction in government financial input. However, the company still decided to abolish the IBM compatible/reliant System 4 technology and produce its own. The decision was then made not to develop further machines from its now disparate computer range but to start afresh, drawing on the experience and ideas of its computer base. Nineteen ICL engineers then became involved in the next Manchester computing machine, the MU5, supported by a significant research council grant that enabled the university to operate its own team of sixteen staff and twenty-five research students.

The 2900 series was delivered two years late in 1974 but was a relatively successful machine, and sales of the 2900 series and its small business systems 2903 were good throughout the 1970s. It also achieved good sales of its System Ten Point of Sale (POS) equipment, which it acquired from a takeover of the Singer sewing machines computing division (Singer Business Machines). Through these activities, the company achieved an initial annual growth of 20 per cent. The problem for ICL, however, was that it specialised in expensive and large machines, which had a limited customer base, and it tended to rely on large contracts from the public sector such as the Post Office, Inland Revenue, Department for Work and Pensions and the Ministry of Defence. The downturn in the economy in the 1970s arising from the oil crisis led to a downturn in government orders.

Another economic downturn in the 1980s caned sales through lower orders and poor exchange rates.

The company needed a £40 million government loan in order to continue its R & D work, as it was struggling with the rising costs of software and semi-conductors that it needed to compete, and it started to finance its operations through divestment of non-core activities and to market a range of Japanese Fujitsu-made mini computers. To make matters worse, ICL was also starting to face an increasing number of competitors who were finding their own niches in the computer world and who were able to produce more and more innovations through ongoing research. This included eight US companies such as Univac (which eventually morphed into Unisys), GE and Honeywell, but the list was headed by now by the far biggest of them all, IBM. Since the 1950s, IBM had been producing smaller and more affordable computers and complete ranges with magnetic tape storage with which they were able to set industry standards and dominate the global market. To put this in perspective, the Metrovick 950 had captured the best aspects of British science in 1956, but the company only produced six computers, which they deployed in-house. IBM's next generation of these types of machine, the 1401, sold more than 10,000 units, or around a third of the world market between 1960 and 1964.

US companies also took forward more quickly and more successfully some of their other scientific advances. In 1958, Jack Kilby at Texas Instruments developed the first integrated circuit (which Britain's Geoffrey Dummer had conceived in 1952), and Intel developed the 4004, the first integrated circuit chip, which enabled a branch of smaller computers unencumbered by wires to be developed. A new breed of US innovators took these developments forward. They were less focused on the more traditional, technology-driven approach of achieving bigger, better, faster and more powerful machines but were engaged instead on making computers more accessible. Based in small university spaces and garages, they began producing simpler, more user-friendly and cheaper computers. These personal computers (PCs) started to come onto the market as kits and included in 1975 the MITS Altair 8800 using a Microsoft basic compiler written by Bill Gates and Paul Allen, and in 1976 the Apple I designed by Steve Jobs and Steve Wozniak. The Apple II, TRS-80, Commodore PET and ZX80 all followed. IBM produced its own

PC in 1981 but its previous agreement to let its PC-DOS be used as an industry standard was starting to allow for widespread, low-cost competition that
was beginning to undercut even IBM. By 1983, there were 10 million PCs,
but these were increasingly from low-cost PC producers such as Dell and
Compaq. As the PC industry grew, so IBM started to defer its leading global
position to Microsoft and Apple and by the early 1990s it was posting an
$8 billion loss – the largest in US history.

While IBM would reform to become a solution rather than hardware
provider, ICL would fail to survive at all. ICL attempted to enter the PC
market, but it was too little and too late. By 1981 it was struggling to compete even in its miniframe market with the IBM 4300 series undercutting its
2900 range and the government was forced to step in to stop a takeover bid
from the US Unisys company. The government provided a loan guarantee
and new Chief Executive Robb Wilmot attempted to lower the cost base
by cancelling work on large-scale integrated circuits and buying in technology from Japan's Fujitsu, although ICL's independence was emphasised to
maintain its credibility. It subsequently produced the Series 39 level 30 and
80 computers.[2]

In 1984 the British company Standard Telephones and Cables (STC)
took over ICL. STC had a long track record of electrical and electronic
innovation, and were pioneers of digital signalling equipment, including
pulse-width methods and the development of fibre optic cables that enabled
the large-scale movement of data. The rationale for this takeover was apparently the expected convergence of computers and telecommunications, but
it was instead followed by a financial crisis at STC itself. STC's attempt
to pioneer 'digital convergence' was at a cost that was too prohibitive for
the company and too far ahead of the market. It ended up instead being
propped up by the flailing ICL company that it had taken over. A planned
ICL flotation never materialised and in the end STC began to sell more and
more of ICL to ICL's former trading partner, Fujitsu. Fujitsu took complete control of the company in 1998 and dropped the ICL brand, while
STC itself was then bought out by Canadian company Nortel.

Britain had pioneered many aspects of computers and the computer
business, and through the work and ideas of Tim Berners-Lee went on to
give the world the idea of the worldwide web. Given Britain's computing

heritage and the conglomeration of expertise, the country might have expected a stronger industry today. That should have happened. In the US, for example, tech companies such as Amazon, Alphabet (owner of Google) and Microsoft, along with Apple, would overtake the country's traditional manufacturing base to become the four largest US public companies, with Facebook, Apple, Amazon, Netflix and Google ('Alphabet') becoming known as the FAANG group.

This was not to be in Britain, however. The British Bell Punch Company – producer of the world's first electronic calculator – sold off its calculator business in 1973 to Rockwell International, who closed it down three years later, while Bell Punch itself was broken up following its takeover by Control Systems and then the Incentive Group in the 1980s. The remaining parts of Elliott Brothers (the parts not absorbed by the ICT company, which would become ICL) produced a number of programming innovations and built semiconductors and control systems but the company – or its employees at least – would eventually be absorbed into a number of other concerns including IBM, Hewlett Packard and the abyss that would become English Electric and GEC. Lyons tea houses gradually declined and the company was acquired by Allied Breweries in 1978 and gradually broken up.

ICL was always Britain's main computer hope and it once employed 24,000 people. It was, though, never able to achieve the commercial success that it might once have promised. However, it was not the only British computing company on the scene. Britain's answer to the home-built PC revolution was the Sinclair Spectrum and BBC Acorn Micro, which were only faintly IBM compatible, if at all. Amstrad and Tiny flared briefly as Britain's low-cost PC manufacturers but, like many early PC producers, succumbed to cheaper competition.

There were legacy benefits that derived from the British tech pioneers, and they would at least have helped to enthuse a generation of computer specialists that support Britain's current computer industry and which still includes pockets of world-class expertise in programming, consulting, and digital technology. The Raspberry Pi enterprise spilling out of Cambridge University's expertise is still helping to enthuse programmers like the BBC Acorn Micro before it. Research Machines, Viglen, and other technology companies have emerged as niche players in the market. ARM semiconductor also emerged from the roots of Cambridge University, Acorn Computers and Apple to become a major supplier of chips in mobile phones and other Internet applications.

Perhaps, though, the finest moment of British computing will remain always in the past, with the knowledge that the Bletchley Park team behind the Colossus may have foreshortened the Second World War and helped, it is said, to have saved the lives of 13 million people, if not large portions of the world, from the spectre of a Nazi ideological dictatorship.

Part Three

Britain's Industrial Decline and Future

12

Looking Back

The corporate biographies presented in the previous chapter described some of the great British industrial companies; how they started, why they might be considered great and why they failed, where failure is defined as either closing down, being taken over, or no longer operating under their own name or ownership. A timeline shows they generally did not fail straight after the Second World War, belying this as the sole cause for industrial collapse. Nor did they generally make it into this century, before China's meteoric industrial rise, belying this too as the root cause problem. Instead, companies failed mostly during a fifty-year period towards the end of the twentieth century.

They collapsed for a whole variety of reasons broadly in line with the reasons that other writers have conferred on Britain's industrial decline:

> Fuddy-duddy management, failure to invest, outdated working practices and head-in-the-sand trade unions … Short-termism in the City and the Treasury; the sterile and destructive cycle of nationalisation and privatisation; poor decision-making by government; inadequate market size at home; an obsession with size; the transfer of jobs to the developing world; takeovers driven by boardroom egos; boardroom disdain for manufacturing as such; the lure of Wall Street; sheer bad luck – and good old-fashioned incompetence.[1]

It is problematic to draw too many additional conclusions from these biographies, which are a small sample drawn from a subjectively random

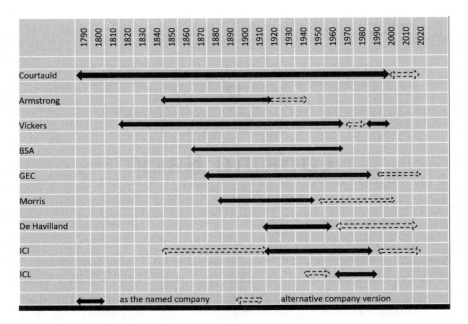

Failure timeline of the British companies described in previous chapters. (© Author)

but potentially biased selection of companies. They are also summaries of complex events around long company histories where the failure mechanisms are also interlinked, so it is also hard to try and identify a single, root cause failure for each corporate collapse. More nuanced insights might come from talking to people who were involved directly in the decision-making or by looking at the more complete and often outstanding corporate biographies that many passionate writers have researched and evaluated. Nevertheless, it is still worth trying to draw some collective conclusions around key points such as strategy, organisation, leadership and innovation in an attempt to induce some broader lessons from which we might learn about both past and future management and industrial directions.

Strategy

The attempts made by ICI and GEC to replace low-value business propositions for higher-value activities look with the benefit of hindsight to have
been strategic mistakes. What makes these seem positively foolhardy is the
fact that the business sold off continued to do so well. GEC's offshoots
have continued to trade well in new hands, while Jim Ratcliffe's Ineos has
become the country's biggest private company with the help of the cast-offs
that ICI considered of low value or loss-making.

What can be said on behalf of this strategic approach is that moving into
new markets to add value can not only work but can be essential as part of
the more modern label of adapting to market conditions and being 'agile'.
Nokia, for example, started as a lowly rubber boot company before evolving into higher-technology mobile phone products. Shell was a company
that sold shells before it moved into oil! High-profile investment company
Berkshire Hathaway started life as a textile producer known as Berkshire
Fine Spinning Associates. Multinational marketing giant WPP started life
as a producer of wire baskets. American Express was a delivery company.
Nintendo was a playing card company.

The difference is that these companies moved into business opportunities
rather than dead ends, sometimes evocatively described as moving into new
'blue ocean' markets as opposed to battling in 'red oceans', which are bathed
in the blood-letting of competitive practice. GEC might have believed
that technology was a market to get into, but they weren't the only ones,
making this an overvalued dead end and not an opportunity at all – if it was
a blue ocean, it was one where the water was draining out fast. They weren't
the only ones making this mistake. British toy giant Tri-ang toyed with the
idea of moving into garden furniture instead of addressing its own internal
problems, but in the end would do neither and it too would go bust. It
can also be said that even today business leaders continue to make errors
of judgement when it comes to adding value, particularly with respect to
growth through mergers and acquisitions.

What business leaders fail to recognise is the complexity and difficulty
of assimilating new business acquisitions and collaborations to form a
cohesive whole. Certainly, Morris, GEC and ICI were guilty of this. In

contrast, companies like Amazon, Costco and Walmart (and even BSA and Armstrong early in their histories) have also shown how to grow organically through internal innovation and investment through retained profit. Unlike the examples given, however, ICI and GEC risked everything, selling all of the family silver in order to buy a bauble of fool's gold. ICI's and GEC's failures then are not necessarily examples of poor strategic choice, but ones that could be considered as due to poor accounting in underestimating the value of their businesses, poor strategy implementation through corporate overambition, errors of judgement and poor risk management.

Organisation

British industrial thinking and culture were forged in the fires and power of the Industrial Revolution; the workshop of the world, a global superpower, the empire leader, and victor in two world wars. The mindset seemed to be that British companies needed to be the biggest and the best as they always had been. Many of the companies described were hence big, leading in size in their field if not across the whole industrial spectrum. Great size is the position that Armstrong and Vickers would find themselves in, and what business leaders of ICI, GEC and Courtaulds would set out to achieve. It was also the position that successive governments would actively seek to achieve through consolidation legislation.

Big can be a persuasive argument where size means economies of scale, power and monopoly situations. It is self-evident today that large companies can thrive as they are in existence today; Exxon Mobil, Apple, Samsung, Siemens, Lenovo, HP, 3M, Johnson & Johnson, Boeing and Proctor & Gamble, for example. Size, however, does not automatically mean efficient and does not insure against failure. The difference with those companies cited is that while they are big, they are also 'lean', being the term today to describe low-cost and efficient business operations. Many British companies had failed from the Third Industrial Revolution onwards to address the need for efficiency, but they failed spectacularly to recognise this need in a world that was so different after the Second World War. The British economy was shattered, resources and finances were minimal and the empire was receding, while the US – far less affected at home by war – with new ideas, new energy and evolved production were powering ahead. British management and British politicians would, however, time a wnd time again, follow policies of enlargement and consolidation in trying to match US economies of scale but without querying the sense in trying to make such comparisons. In Courtaulds' case, its smaller US plants were more efficient because they tended to service fewer but larger customers, allowing them to operate longer and more efficient production runs. In Britain, the opposite was true, with lots of smaller runs to meet the smaller needs of many customers.

Across the English Channel in Europe, the post-war perspective was also very different. France and Germany knew they were shattered. They had also had long histories of strife, including the Thirty Years' War, which was a Proto-world war, but the horrors and enmity of the two twentieth-century conflicts just could not be repeated. It made sense to collaborate, and there had been periods when the regions had collaborated too, going as far back as Charles Martel and Charlemagne. The subsequent European Coal and Steel Community (ECSC) agreement in 1952 between Germany and France enabled investment, economies of scale and collaboration, and laid the groundwork for the European Economic Community (EEC) and the European Union (EU) to follow. Had Britain been a part of the EEC from the outset, perhaps the mindset of the British towards Europe may have been different – and perhaps it would have retained its industry.

At the same time, in Japan, resourcefulness and the emerging 'quality' movement would also enable industry to produce more goods that people actually wanted, that worked efficiently and which were produced cheaply through, for example, the reduction of high-cost stocks and reduced failures through zero defects. This allowed their businesses such as Toyota to flourish at a time when British cars were gaining a reputation for unreliability. For BSA, the Honda Super Cub, released in 1958, was a small motorbike significantly at odds with the power machines that British companies, including BSA, thought the market wanted. The Cub, however, appealed to a much wider audience than the British bikes and would become the most-produced motor vehicle of all time. This customer-focused approach helped Honda, a small company of twelve staff in 1946, grow to become the world's largest motorcycle manufacturer by

1959 and to hammer British bike companies into near non-existence. Had Britain been less inward-looking, it could have been more inclined to look at Japanese business techniques of quality and efficiency instead of hanging on to their diminishing imperial beliefs. As a result, big car companies like BMW, Volkswagen and Toyota remain operational, unlike Morris Motors. In the US, GE would thrive under the leadership of Jack Walsh, while the British GEC crashed despite having similar business portfolios. BASF and DuPont have survived, whereas ICI has not. In other cases, big companies such as General Motors and IBM have struggled, but they are still big and still running – testament to the fact that big might lead to change but not necessarily failure, which was the case in Britain.

There were other signs that, for some of Britain's companies, the notion of size should have been questioned. Courtaulds was also hit by political interventions, including US Lend-Lease requirements and European tariff shenanigans that cut into its profits. For Armstrong and Vickers these difficulties were exacerbated by managing the growth and decline cycles that followed after two world wars, so that their profits could not sustain their everyday running costs. However, many views on enterprise were rooted in Victorian times, with values around patriotism, employment and conservatism rather than the purely cut-throat enterprise of capitalism. Instead of cutting back, British companies elected to diversify to try and remain big. Once again, this might seem a sensible course of action. The notion of spreading risk by not keeping all of your business eggs in one basket had for many years seemed reasonable and, in the past, sustained many of the companies looked at, including Vickers, Armstrong, ICI, GEC, BSA and Courtauld. At the time, this was not an uncommon business practice. The problem was that in the past these companies had less competition, but as competition grew globally these generalist concerns, particularly Vickers and Armstrong, began to look less and less effective. The influential *In Search of Excellence* study into the most successful companies of the 1980s advised companies simply to stick to what they did best, or 'Stick to the Knitting'.[2] The 1980s and '90s would hence see many companies move away from the model of multi-faceted conglomerate to more slimline operations more focused on their specialist areas.

It was, however, too late for some of these British giants. Such large concerns might now be described by business sources and free-market economists as 'dinosaurs' – dumb, slow-moving organisms doomed to fail in a natural survival of the fittest process – and quite likely to fail at the hands of fast-moving, technology-savvy and privately owned organisations that would nowadays be called 'unicorn' businesses. Accusations of dinosaur-ism, though, might seem a bit rich coming from British politicians working for one of the country's oldest, most archaic and inefficient institutions in the museum-like and inadequate parliamentary buildings. Comparing the House of Commons with the German Bundestag would perhaps in an instant help to explain the decline of the country's governance.

Leadership

There are reams of books written about the shortcomings of British management during this period and our corporate biographies pick up a few. It seems likely, for example, that the British Empire engendered an arrogance among home management that was hard to shake off. Writing of his takeover of the Coats textile business, which unlike Courtaulds would survive today as a British-headquartered company, (Lord) David Alliance wrote that the company was managed 'in a patrician and hierarchical way, rather in the mould of the old British colonial system of governors, district officer and agents', and this was in 1986, not 1886.[3] In fact, production at Courtaulds' US business AVC was always more efficient, which was attributed to better attitudes.[4] AVC also introduced concepts of industrial relations management, including notions of motivation and time and motion study, years ahead of its British parent. In Britain, Courtaulds were content to pay workers above the going rate as a policy for keeping workers happy – which it did not.

It seems evident from so many studies that the business leaders failed to recognise or adapt to the skills needed to manage such large enterprises, Armstrongs being a case in point. Again, it must be remembered that many of them were brought up in the dying embers of the Victorian period.

British management – and workers – would fail to recognise the passing of the aristocratic manager and instead embark on bitter relationship battles, while German workers recognised from the outset of the post-war period the need to pull together.

Where there was successful leadership, there is evidence of succession failures at companies like ICI, GEC, Armstrong, Morris and de Havilland, where they failed shortly after changes at the top. In the case of GEC and ICI, new corporate leads were inducted from outside the companies and in both cases from different industrial sectors. Was this sensible? At BSA, leaders took over from the industry sector, but without the passion and drive the company needed. The management failures at BSA were made tacit by the reports made at the time, and by a host of subsequent authors; there were failures in succession and failures to communicate effectively.

By contrast, the Coats Group, which, unlike Courtauld, has survived as a British-headquartered textile business, cites its near 50:50 mix of older and younger senior managers as getting the balance right between experience and zeal. It is not only experience and zeal that counts, however, but the right mix of technical and business acumen. During the successful years, leaders were either technical like Geoffrey de Havilland or William Armstrong, or commercial like H.G. Tetley at Courtaulds or James Leek at BSA. Corporate history shows that some of the best industrial organisations have benefitted from either a leader who was adept at both the technical and the business skills such as William Morris, or which had two leaders, one from each field, capable of working closely together, such as Boulton and Watt. Many of the companies failed when that vital combination of engineering and business failed at the top. One hypothesis sometimes raised is the fact that British engineering companies have been led by accountants, unlike the US where businessmen have ruled or Germany and Japan where engineers rule – and where engineering is seen as a profession, unlike in the UK where it seems to be linked too often to the image of a grubby apprentice mechanic.

Innovation

ICL failed to innovate away from its core mainframe computer business in the face of the possibilities of new, smaller personal computers. It is speculation that the lack of post-war funds hampered the company's and government's ability to sponsor key research, but despite the difficulties the need to innovate was well understood and in fact 3 per cent of Britain's GDP was spent on R & D in the 1960s, with which only the US could compare. It is possible to wonder that if the government and ICL had foreseen the future scale of the technological revolution that was about to happen, they might have chosen to invest in more than the handful of staff that were available at ICL's inception.

Despite this expenditure, it seems likely that the perilous state of corporate and national finances after the Second World War had some impact on investment in research and development that would not have shown up immediately after, but some years later, when new ideas and new products would fail to materialise. University of Cambridge academics cited underinvestment as the key reason for Britain's industrial demise.[5] Similarly, Frank Woollard, in his 1954 book *Principles of Mass and Flow Production*, suggests that efficient, low-waste production – now known as 'lean manufacturing' – was originally introduced at Morris Motors' Coventry plant in 1923 and was pivotal in increasing engine throughput from 300 to 1,200 two years later, while reducing labour and energy costs by 50 per cent. Such developments were however lost in the fog of war. Lean manufacturing expert John Dennis considers the war time emphasis on mass production numbers lost Britain's wider move towards lean manufacturing efficiency (which the Japanese re-discovered twenty years later and implemented to such good effect). For example, Japanese Dr Genichi Taguchi developed an approach to cheaper research known as 'design of experiments', saving Japanese companies time and money in producing products 'right first time'. This approach is, however, also said to be rooted in British statistical techniques used to maximise crop production during the war.

There is also the argument that Britain's technical expertise was also in short supply, with scientists moving away in a brain drain from austere

Britain to the opportunities available in the US. There were at least two British Nobel prizes every year between 1950 and 1984, but from the 1970s onwards, the number of winners started to decline. These shortfalls might help to explain the case at GEC, where research was increasingly scaled back over time. As the major players in electronics and computing, GEC's and ICL's failures meant that the country lost out in the technologies and areas that appeared from the 1960s onwards and which have since become modern industrial sectors: wind turbines, solar panels, batteries, mobile phones, consumer electronics such as microwave ovens, space exploration or rapid prototyping.

The problem with the research that was taking place was also that too often the business leaders could either not see their way to exploit the research ideas realised, or that it was 'the wrong type of research'. British scientist C.P. Snow famously exclaimed in his 1959 Rede Lecture that Britain's social and political rulers were 'natural Luddites' opposed to science. Again and again, too many companies failed to drive through new ideas that would have sustained their business, choosing instead to look for small-scale efficiency gains or to diversify when the going got tough. What would the British car industry be like today if Morris had been allowed to take on the Beetle? Sometimes the science was lost in other ways. In 1961, for example, East German MV motorbike rider Ernst Degner defected to the West, bringing with him two-stroke engine technology that was itself derived from German V1 pulse jet engine research. A Japanese musical instrument company would refocus its production towards motorcycles based on this information, allowing it to grow into the multinational producer of instruments, motorbikes, semiconductors, consumer goods and robots known as Yamaha.

In some cases, British innovation was simply gifted away, including, for example, penicillin and antibiotics, gene discoveries, swept wings, metal fatigue and later the World Wide Web. In the case of the jet engine, the US had discounted turbine as a source of aviation power, but were astounded when gifted a working jet engine developed by Frank Whittle. The decision to do this was partially a need to spread British expertise to the US in case of German aggression, but it gave away massive long-term benefits to US companies GE and Pratt & Whitney. After the war, Britain gave the Russians a Rolls-Royce Nene engine, from which they developed the powerplant for the MiG-15 – one of the most successful fighters and a major threat to the West. The US policy was also to bleed Britain dry, as typified by the comments of the US ambassador to London; 'Great Britain is a goldmine of information of a technical nature which should be worked to the limit.' In other cases, innovations were given away as part of the government's tacit repayment of its Lend-Lease war debts to the US, and many of these were transferred by the British Technical and Scientific Mission, which was better known from its instigator as the Tizard Mission. These include the cavity magnetron. The magnetron formed the basis of radar, which helped the Allies during the war, being used, for example, to find German U-boats, but it also then helped to found the MIT Radiation Lab, which would go on to develop world-leading expertise in electromagnetics, including, for example, ground control approach equipment for the blind landing of aircraft. It was these developments that helped to lead to the demise of Vickers-Armstrongs noted earlier. US company Raytheon would also use the properties of the magnetron to develop the world's first microwave ovens. Other research gifts included the Miles M.52 aircraft with its movable tail design and sound transition theory – which enabled flights faster than the speed of sound – sonar, anti-tank weaponry, rockets, superchargers, gyroscopic gunsights, self-sealing fuel tanks, plastic explosives and nuclear know-how (from the British MAUD Report to the US Manhattan Project).

In our corporate stories, we can also see the other end of the innovation spectrum. De Havilland could hardly have been accused of failing to innovate, but its high-risk, revolutionary rather than incremental approach to innovation was bound to fly too close to the sun and, when a succession of failures like the DH.108 and Comet came along, the company was doomed – and with it went any technical advantages the country could have aspired to with rocketry or missiles. Courtaulds' Tencel development was similarly bold, but took too long in coming and was too expensive.

Government

The government's treatment of pioneers Frank Whittle and Alan Turing was shocking, and was detrimental to Britain's long-term economic development, as was the decision to give away technologies in order to induce the US to join the war. At the time, the mindset (assuming the Allies won the war) was that Britain would return to its empire, would continue to innovate and continue to act as a workshop of the world. That mindset, however, was caught out by the change of US policy towards Germany and Japan after the Second World War, which saw it boosting both countries in order to combat its perceived threat from Russian communism. At the same time, Britain's war debts were becoming increasingly less serviceable by shortages in resources and the decline in its traditional empire markets. US hegemony made it difficult for the British government to meet these international developments, but could it have undertaken more effective actions at home? The tools available for government are, after all, extensive and powerful: using tariffs to raise the price of imported goods; nationalising or privatising core business sectors; financially supporting businesses or not; cajoling through argument or legislation for consolidation; enabling tax breaks and incentives for investment; and introducing training schemes for effective employment and management.

The immediate post-war action of the Labour government was to nationalise many industries: aviation, telephones, railways, utilities, mining and steel. These were, however, already creaking with poor efficiency and management. British train engineers, for example, had been allowed to innovate and strive for the fastest and most powerful machines, which were often classy locomotives, but they were produced in small batches. When the big four train companies of GWR, LMS, LNER and SR were hence nationalised under the 1948 Transport Act, the newly formed British Railways took over a hotch-potch of 448 different types of steam, diesel and electric locomotives, with some dating back to the 1870s.[6] This might be contrasted with the German Deutsche Reichsbahn, which, although (or even because) it was decimated after the First World War with 5,000 trains moved abroad as part of the war reparations, was built under a model of standardisation, allowing trains to be mass-produced efficiently with an emphasis on low cost and easy build and repair instead of power and speed. Britain's highly regarded Class F and West Country Light Pacifics, for example, were produced in numbers of 251 and 40 compared to 7,000 German Class 52 2-10-0s. Nevertheless, even the now nationalised British Railways would continue to make errors, ditching steam trains before their time in a headlong drive for modernisation.

Although railways struggled, and most of the large nationalised bodies struggled irrespective of their nature or industry, it has still been argued that greater consolidation, reorganisation and planning at the same point from the government could, for example, have saved the entire car industry from the slow demise that followed, and which was symptomatic of the entire industrial landscape.[7] The government focus was, however, less on industry and more on dealing with many of the other issues of the day, including austerity, reorganisation, rebuilding Europe and maintaining its global presence in the face of new world orders. In this latter case, with less funding available, it was just not able to provide the aid to other countries that was now being provided by the US, which began to assume the political control and influence it has retained to this day. The British government instead became even more jingoistic after the war than at any other time as it fought to maintain global relevance – wasting 10 per cent of GDP on military spending in the 1950s. Ernest Bevin resigned from his government role at the introduction of costs for false teeth and spectacles, which he viewed were introduced to pay for arms. British impotence in the support of post-war Greece and the Suez crisis of 1956, however, dealt death blows to British esteem and global influence. It has also been argued that with its eye off the industrial ball, the post-war socialist government enabled too much power into the hands of the unions, which would come back later to haunt business.

The Conservative governments of Harold Macmillan (1957–63), Sir Alec Douglas-Home (1963–64) and the Labour government of Harold Wilson (1964–70) seemed even more focused on these political rather than industrial matters. Wilson made a famous 'White Heat' speech that recognised the crucible of innovation as the driver for industry, but it served as a means to differentiate Labour from the older world Tories, and Wilson never followed up with successfully supportive actions. Why this lack of attention?

Probably because industry had, after all, always done its bit for Britain and it was inconceivable that it would collapse, and actually because during this period of the global economic 'Long Boom', the country was growing at an average of 2.9 per cent. The problem, however, was that Germany and France were growing at a much faster rate, and this would become evident when the Long Boom ended with the oil crisis of 1973. The political motivations of the Organisation of Petroleum Exporting Countries (OPEC) saw oil prices rise fourfold, putting immense pressure on manufacturing costs and reducing global demand. Only the efficient businesses in Western economies would survive, and British companies were not that. The government policy of maintaining sterling was also linked to a system of sterling loans that facilitated the trade of British goods for empire resources, but it produced high interest rates and high sterling values that were equally not helpful to industry. By 1976, the government was having to call on the International Monetary Fund for support.

The Bretton Woods system discussed at the beginning of the book also broke apart when the costs of the Vietnam War and trade deficits began to put pressure even on the US dollar. Gold, too, which acted as a buffer control, was becoming insignificant when compared with the rise in global trade. The US broke the link between the dollar and the gold standard and devalued in 1971. As a consequence, the system of fixed exchange rates was replaced by a floating system determined by free-market trading. During the 1970s, this variability led to changing levels of inflation and monetary instability, which hit Britain hard. Over time this floating system and accompanying deregulation have led to an ever-increasing level of financial globalisation with few controls and which has since become unstable and overcome the resources of countries and the institutions capable of helping them. Reform is required – but is not in sight.

As the oil crisis began to reveal the perilous state of the nation, Britain's industrial organisations began to fail and, as the companies were often highly interlinked, as one company failed so it had a domino effect on others. As firms reduced orders, so demand for British steel fell, so the price for steel went up and up went the price of British products. As companies started to go under, they took with them second-tier machinery suppliers and equipment suppliers, which included first-rate businesses in their own right. Lucas Industries, for example, started in the 1860s and in the 1980s was the biggest aircraft and motor components company outside of North America, employing 50,000 people and servicing companies including Morris Motors and de Havilland. As trade declined, it tried to spend its way out of trouble rather than cutting costs and reducing its staff base, but the ongoing nature of the decline made this a doomed policy, and it was taken over at a snip by US company Varity in 1996. (The company later moved overseas and was broken up, with the brand now maintained by a German firm.) Pilkington, founded in 1826, was a pioneer in the production of plate glass and vehicle safety glass, yet it too would succumb to takeover. Other similar stories come from companies such as Beardmore, Doughty, Murex, British Oxygen, Turner & Newall, Pinchin Johnson, Alfred Herbert, Bonas, Coats, Dunlop Rubber, Murex, Rolls-Royce cars, United Steel, Leyland Motors, Swan Hunter, Rexam, Hanson Trust, LucasVarity and Tube Investments. Supporting industries such as toolmakers, parts suppliers, transport and packaging went too – even the sandwich makers that supplied the workers' lunch. The London Docks were closed in 1969, despite the fact that they had been part of the world's busiest port and river for over 200 years.

As policy and empire crumbled, industrial complacency was revealed and the door opened to the new generation of low-cost industrialising economies, including China. China's rise is usually attributed to the economic reforms of Deng Xiaoping, which introduced the concept of the free market to a young and enthusiastic Chinese people. The reforms took place from 1979 onwards, starting initially in a small corner of China known as the Pearl River Delta in Guangdong, which included the cities of Shenzhen, Guangzhou and Dongguan, before spreading. Ironically, GEC and its partner Alstom provided the nuclear power station that helped to transform the region. What is important to note, however, is that the Chinese economy did not start to grow massively until the turn of the century, and many companies failed or were failing long before China took off as an industrial power and for reasons other than China's low-cost sledge-hammering of the market.

As companies failed and unemployment increased, underlying social discord began to ripple through the country. The Conservative government of Edward Heath (1970–74), despite an election promise of less industrial interference, tried to intervene and support failing business through a confusing mix of the National Economic Development Council (NEDC), the Selective Assistance programme or under the 1972 Industry Bill (or its predecessor Science and Technology Act, which it used to prop up ICL). Supported companies were, however, still inefficient even when turned into larger concerns or more worker-friendly labour co-operatives. Heath's government was investing money in companies that were badly run and which simply poured money into extending their lives. They should have put money into companies that offered better futures, or which offered general programmes of reform and improvement. The simultaneous action adopted by companies and government of amalgamating companies to make them bigger was simply piling together badly run organisations that were still – if not more inclined – to fail. The government and its trade department should have invested money into national programmes looking to improve efficiency, improve labour relations, and improve management practice. The Labour governments of Harold Wilson and James Callaghan (1974–79) just seemed entirely unable to cope, particularly as the declining economy led to increasing levels of social unrest. This was not helped by the fact that up to 20 per cent of the leading officials and executive committee members of thirty-four major trade unions were considered by the Secret Service to be communist, with subversive threats.[8]

By 1979, at the point of the Conservative Margaret Thatcher's rise to power, one-third of housing in Britain was owned by local government and the NHS was a fully state-run organisation. Utilities were also state-run, including power stations, the national grid, coal mining, gas supply, water, sewers, refuse collection, telephone systems and the postal service. Publicly owned transport included roads, the majority of the car-making industry, railways including track, trains and train services, airports, air traffic control, British Airways, Rolls-Royce jet engines, aircraft companies, ports, shipbuilding companies, Sealink ferries, and buses. Other government-owned companies included Cable & Wireless, Royal Ordnance, Trustee Savings Bank, Ferranti and most steel companies.

Thatcher was sceptical about this degree of governmental interference. She had seen taxpayer investment of £25 million in the motorbike industry, £50 million in Concorde and around £600 million in the aluminium-smelting industry all fail, with an emerging view that politicians should not 'play God in the marketplace'.[9] She and her economic advisor, Sir Alan Walters, were influenced by the writings of Friedrich Hayek and Milton Friedman, and sought a policy of privatisation of these publicly owned organisations, aiming to reduce their dependency on centralised government control and support, and to break up the unions who were perceived as wielding too much power and enabling over-staffed and inefficient practices. The problem was that Thatcher had not perhaps understood the politics, chaos and foolishness of previous government industrial interventions. If she had, she might have looked towards smarter investments, but instead she went with ideas that were unproven. Hayek's thoughts, for example, were heavily influenced by his proximity to the totalitarian movements of Communist Russia and Nazi Germany. Thatcher applied this ideological thinking wholesale, developing a political dogma referred to as Thatcherism, but without evaluating the pros and cons or more intelligent action for each industrial situation. The position then saw a number of solid companies fold because the government failed to tide them over during a bad patch. Babies were effectively thrown out with the bath water. In some cases, the medicine worked – in others, the patient died. Thatcher only had to look back in history to see the fallacy of this absolutism. During the 1930s, de Havilland pleaded with the British government to help them develop the air passenger industry, but they were refused. They had to watch on while the US and European countries such as Germany and Holland were supporting their industry with subsidies, enabling plane development to catch up with the British. Thatcher's chancellor, Nigel Lawson, indicated the government's indifference to industry in deference to the free market when he commented that the case for manufacturing was 'special pleading dressed up as analysis' and his comment in 1985 that services would take up the slack.

Thatcher's ideas also required the people to inherit through shares a community stakeholding in the newly privatised companies, but this too failed, with small stakeholder ownership diminishing and inequality rising. British workers turned overnight from being the salt of the earth into faceless 'human resources' colloquially known as 'chavs' or other derided terms.

Privatised companies eventually became owned by large-scale organisations that were increasingly foreign-owned, seeking no longer to support employees, but to maximise profits and maximise executive earnings. The irony of a right-wing and patriotic Conservative government overseeing an advocation of foreign ownership is still somewhat mind-bending. A long-standing sense of British fairness, pride, community and sense of shared ownership died with this. The Thatcherite monetarist policy of using monetary supply to control inflation, recession and unemployment in response to the OPEC-inspired economic recession also raised interest rates to record highs that undermined investment and bankrupted alike businesses and homeowners unable to service their debts. This would also let richer, newer or lower-cost industrial nations become even more rapacious. Famous British brands and assets would all be sold off: British Airports Authority (Spain), Boots (Italy), Cadbury (US), P & O Ports (Dubai), British Energy (France), Rolls-Royce cars (Germany), Lea & Perrins (US), Tetley (India), Tate & Lyle (US), United Biscuits (Turkey), Financial Times (Japan) and so on. This same approach allowed non-oil-producing countries to recoup some losses by re-exporting goods, but developing countries simply accumulated debts that they could never then afford to pay back and which they are still saddled with today.

Thatcher served as prime minister until 1990, but despite the rhetoric of an industry-centric leader, her laissez-faire and reprivatising approach to the support of industry failed. During her tenure, manufacturing assets were sold off wholesale, and the nation's manufacturing imports increased to a level greater than its exports. After Thatcher's fall and following on from the Conservative John Major, Tony Blair's and then Gordon Brown's New Labour government governed from 1997 and continued the theme of building a service-based economy with a particular emphasis on the creative industries but with little to offer traditional industry. When Thatcher came to power in 1979, manufacturing still accounted for almost 30 per cent of Britain's national income and employed 6.8 million people. By the time Gordon Brown left Downing Street in 2010, British industry was down to just over 11 per cent of the economy with a workforce of 2.5 million.

Thatcher's open door, free-market policy pervades still in today's government, allowing overseas companies to predate on British organisations.

Section 172 of the Companies Act 2006 makes some mention of the need to consider customers, workers, suppliers, communities and the environment in a takeover bid, but the law is very clear that shareholders' interests are paramount. This is made all the easier when the exchange rate is favourable, as seen in the takeover of the UK's ARM semiconductor business by the Japanese firm SoftBank in 2016 (SoftBank would sell a one-quarter stake to Saudi Arabia one year later). Conservative Prime Minister Theresa May described this as being in the country's interest but did not explain why.

It is much harder to do this in Germany, where a dirigiste approach of intervention and support is writ large. Nowadays, there are strict rules on market listing for non-European companies, a 75 per cent approval rate required by shareholders and preference for joint venture operations. When Chinese companies began to move in on German aerospace companies in 2018, it simply legislated against foreign deals in certain sectors. Unsolicited takeovers in Germany are hence very rare. Commentators on the emerging German industry back in the early 1900s described its company and government behaviour as 'unscrupulous'[10] and would no doubt be unsurprised by current industry scandals at Audi and Volkswagen, for example.

In France, the approach tends to be more liberal, but there is still a much more open perspective on state intervention and ownership of commercial bodies, which has included huge state-owned, or partially owned, bodies such as Renault, Thales and the chemical giant Rhone-Poulenc, which was turned round under state ownership. Under the chairmanship of Jean-René Fourtou, the company increased profits by 72 per cent within a two-year period, and this would be far from unique. The French government was collectively able to limit wage rises across its nationalised businesses, encourage innovative business practices, and scrutinise chairman performance every three years to ensure effective management and results. If we look at the aircraft industry, by the 1960s US companies such as Boeing, McDonnell Douglas and Lockheed were establishing a stranglehold over the airliner market. Britain responded by consolidating all of its smaller aircraft companies under the 1977 Aircraft and Shipbuilding Industries Act, having disagreed with France over international collaboration. France and Germany instead collaborated in 1970 to form G.I.E. Airbus Industrie. The company was formed with astute and clever political support based on an unlimited partnership, which allowed everyone to act unless everyone disagreed (unlike other collaborations, which needed agreement by all to act). The company then grew to become a global aircraft superpower. Hence, while France and Germany developed a business model capable of growth, Britain, like its European approach generally, would dither, opt in to bits, then opt out and ultimately lose out.

These factors help to explain why so many British companies failed while their European equivalent competitors, including many that were involved in Germany and France during the war, thrived: VW, Krupp, Siemens, BMW, Daimler, Bayer, Carl Zeiss, Hugo Boss, Miele, Bosch, Henkel, Renault, Citroën, Alstom, Dassault, Lafarge, Michelin and Salomon as examples. In fact, none of the companies listed in the British FT 30 shareholder index of the 1930s are now listed in the current index equivalent, the FTSE 100, and there are now very few engineering-type companies in FTSE 100 at all; perhaps just 15 per cent are industrial engineering if civil engineering and mining are excluded. It is difficult to relate this directly to other indices but in Germany around 237 out of 300 top companies, around 80 per cent, can be considered as having an industrial nature, including technology, chemical, utility and consumer goods. The US Dow Jones Industrial Average (DJIA) Index lists thirty of the top US companies, but it is industry-focused and does not include market capitalisation, so is more inherently stable. However, by way of contrast, it can be seen that the DJIA still has four companies listed that were established in the 1930s at the same time as the FT 30, and still has over 50 per cent (currently seventeen of the thirty) of companies listed that relate to engineering or technology.

13

Does it Really Matter?

Industry and the Economy

There is an economic argument that the decline of Britain's industry is less important than it might seem. The liberal, free-market argument is that slow, poorly run and inefficient British companies lacking invention deserve to fail and be replaced instead by ones that can provide better goods and services more cheaply and more effectively. It is an argument advocated by right-wing politicians, economists and think tanks. The dichotomy is that those on the right who hold a strongly nationalistic view of Britain are equally happy to see parts of the country sold off as part of a right-wing, open market philosophy. Others on the right might disagree and consider that to be great, Britain must hold a strongly domestically owned infra-structure. This conflicting logic is, however, equally muddled on the left, where similarly polar views can be held by advocates. Some left-thinking, for example, consider it is acceptable to sell out because notions of nation-alism can be dangerous. This polemic thinking within the political sector and parties is not actually helpful as it leads to argument and confusion that does not help to find clear and common ways forward. Equating Darwinian notions of survival of the fittest to economics is equally unhelpful. Both left and right can, however, avoid having to think this through too deeply in the belief that it doesn't really matter on the grounds that Britain's economic muscle is now provided by a service-based economy, including the law, creative media and advertising, management consultancy, petrochemical, banking and finance industries.

However, this thinking is wrong, and yes, it really does matter economically that Britain produces less than it used to. British citizens still need goods, and if these are no longer being made in-country then they will be made elsewhere. They must then be imported, to the financial detriment of the nation. Britain imports from the US power generation equipment, aircraft, science equipment and electrical goods but at levels slightly below exports, giving us a net credit (although the figures differ widely between the US and the UK statistical offices). In fact, China is only ranked fourth in countries importing goods and services to the UK, behind Germany first and then the US and the Netherlands. There is a new trade deficit with Germany, France and the Netherlands, which are the top destinations for exports, while China is only the ninth biggest export destination.

The deficit in visible trade (that is, goods that are made) was £60 billion in 2006, or 5 per cent of GDP, larger than at any time since 1945. In 2014, the deficit in goods was £123 billion and the vast majority of this, £63 billion, was in the import of finished products as opposed to semi-manufactured goods that might be assembled here.

When the visible trade in goods is combined with the trade in services and investment income, the net result is known as the UK's 'current account'. Although services and investments income has grown, it has not grown enough to offset the deficit in goods. In 2014, for example, there was a services surplus of £89 billion, but this was not enough to offset the £123 billion deficit in goods. The nation's current account has hence been in deficit since the mid-1980s. In 2015, the total current account deficit was £96.2 billion, which is around 5.2 per cent of the country's GDP, a particularly high figure and much worse than Germany or China, which operate current accounts with surpluses of around 5 per cent.

When capital account trading (capital and financial flows including capital investments) is added to this current account trading of goods, services and investment income, then the combined figures define the nation's overall balance of payments (BoP) and it is the shortfall in goods that has contributed to a BoP that has run at a deficit for many years. A poor BoP will ultimately result in a range of problems. In everyday terms, that might mean lower standards of living and more austerity: families on below-average incomes were actually earning less in 2016–17 than they were in 2003, with a corresponding rise in poverty levels.[1] It also leads to much more hidden longer-term problems; there are more potholes in the roads, longer NHS waiting times, poorer BBC programmes, smaller police services, and so on.

Borrowing to cover losses can lead to high debts with high interest rates that burden a country's chances to invest and grow. Overseas investors are courted to invest in the country to help balance the figures, and Britain is good at attracting inward investment because of its flexibility, stability, command of English and solid legal base. US investment in the UK is second only to that of the Netherlands, and the UK hosts more than half of the European, Middle Eastern and African corporate headquarters of American-owned firms. Eighty per cent of the electronics activity in the country, for example, comes from foreign direct investment. However, investment comes with strings, including, for example, the loss of national assets. Inward investment also risks the sudden removal of these investments, leading to devaluation, depreciation and further lowering of standards of living. Overseas ownership also presents a curious conflict of interests, such as the position where citizens might want a foreign company to outperform one in their own country so that they can enjoy a better retirement. This is also true of better-performing companies in more vibrant overseas economies. Many British pension funds, for example, are invested in Apple or Siemens, and pensioners might therefore want Apple to perform better than their local IT business. Similarly, BMW's biggest institutional shareholders are British, with, in 2018, a 15.9 per cent stake that is larger even than Germany's own institutional shareholding of 15.1 per cent.

While the service sector has grown to mitigate some of the effects of current account and balance of payment shortfalls, it seems unlikely that this can ever grow sufficiently to cover the whole trade imbalance. What is perhaps also less well considered is that industry actually supports and enables the services sector, and further decline in the industrial sector will be doubly bad for Britain. Economic theory only works, like the board game *Scrabble*, when there is equal competition with players all competing and the winner gaining an advantage. The actuality is more like the board game

Monopoly, with one winner and everyone else losing, and Britain cannot afford to keep losing.

According to some economists, successes in the service sector are actually being overblown and that rather than success being based on added value and business acumen, successes in the service industries are actually being supported by government spending, house-price rises, high consumer credit, spending and taxes arising not from profit margins but from population increases typically from more people actually working in lower-paid call-centre- and barista-type jobs. Some commentators have therefore described the transformation of Britain away from the production of artefacts in favour of more thoughtful and vocal industries as 'Bullshit Britain'.[2]

It is also foolish to rely just on service industries to bail the country, out as they are just as vulnerable to the decline that industry has seen. Earnings from the much-lauded design and creative industry declined from £1.4 billion in 2000–02 to £699 million in 2004–05.[3] Who also would until recently have predicted today's retail industry troubles, with many famous high street names disappearing under the attack from online retailers such as Amazon. Britain's drug and pharmaceutical industries are strong and yet issues around generic drug manufacture can easily reduce this strength overnight. The finance sector has often proved itself incompetent and dishonest in the face of mortgage lending disasters, money laundering and accounting failures, showing that Britain's service sector is just as capable of making the same failures made in its industrial sector.

If this all seems esoteric, remember this when considering the demise of ICL: by 2020, the stock value of US tech companies was worth more than the value of the entire European stock market, and Apple alone was worth more than the entire value of companies listed in the British FTSE 100. If Britain is, therefore, to 'make it' as a nation, it must 'make' things.

Industry and Culture

There are, however, other social arguments to suggest that Britain need not be too upset at its industrial decline, and it would be just as easy to write a series of corporate biographies to showcase why these factories and companies weren't great. For millennia, the land had been a common place of mutual benefit, but the drive by the wealthy to graze more and more sheep to make profit from the burgeoning wool trade led to increasing notions of land grabbing, culminating from the 1760s to the 1870s with the Enclosure Acts. People poured out of the countryside, hit by reducing common land and increased mechanisation, to live in deplorable and shocking urban living conditions. London, for example, doubled in population between 1800 and 1840. The industries that they increasingly worked in were often harsh places. Armstrong had his share of industrial disputes with his employees, as did Morris, who had his own vicious purges among senior staff. There are rumours and stories about the business as well as personal practices and behaviours of some of these company leaders.

Industry was also a dirty, polluting and dangerous business. Courtaulds was noted as being a particularly bad place to work and even by the poor working standards of factories in the 1800s:

> It was noted in 1890 that emerging industries were not unduly worrisome – apart from the Courtaulds viscose plant with an unpleasant and dangerous atmosphere.
>
> Thoms, D.[4]

ICI's environmental legacy needs some considerable consideration, particularly with respect to the scale of plastic pollution in our seas that are only now coming to light. Plane companies are depositing high levels of pollutants that are helping to cause both global warming and global dimming, while car companies are leaving a legacy of pollution including carbon monoxide, hydrocarbons, nitrous oxides and particulates, causing greenhouse gasses, ozone depletion and injuries to human health. For the car and bike industry, pollution caused by traffic each year in London alone is reported to cost the NHS £8,000 and cause 10,000 premature deaths.[5]

It is also true to say that notions of 'Britishness' are not what they were fifty years ago. British companies today might be run by foreign executives, serviced by foreign investment and buying in foreign components. The whole notion of global supply chains makes the concept of 'Made in Britain' less relevant than it used to be. On the citizen side, only 15 per cent of 18- to 24-year-olds are likely to be 'very patriotic', compared with 49 per cent of over 60-year-olds.[6] Young people may have more allegiances with global youth and music, for example, through social media than previous generations. British society is more multicultural than it was prior to the Windrush generation arriving from 1948 onwards. The industrialist William Morris had worked out that all of the cars imported into Britain in 1936 would cost 10,800 British workers their jobs, but that view did not stop Britons buying from the same German and Japanese car companies that made war equipment in support of the worst of humanity's behaviour.

Even if somebody is patriotic, does that patriotism really transmit itself into corporate entities? After all, many Britons get massively excited during the football World Cup, with record television viewing figures, but there is barely a murmur when a British business such as ARM or GKN is taken over. And why should they get excited? A number of laws were passed during the Industrial Revolution, starting with the Joint Stock Companies Act of 1844, which gave companies legal identity, conferring on them juristic personality, but they are not real in the sense of being transient and living, so should we grieve for them or even care if they disappear? Many large companies are, in any case, now simply holding offices that outsource design, manufacture, transport, finance and any other business function, and are not, therefore, the same as the business entities of previous generations. Such modern concerns are promoted through branding, the branch of marketing that emerged in the 1960s as a more impactful way to achieve consumer loyalty through emotional and value-based 'partnerships' endorsed, for example, through brand identity elements and celebrity endorsements. This can produce tribal loyalties in some consumers, who would happily wear branded clothing or even tattoo themselves with logos to signify their brand allegiance. To others, however, this simply creates a 'ghost business' made tacit through 'hollow branding':

> A great many corporations that did not embrace this [branding] model were bloated, oversized; they owned too much, employed too many people, and were weighed down with too many things. The old-fashioned process of producing – running one's own factories, being responsible for tens of thousands of full-time, permanent employees – began to look less like the route

to success and more like a clunky liability. The goal was to become a hollow brand – own little, brand everything.

Naomi Klein[7]

What then does it mean to be British, and does it follow to be proud of branded images of dubious corporate entities? Does it matter to British people if the goods they buy are made by foreign-owned companies? Does it matter as long as the taxes paid by these companies that pay for our public services are British or foreign-owned? Does it matter if the goods you need are provided by one large, well-known company, or several smaller, more anonymous companies? If the answer to these questions is 'no, not really', then Britain's industrial decline doesn't matter.

There are parallels to be had at this point with football. Like industry, Britain gave the world association football; it developed the rules, top-flight football, the leagues system and was a football powerhouse internationally in the 1960s. Thereafter it has failed to compete at international level. The point was made that multinational industry, like our multinational football, is not quite the same game. Top-flight English football is staffed with foreign players, run by foreign managers and owned by foreign owners, broadcast by foreign television companies, and watched on foreign television sets on foreign settees. It is successful, and entertaining, but it is quiet and lacking in atmosphere. It is no longer the people's game, giving entertainment and hope to the lower classes, and it is not in the interests of home-grown players or the national team. The more successful German model has more home- and fan-based ownership – in both football and industry.

There is another view to these philosophical arguments. If Britain does not contribute to global production, or declines further, for example, then it risks being excluded from any global-style industry summits. These discussions are inevitable for the future as the world grapples with diminishing resources and environmental concerns but increasing demands. Is it best to let other countries decide these matters without an input of British perspective and values?

There is also an argument that industrial work is better. While jobs have actually emerged, they are not as value-adding as industrial-based employment. The proportion of people working in domestic service jobs such as cooking, cleaning, child care and gardening is the same today as it was in the 1860s, while between 1992 and 1999, hairdressing was the fastest-growing occupation. There are many people who aspire to work, and work best, in practical, creative, physical, problem-solving employment that industry provides through engineering and manufacturing. A network of small, medium or large industrial businesses benefit the job aspirations and career paths of this large section of our working society. They benefit the community through training and educational connections, and they benefit the country through a shared sense of pride in the goods that Britain as a nation could provide.

Finally, there is a question over well-being. The Covid-19 pandemic demonstrated how reliant the country was on China and Turkey for masks and diagnostic products. There is a similar vulnerability around security. Companies that were vital to Britain's South Atlantic battle over the Falkland Islands in 1982 included Ferranti, Marconi, Westland and Thorn EMI. Ferranti went bust in 1993. The long-standing Marconi company went defunct in 1987, before limping weakly on. Westland went defunct in 2000, now being part of Italy's Leonardo S.p.A. Thorn EMI's defence businesses were sold off in 1995. It is vital that Britain retains some measure of home-based industry to secure the safety of its citizens. The emerging spread of Chinese autocratic doctrine underscored by its ability to dictate positions through its economic and manufacturing power is something that the world is only now waking up to, and something to be very concerned about indeed,[8] while the Russian invasion of Ukraine in 2022 has clearly demonstrated a need for national self-sufficiency.

14

Where is Britain Now?

Turnaround

Although many companies failed from the 1960s onwards, leading to a catastrophic industrial collapse, at the same time some of the seeds were sown that would help form a partial future industrial recovery. In 1934, the government had nationalised the country's oil reserves under the Petroleum Production Act as part of a continuing search for oil for the armed forces. This was a prescient act because significant oil was discovered in Sherwood Forest, which provided high-grade fuel for the RAF's Merlin-engined fighters and bombers during the Second World War. In the late 1950s, it became clearer that there was a connection between onshore oil and oil reserves under the North Sea, and from 1965 offshore drilling commenced. Vast oil and gas reserves were tapped, with 39 billion barrels of oil being extracted over the next four decades, making Britain second only to Norway as the leading European producer of oil and gas, and ranking it fourteenth worldwide. This production contributed around £350 billion in current values in tax revenues and provided much relief for the British economy. It allowed the government some freedom in how it chose to finance government spending, provided a financial source for research spending, and avoided the need to overtax industry, allowing companies to reinvest. When Britain exited the European Exchange Rate Mechanism (ERM) in September 1992, the value of sterling dropped, and this helped business to become more competitive and buoyant overseas.

Industry was, however, also undertaking its own period of self-help by becoming more productive. In fact, this trend had started after the war and despite all of the reductions in size, employment and national performance, British manufacturing has actually increased in production and value since 1945.[1] The fact that manufacturing employed one in four workers in the 1980s but now employs one in ten might be viewed as disappointing and indicative of the move towards services, but is actually also indicative of more efficient working (jobs lost in industry are mostly lost through productivity gains rather than through trading losses).

That further emphasis for improved performance was brought on partly by the awareness that things had to change, as some of Britain's biggest companies began to stutter, partly because of the oil crisis, which had highlighted Britain's industrial inefficiency. There was one other reason, too. In 1951, Belgium, France, Italy, Luxembourg, the Netherlands and West Germany created the European Coal and Steel Community (ECSC) as an economic alliance for coal and steel and as a political movement to help prevent further European conflict. In 1957, the ECSC collaboration was expanded with a customs union to enable further integration known as the European Economic Community (EEC), which in time morphed into the European Union (EU). Britain joined the EEC in 1973, spurred on by fear of isolation and the vision of German and French industries succeeding where it was not. It brought home the realisation that the country could no longer rely on the illusion and protection of its own private trading empire.

One of the consequences was that, in the 1980s, British companies started to adopt the 'Quality' principles applied in Japan to start making products that better met consumer needs, which failed less often, and which helped staff and management communicate better. The words 'Total Quality Management' (TQM) and 'Quality Circles' started to appear, along with a drive to make products with 'zero failures' rather than the 2 per cent that was normally accepted. This helped to accelerate efficiencies. The British steel industry, for example, increased its productivity eightfold between 1978 and 2006, and labour productivity generally rose 50 per cent between 1997 and 2007.[2] Hence, although Britain's manufacturing declined in importance and employment relatively when compared with services, and its global position dropped because of the increasing output of foreign competitors, its internal performance grew in actual terms over this long period – by 1.4 per cent per annum since 1948[3] and gross added value was considered to be double in 2007 what it was in 1958.

Current Status

Although British industry has, therefore, suffered the worst period of stagnation for 150 years, it is not all bad news. Britain still has a large manufacturing base of around 88,000 manufacturers and manufacturing accounts for around 13 per cent of the country's economic output, with engineering generally accounting for around one-quarter of UK turn-over.[4] Nearly 5.5 million employees work in the industrial sector, split roughly equally between engineering and manufacturing, which accounts for around 8 per cent of the UK workforce. Britain is, hence, still a great industrial nation and is ranked between seventh and ninth in the world as an industrial producer depending on the factors chosen to make the ranking: by profits, tonnage, units produced or employment numbers. The Engineering Employers Federation, for example, ranks Britain ninth for manufacturing output,[5] and in 2018 the United Nations Conference on Trade and Development (UNCTAD) considered it eighth largest.

Many big companies of long-standing are still doing well, such as the general household and product-based companies Reckitt Benckiser and Unilever, the latter of which has roots back to 1885. Other examples of engineering-oriented companies with long-standing or legacy roots include BAE Systems, with 83,000 employees, and the Smiths Group, founded in 1851 and employing around 22,000 people. Many of these older companies have reinvented themselves. Coats Group Plc, for example, started as J. & P. Coats, a weaving business, in 1802, and would merge with Patons & Baldwins, and then Vantona Viyella, before becoming a private business, then a public business again in 2015 as the Coats Group. It maintains a leading British place in the textile industry as the world's largest producer and supplier of sewing thread, with sales of $1.5 billion in 2017. These include industrial threads such as polyester and nylon and engineering yarns such as fibre optics. It is also a leading zip and fastener manufacturer, although the

Japanese YKK company makes over half of the world's zips (along with the machinery that makes zips) and the Chinese SBS company founded only in 1984 has risen fast with low-cost offers.

Triumph motorbikes, as another example, began as a bicycle company in 1893 but would produce its first motorbike in 1902 from its Coventry site. This original bike, largely copied from other designs and using a Belgian Minerva engine, sold 500 units and encouraged the company to produce their own design three years later. Triumph produced 30,000 bikes during the First World War. In the 1920s, the company took over the Hillman car company and started to produce Triumph cars alongside its bicycles and motorbikes with a strong track record of sales overseas – particularly for bikes in the US. The depression of the 1930s caused the company to sell off its bicycle division to the Raleigh Bicycle Company and its car division to the Standard Motor Company. The motorbike business was then bought by the Ariel Motorcycle Company and began to improve its sales through exports to the US market. Following the destruction of its Coventry plant in the Second World War, the company relocated to Meriden in the West Midlands and continued its export-driven business. Seventy per cent of Triumph bikes were exported to the US to help with the Lend-Lease debts. The bikes were good – and a Triumph 650cc-engined bike held the bike land speed record from 1955 to 1970. The trouble was that Japanese-made small bikes were infiltrating the market and were assumed by Triumph and other British companies to be inconsequential – in much the same way that British supermarkets have underestimated the low-cost Aldi and Lidl supermarkets to their cost. Honda started to build bigger bikes that were no match for the speed and power of Triumph bikes, but the Japanese models had more modern features such as electric starters, and they were easier and cheaper to maintain. In other words, the quality approach was delivering what consumers wanted. Triumph sales would decline, and it would struggle on under a variety of owners, and as a worker co-operative, but would go bankrupt on 23 August 1983. The company was, however, bought out of receivership and the Triumph marque would re-emerge as Triumph Motorcycles Ltd under the patronage of John Bloor. The company now employs around 1,000 people and 85 per cent of sales are overseas, along with much of its yearly 130,000 bike production capacity.

While these larger companies tend to get a higher profile and limelight as part of the FTSE and general press coverage, they actually account for only 1 per cent of UK business activity and most businesses are small or medium enterprises (SMEs) that have fewer than 250 employees. The engineering consultancy market, for example, is valued at around £50 billion, growing at an average of over 4 per cent for the past five years,[6] while 2015 saw a 7 per cent rise in the number of UK engineering enterprises. In some cases, long-standing companies have been down but not out. The 150-year-old Lister Petter company, for example, has its own illustrious but chequered history and is now effectively starting afresh as a small specialist engine operation. Other businesses are completely new, and Britain is significantly ahead of the US, Germany, France and Italy in business start-ups, with a good record in engineering. Thirty-four per cent of the country's engineers report having an entrepreneurial foundation, as opposed to 27 per cent in the US.[7] Some of these new starts have grown to become large, and Dyson is an obvious example, having been founded by James Dyson in 1991 and now employing 8,500 people (although Dyson controversially moved its manufacturing base to Malaysia in 2002).

Across these businesses, the general engineering sector accounts for around 30 per cent of British manufacturing (by value added). General engineering includes the transport sector and Triumph Motorbikes, McLaren, Caterham Cars and a number of specialist companies and suppliers contribute to British-owned businesses in this sector. British-based manufacturing under foreign ownership is well-represented by companies including Nissan, Toyota, Jaguar Land Rover, Vauxhall Motors and Leyland Trucks. These account for 250,000 jobs directly and indirectly. Aerospace is also a strong sector with over 250,000 related jobs at British companies such as BAE Systems and Rolls-Royce but with European companies such as EADS also heavily involved with British manufacturing. There is, for example, almost a decade's worth of aerospace work in hand with an order book of more than 13,000 aircraft components such as wings and engines, worth up to £195 billion to Britain.[8] Gatwick Airport is the world's fourth-largest airport and enables both large- and small-scale related industries, which, in conjunction with Heathrow Airport as the world's busiest international airport, generates around them a large, world-leading aerospace cluster. Productivity in the aerospace sector is reported to have improved 30 per cent over the past five years, and 15 to 18 per cent of global aerospace is British, making it the second-largest player in the world behind the US.

Britain also has a leading role in pharmaceutical products due to companies such as GlaxoSmithKline and AstraZeneca (ranked second and seventh in the world in 2020), while hosting many foreign-owned companies such as Novartis, Pfizer and Hoffman-La Roche AG. It provides over 150,000 direct jobs but also supports a further 500,000 indirectly through supply chains. Textiles may no longer be a national behemoth, but it still supports 340,000 jobs and adds over £11 billion to the economy every year. Within shipbuilding, Cammell Laird and Abel are British. Companies such as Harland and Wolff, Sealine, Sunseeker, Princess and Fairline are no longer British owned but still contribute to a vibrant sector. British electronics is the world's fifth largest in terms of production, supported by 6,000 businesses, 95 per cent of which are SMEs. Fourteen of the world's top twenty semiconductor companies have established design and/or manufacturing sites in Britain. Within the polymer industry, Britain has over 6,000 companies employing 170,000 people.

Britain hosts some contentious industries, including, for example, the arms trade of BAE Systems, tobacco companies such as British American Tobacco Plc (B.A.T.), and resource extraction companies such as BP Plc and Rio Tinto Group. While they are undoubtedly contentious because of the nature of their work, they are successful and world-leading in what they do. The Rio Tinto Group, for example, is the third-largest mining group in the world, employing 50,000 people and turning over £40 billion. BP is the seventh-largest oil- and gas-producing company, turning over around £200 billion and employing around 74,000 people. B.A.T. is the largest tobacco company in the world, turning over £59 billion (2017), employing over 90,000 people and contributing significantly to government revenues.

'Luxury' is a less well-recognised UK sector, with luxury, heritage and craft industries, including brands such as Burberry and Mulberry, accounting for 6 per cent of all new jobs created in Britain. Britain has a strong brand image abroad that encompasses luxury, creativity and craftsmanship. For example, Savile Row, Rolls-Royce jet engines, Aston Martin, Arthur

Brett furniture and Vertu phones might all typify British craftsmanship. However, it is pharmaceuticals that are Britain's largest export sector, and they add some £60 million to Britain's balance of trade every day.

Nearly half of British production, around 44 per cent, is exported, with strong performance in mechanical and precision engineering and 25 per cent in hi-tech goods (a bigger percentage than the US, France or Germany). Britain's biggest trading partner is the US, where its biggest exports are pharmaceutical and medical goods, cars and power generation equipment. British overseas investments are also biggest in the US, where holdings above 10 per cent are recorded as Finance Direct Investments, or FDIs.

The often-stated belief that everything is now made in China is therefore very wrong and many of the products you buy still have the potential to have been made in Britain by British companies, or made in Britain by foreign-owned companies (or made overseas by British-owned companies). Imagine, for example, a young professional getting ready to leave for work on a Monday morning: the radio alarm (Roberts) kicks in. Our man is tired after mountain biking (BTR) all day yesterday and would like to snuggle back into the enormously comfy mattress (Harrison) but he must get moving as he has a plane to catch today for a business meeting. Entering the bathroom, he shaves (Edwin Jagger), brushes his teeth (Wisdom) and washes before dressing (Rohan) and putting in his contact lenses (Rayner Intraocular). He heads downstairs and grabs some toast from the toaster (Dualit) while checking his laptop for some last-minute financial details (Sage) and virus checks (Sophos) ahead of his meeting. After a few minutes, he washes his crockery (Denby) and cutlery (Viners) in the sink (Leisure Sinks), and picks up his mobile phone (including components, for example, from Parafix and Qinetiq) from the worktop (made in Chirk) and unplugs (Volex) the charger. He tidies his house with a quick run round with his Dyson, putting his dirty clothes into his washing machine (Ebac), the packaging (DS Smith) from an online order in the bin (Addis) and straightening the furniture (Ercol) before grabbing his suitcase (Antler) and heading outside. He then heads off in his car (made in Sunderland). There is a short delay en route for a digger (JCB) to attend some road works but he remains on time. At the airport, he checks in and visits the toilet, drawing soap from the dispenser (Brightwell) and drying his hands (Dyson) in the surprisingly fresh facilities (Vent-Axia) before he passes through the security scanners (Detectnology) and boards the flight. Finally he can relax as the captain starts up the engines (Rolls-Royce) and he tunes in to the in-flight entertainment (Inmarsat).

The Economy

The problem for British industry is that its national context – the context that caused so many problems for post-war Britain – is still troubling. The 'Great Recession' is the name given to the economic downturn that swept across the world during the 2000s. In 2008–09, Britain experienced six consecutive quarters of negative growth, its worst recession since the Second World War, and the Bank of England cut interest rates to their lowest ever to help the economy recover. It also spent £435 billion on a policy of buying government bonds to put more cash into the economy, a process known as Large Scale Asset Purchasing, or Quantitative Easing (QE). A total of £133 billion was spent on cash support and a further £1 trillion in guarantees. The 2010–15 coalition government also implemented a policy of borrowing to finance debts with austerity and cutbacks to reduce expenditure, and there were significant public sector job losses. Unsurprisingly, there was a big rise in government debt from 52 per cent of GDP to 76 per cent in the same period. The overall national debt, including household and business debts, rose to 420 per cent of GDP in 2011, more than Japan or France and twice that of the US or Germany.

The policies did help to avoid a full-scale depression (noted simply as being a nasty recession!), and there would actually be some job growth in the industrial sector, but manufacturing had a much more pronounced fluctuation in its performance than services, where the effect on production costs was more easily affected by commodity and power costs. Following the Great Recession, as Britain moved into the current decade, GDP initially then grew again and at a faster rate than other leading economies but not fast enough to offset the rising current account deficit, which rose to over 7 per cent of GDP by the end of 2015 – the highest rate in the developed world and the highest since records began in 1772. Only increasing foreign investment helped the nation's balance of payments as more of the country's silverware was sold off, and Britain is now among the highest for direct inward investment. Although this can be seen as being good and bad, the reality is that four large UK businesses are actually foreign owned, alongside a great deal of the country's infrastructure.

Trading losses were then poor, not just with low-cost economies but with European partners, too, suggesting the issues have been more entrenched and structural rather than random or cyclical. One of the problems has been efficiency. For industry, productivity crashed after the Great Recession, and its mysterious failure to recover at any significant rate is known as the 'productivity puzzle'. Industrial productivity stagnated between 2007 and 2015, growing at 0.6 per cent in the decade following 2008 compared to 1.6 per cent in the preceding decade. Output per hour worked dropped to levels not seen since the 1800s and was not growing fast enough to keep pace with competitor countries, with productivity being on average 18 per cent higher in Britain's G7 partners, and notably 28 per cent higher in the US and 35 per cent higher in Germany. That means a car built in a week in Britain can be built roughly in four days everywhere else. To overcome losses and shortfall, many companies have taken the opportunity to draw on low interest rates to take out loans; at the same time these companies are accruing large debts. Worst still is the use of this money to pay dividends rather than investing in new innovation and production efficiencies. The level of investment in research and development in Britain today is around half of that in the 1960s.

For the general population, the post-'Great Recession' has seen employment rise to record highs, but wages in real terms fall by 10 per cent during the eight years leading up to 2016. Across the other Organisation for Economic Co-operation and Development (OECD) countries, wages rose by an average of 6.7 per cent. Workers have seen wages gradually buying less and less while house and rent prices and debts have soared. Consumers turned to credit more to buy the goods they needed and wanted; this would amount to an unheard-of level of 3 per cent of GDP and in 2018 this stood at a record debt level of £200 billion. It would be consumer spending that accounted for growth in 2016, rather than true economic growth.

We can summarise this section by saying that Britain ceased to be the world's leading industrial nation over 100 years ago. It slipped further down the list in the mid-twentieth century, but collapsed in a steeper decline from the 1960s onwards, shedding jobs and shedding traditional companies alongside its descending league position. It did not collapse completely, though, and there has been a significant turnaround. However, that turnaround has been threatened by the nation's perilous position. Among leading industrialised nations, Britain has almost the worst balance of payments, the worst research spending, the lowest production efficiency, the highest national and consumer debt and the highest trade imbalance. It means that the future of industry is more important than ever.

15

Britain's Industrial Future

Strategy and failure

Earlier chapters looked at companies and governments striving to be the biggest and the best, growing through acquisitions and trading low-cost core business for higher-value activities but ultimately throwing away industrial leadership through a range of poor practices, including poor business integration and poor decision-making.

There are still plenty of recent examples of this type of doubtful corporate dealing seen in the earlier case studies, driven on by seemingly overambitious company executives and shareholders as well as city financiers perhaps keen for a large stake in these trading deals: Vodaphone's takeover of Mannesmann, for example, included eye-watering, one-off losses of £23.5 billion.[1, 2] Glaxo Wellcome's takeover of SmithKline Beecham lowered Glaxo's share price by one-third.[3, 4] Six thousand investors took Lloyds Bank to court following a takeover of HSBC that they considered to be disastrous.[5] The RBS takeover of Dutch bank ABN Amro cost a record-breaking £49 billion, but just six months later it needed a £45 billion taxpayer bailout and reported consecutive losses for the next ten years.[6, 7]

There is a similar story of failed decision-making today, for example, around pension funds. From 2006 to 2017, companies reduced the equity in pension portfolios from 61 per cent to 29 per cent while increasing bond shares from 28 per cent to 56 per cent. This situation locked some companies into paying high interest rates during a period of high inflation coupled with excessive payouts and reckless guarantees leaving big holes in their accounts, encumbering companies with debts that have hit British companies hard. The pension deficit of Britain's leading companies, for example, has been equivalent to 70 per cent of their profits, amounting to £62 billion for FTSE 350 companies. These debts are also hard to shift. The ageing population means there are growing numbers of pensioners, which have to be funded by an increasingly smaller number of workers. Pension scandals have followed, such as that at Equitable Life, which saw a company founded in 1762 and once the second-largest life insurer flounder after developing a £4.3 billion hole in its accounts.[8]

There is, hence, no evidence to suggest that British managers are intrinsically any less likely to make fundamentally poor decisions than their predecessors. What might optimistically be said is that they are no more or less likely to be worse than managers in other countries, where there are plenty of similar corporate decision-making failures to be seen. With regard to mergers and acquisitions, for example, Microsoft wrote off $7.6 billion after its acquisition of Nokia and the subsequent failure of the Lumia phone.[9] Hewlett Packard would rue its $11.1 billion takeover of Autonomy with a $9 billion write-down.[10] Motorola's purchase by Google was an apparent disaster.[11] *The Wall Street Journal* cited Bank of America's acquisition of Countrywide as 'the worst deal in the history of American finance', and it cost the company around $40 billion.[12] Alongside these takeover disasters, mergers of AOL Time Warner, Daimler Chrysler, BMW Rover and Kmart Sear contribute to a seemingly endless list of doomed collaborations.[13] It is also a similar picture for pensions, where the twenty largest OECD countries have around $78 trillion in pension obligations, about 1.8 times the collective national debts of these countries.[14]

What might also be said more positively is that British managers no longer have the illusion of an empire and track record of success to rely on, and therefore have less complacent myopia about failing. Indeed, there is less capacity to actually do so. The UK Corporate Governance Code (2010) guides larger companies into having a majority of non-executive members from outside the business appointed by shareholders on the directors' board. This aims to generate a wide variety of experience and specialism in the senior management team – similar to the system of interlocking business relationships in Japan known as *Keiretsu*. This system enabled Japanese companies to better plan and manage long-term projects, particularly in the second half of the twentieth century. Smaller companies should have at least two independent non-executives on the director board. This 'unitary board' should be a forum for healthy debate and is perhaps a better set-up than the German model where the non-executives form a separate board. UK companies should also have a separate chief executive and chairman, again seen as an improvement on the US model where the roles can be combined. UK companies should also have an appointed senior independent director (SID), who can provide an intermediary route for, say, shareholders who have concerns about the direction of a business. There are other rules that might help to instil some confidence in business leaders having less ability to run amok. These include Stock Exchange listing requirements, the OECD Principles of Corporate Governance (2004), the revised Corporate Governance Code (2018) and even the Competition Commission (formerly the Monopolies and Mergers Commission) blocking the kind of growth and dominance model once striven for by ICI and GEC. Auditing, too, might be supposed to ensure that companies are being effectively managed, but a litany of high-profile failures by the four accounting firms that dominate the audit market suggests that this is not always the case. 'I wouldn't trust you to audit the contents of my fridge,' said the MP Peter Kyle at a ministerial Business Committee chaired by Rachel Reeves in 2018, following the government's investigation into the latest auditor failure, this time at Carillion, one of Britain's biggest construction companies. At a Committee meeting of the Department for Business, Energy and Industrial Strategy, Reeves added that the auditor's work appeared a 'colossal waste of time and money, fit only to provide false assurance to investors, workers and the public'.

Strategy and the Environment

One area that past companies did not have to contend with, and which many current companies seem unable to contend with but which is critical for future industry, is that of the environment. Failure here means not just a decline in industry and living standards but a potentially catastrophic destruction of the planet's flora and fauna and ultimately the planet itself. Industry is, however, in the business of making money, not saving the planet. The priority is, therefore, one of profit through making products that function well, look good and are cheap and safe, and these factors have tended to take precedence over environmental issues, in particular where consumers and government have failed to exert any pressure to do so.

In fairness to business, there have also been challenges and uncertainties as to how to be greener. However, this is changing. Environmental Management Systems (EMS) have made progress in tracking environmental data, and environmental benchmarking tools such as Life Cycle Analysis (LCA) are making it possible to formulate informed changes to make goods and services greener. Over two-thirds of FTSE 250 companies had a formal EMS in place by 2006 (BSI survey 2006), with a 10 per cent increase in EMS adoption between 2005 and 2007 by SMEs (NetRegs Environment Agency survey). Investors are also now actively seeking information on business environmental issues before they invest, requiring effective EMS.[15] The twenty-sixth UN Climate Change Conference in 2021 (COP26), if not finding solutions, at least took some small steps in the right direction.

Industry is realising it has to change, albeit it is doing so very slowly. Shell, for example, is spending around £1.5 billion a year on green energy projects, but it needs a green licence to be able to sell non-oil-based fuels, and the outcomes of its research are not exciting. However, there may perhaps be some green shoots. Automotive companies Ricardo and Williams are shifting expertise respectively towards water technology and aerofoils. Orkney has also developed into a major centre for sustainable energy research and is the world's leading centre for wave power research. Within the environment, Swedish power company Vattenfall is deploying eleven of the world's most powerful 8.8 MW offshore wind turbines from the new European Offshore Wind Deployment Centre in Aberdeen Bay.

New business models are emerging, too, such as Product Buy Back, which look towards organisations taking back goods at the end of their lives to reuse materials. Product Service Systems enable organisations to fulfil consumer requirements, perhaps through a service-based system or rental approach. This allows companies an opportunity to design better-made goods that last longer and which are more efficient than consumer-purchasing-based models. DuPont, Herman Miller and Xerox are often cited examples, and there are British examples, too, such as Hydro Industries. However, these companies do tend to be less well recognised for these practices, and academic research suggests that the take-up is less than expected despite both sustainable and economic benefits.[16] The suggestion, therefore, is that industry is starting to wake up to the environment, but the best exemplar companies are US or European, and British businesses need to do more.

Organisation and Efficiency

The corporate biographies picked out big companies such as Armstrong and Vickers that were undercut by overseas companies with lower cost overheads and more modern products, and this was seen as allegorical for British industry as a whole. The arrival of low-cost industrialised nations has meant that British business would always struggle to compete on pricing based on labour costs alone. The problems are, however, not just about labour rates, which are significantly lower overseas, but also about efficiency. As a result, Britain currently ranks seventeenth out of the top twenty industrial nations for productivity.

This is not a hidden fact. Rolls-Royce Holdings, the company behind Rolls-Royce jet engines, has about 55,000 staff worldwide, with 26,000 based in the UK. In the 2018 Annual Report, Chief Executive Warren East inferred the company as being first rate in technology but second rate as a business, 'We must create a commercial organisation that is as world-leading as our technologies. We need to modernise the way in which we do business.' GKN, Britain's last remaining historic engineering giant, was taken over in 2018 when investors stopped believing that the GKN management were able to produce an efficient organisation.

Incredibly, smaller British-owned companies tend to perform even worse than large companies!

The reasons for inefficiency seem to include cultural legacies, a preponderance of smaller companies less able to manage risk and investment, and a dearth of take-up of the type of automation that can boost production efficiencies. Culturally, some British-owned companies still place their emphasis on efficiency of machine utilisation rather than overall business effectiveness. There are clearly still some best-practice lessons to be learnt, including the principles of 5S, kaizen (Japanese for improvement) and lean manufacturing, all methods of achieving maximum value for minimal input pioneered by Toyota as part of the Japanese quality movement.

In terms of automation, the investment in robots has contributed to a 10 per cent rise in GDP in OECD countries, but in 2012 Britain was ranked just nineteenth in terms of production robot density. Britain only has 71 robots per 10,000 employees, compared to 309 in Germany, and is moving backwards compared to countries like Denmark and Korea.[17] There is some sign of an upward trend, with 58 per cent of British manufacturers investing in automation and robotics, but that is still behind Germany's 66 per cent.[18] The challenges, particularly for small companies, are in finding the necessary investment money coupled with uncertainty and the difficulties in predicting the future and therefore calculating the returns on investment (ROI). Confidence is the key, and there is often a shortage of this. This could and must be better; a £1.24 billion investment across the country in automation could improve productivity by 20 per cent and add £60.5 billion to the economy. It is not only vital to keep up but also not to fall behind as the automated factories start to become integrated 'smart factories' through the approach being termed the Fourth Industrial Revolution (IR 4.0).

It also needs to be recognised that productivity is not just about automation and systems, but about good management of people. There are low levels of industrial action today – 276,000 working days lost in 2017, the sixth lowest since the start of record-keeping in 1891 – but this can simply be an indicator that it is harder for unions to act today than it has been.[19] The Office for National Statistics actually shows that the wage differentials have increased, with higher earners receiving an average 117 per cent increase over the past twenty-five years compared to 60 per cent for the average earner and 47 per cent for the lowest earners. Analysis by the Chartered Institute of Personnel and Development (CIPD) and the High Pay Centre show that FTSE 100 chief executives earn a median average of 120 times more than the average worker. At the same time, the turnover of chief executives is now at an all-time high, reaching 16 per cent of the FTSE top 100 companies in 2018. The blatant financial and career ambitions of some of Britain's industrial leaders will inevitably continue to demotivate staff.

To be more efficient and to compete globally, industry must, therefore, address issues of culture, systems, automation, investment, risk, labour and fairness, but these are not easy to resolve. Where then is this drive going to come from? Manufacturing consultants argue that too many British efficiency programmes are still driven by overseas companies that produce in the UK (particularly the US and the Japanese) rather than British companies themselves. One problem may be that Britain's top 100 firms account for one-quarter of total UK revenue and this lack of competition in the internal market is unhealthy and failing to drive the need for better efficiency.[20] While industrial inefficiency is hence well recognised, there is no sign that this is about to change in the future.

Production: Home or Away?

The alternative to trying to become more efficient as a UK-based manufacturer, at least for companies producing goods that are not too massively complex, heavy or bulky, is to operate or subcontract to production plants overseas in countries where labour costs are lower and efficiency can be higher. Since 1992, corporate taxes have also tended to undercut traditional industrial economies.[21] Hence, when Dyson moved production to Malaysia, its costs were said to be reduced by 30 per cent. Raleigh Bikes moved production overseas from 2003 onwards. 'It's the only way we could survive,' it said. Triumph bit the bullet in 2009. If any motorcycle manufacturer said, 'I'm going to source 100 per cent from my home country, and I'm going to manufacture 100 per cent in my home country', they'd never compete.[22] Triumph have, however, also vertically integrated the business more by actually bringing in-house some manufacturing that was previously outsourced, such as fuel tank production.

Not only are costs overseas lower, but plants can then be located closer to customers and overcome any trade restrictions or import tariffs in these countries. Triumph moved production to Thailand. Coats Group transferred production to overseas plants in Asia, South America and south-east Europe. Raleigh bikes are made in China, Bangladesh, Mexico and Sri Lanka. Increasing currency and foreign exchange volatility (FX volatility) allows multinational production to be tailored to suit these fluctuations to best economic effect. In the past, currencies were often pegged against more fixed standards – such as gold or the dollar – but they are mostly now floating freely. There is no particular reason that lies behind currency fluctuations, but it seems likely that a world of increasing environmental and political uncertainty would tend towards a more volatile currency market and recent indicators, such as the Deutsche Bank Currency Volatility Index, are starting to indicate an increasing level of implied volatility.

However, this approach is not a panacea, and there are ethical questions around overseas production. Is it ethical to pay foreign workers minimal wages producing goods they are unlikely to be able to afford under conditions that may not conform to British law? Is this a modern form of slavery? In Triumph's case, the company chose to establish its own plant rather than subcontract, and by retaining control they have been able to ensure workers' rights are met and quality is maintained. But philosophical questions remain. Is a Triumph motorbike made in Thailand really a Triumph? The answer is, of course, that it is better than no Triumph at all and as Triumph's chief product officer Steve Sargent would say, 'As far as we're concerned, Triumph manufacturing is Triumph manufacturing – whether it's UK based or Thailand based, it's a resource that we have available to us that we can use in the best way we can. It's not an "us and them" situation; it's all one company.'[23]

It is noteworthy that some companies have come unstuck, particularly with subcontracting. Frank Hornby patented the metal construction toy Meccano in 1901, and followed with trains from 1920. Hornby trains and Meccano were bought out by Lines Brothers under their Tri-ang name in 1964. When Lines Brothers failed in 1971, Hornby was sold on but became independent again as Hornby Hobbies in the 1980s following a management buyout. The company would make a number of acquisitions, including the Airfix, Humbrol, Corgi and Scalextric brands. In the face of growing competition, Hornby production was moved to China. However, the company has always struggled in the face of newer toys and activities for its target users. In 2017, its largest shareholder, Phoenix Asset Management, took control of the company and has since been attempting to review its fortunes. Throughout its troubles, the Chinese production has been a constant thorn in the company's side, with issues over quality, delivery, contracts and management. In other cases, companies have complained that Chinese manufacturers have plagiarised their products and subsequently produced their own versions. China has ranked twenty-fifth in the US Chamber of Commerce's index for countries' commitment to protecting intellectual property rights (IPR), which includes legal protection such as patents, copyright and design rights. The US claimed this costs it between $225 and $600 billion annually.[24] The message from businesses that outsource production has been to spread it over different companies, areas and even countries to reduce this risk.

Nevertheless, the issues concerning offshoring are not just around ethics, philosophy, quality and management. Rising transport, rising power and rising labour costs are making overseas production less of an automatic option, particularly within China itself. Energy costs look set to rise through rising demand and dwindling and harder to access resources, and since around 80 per cent of the growth in demand is from India and China, then industrial costs in these economies will only rise further.[25] At the same time, renewable energy production rose 10 per cent between 2015 and 2016 but cost 25 per cent less in investment. If Britain can continue its rising profile of renewable energy, then the case for reshoring will continue to become stronger. Travelling to and from Britain to China and dealing with language barriers can be exhausting for managers and staff.

Given these types of issues, some companies do consider bringing production back to the UK. One-quarter of companies considering this move cite that increasing costs of overseas production were driving this possibility, while around one-fifth cited quality issues and lead times.[26] Hornby, Aston Martin, Clarks and Trunki are examples of British businesses that have sought to reshore some UK production. This is particularly being driven by SMEs, who consider that 'Made in Great Britain' and British brands still have a cachet. Cello Electronics makes British televisions in County Durham and is bringing back the Ferguson brand name. Norton Motorcycles would emerge from the wreckage of the British bike industry and from various owners as British-owned once again in 2009 when it was bought by James Garner and would partially re-establish itself as a manufacturer based in Donington Park. Other transport examples include Morgan and Caterham and within furniture examples include Ercol or the Chesterfield Company. Here it is hoped that being niche or crafted offsets some of the difficulties of not being the cheapest.

The government's Reshoring UK initiative aims to help companies looking to bring manufacturing back to Britain to find the necessary supply chains and expertise, and it is run by the government's contracted-out service Innovate UK. The future outcomes, however, could be that SMEs and businesses with high value and branded goods will look increasingly more towards Britain, while larger businesses will look increasingly towards a mix of home- and overseas-based multinational manufacture, with low-cost, mass-produced components and products still tending towards the low-cost economies but higher-value production in Britain.

Organisation

The evidence suggests that the combined Austin and Morris company failed to integrate their businesses sufficiently to make an effective whole, resulting in a management failure that not only doomed the company but laid open the failure of the whole British car industry. There are elements of organisational failures seen in the other case studies, including ICI, GEC and Courtaulds. Today, the need to organise effectively is even more imperative given the dynamic nature of the world. Among the terms that business professionals cite that modern and future industrial organisations need to be are: dynamic, open, rule-bending, networked, communicative, global, fast, lean, flexible, informed, more diverse, more global and more linked. There is too an increasing tendency to reject public ownership in place of more private control. Companies like the US Uber, for example, have chosen and been able to become large multinationals without recourse to the stock exchange. In other examples, there is more partnering between bigger and smaller companies, and this would be a good model for Britain. There are also arguments that more employee-owned companies should pioneer a new future, or that growth-based econometric models are simply no longer appropriate for a world that has grown itself into an environmental mess.

The good news is that British businesses recognise this. Eighty per cent of businesses believe that building an organisation for the future is important. The bad news is that, according to the Manufacturing Advisory Service, only 11 per cent say they know how to do this:

> The way high-performing organisations operate today is radically different from how they operated ten years ago. Yet many other organisations continue to operate according to industrial-age models that are 100 years old or more, weighed down by legacy practices, systems, and behaviours that must be confronted and discarded before true change can take hold.[27]

Leadership

There will no doubt be many employees who consider that their business leaders and managers are there by dint of personalities and egos, rather than intellect and ability. What might be argued is that at least Britain's leaders are now less likely to be there due to their aristocratic connections through the traditional British old boy network. Leaders do also now have access to better education, with nearly half of school leavers moving on to university education compared with 5 per cent in the 1960s. There are also Master of Business Administration degrees and in Britain there is a massive upswing in industry-specific MBAs taken online through Massive Open Online Courses (MOOCS). This form of business-training-while-working looks to be successful, although Bob Lutz, vice chair of US car giant General Motors, would make the connection between the number of MBAs coinciding with the decline of the US motor industry. His point was that experienced engineers are best at running industrial businesses. For 'good leaders', Morris Motors, for example, appeared to be a company that failed to manage its leadership succession. Since the collapse of the Bank of Credit and Commerce International (BCCI) and Robert Maxwell's publishing empire, both from 1991 onwards, there are now better safeguards with respect to succession and companies must now produce a succession plan.

With better educated, more merit-based leaders comes better management. Unions and management are working more closely together – certainly more closely than in the strife-torn era of the 1970s and '80s – and only 276,000 working days were lost in 2017 due to labour disputes, which is the lowest number since records began in 1891. It should also be noted that today's and future British management leaders should not suffer the same type of Victorian attitudes to enterprise and jingoism. The millennial generation – also known as generation Y, or the echo boomers – are noted as being more narcissistic and more achievement-focused.[28] While this is somewhat stereotyping, it seems true that this emerging business generation has been brought up in the Apollonian culture of Thatcher capitalism – cold, rational, self-interested. This is good, or bad, depending on your perspective.

On the other hand, while there is less aristocratic involvement at the top, the argument can still be raised that too much career progress within Britain is still based on privilege rather than merit, notably now through the increasingly privatised secondary school system. The Fair Access watchdog noted that bright students from poor backgrounds are seven times less likely to go to university than their richer peers. Senior management roles are also still white-male dominated, with, for example, less than 30 per cent of women in senior management positions in FTSE 100 companies and gender pay inequality still rampant throughout corporate culture, potentially disenfranchising up to half of the UK's employees. While there has been less union action, it is also evident that it is harder for unions to take industrial action now, and harder still following the Trade Union Act (2016). There is still also a polarisation of union and management perspectives. Unions still relate production to the stability of jobs, whereas business leaders recognise that company performance is linked not to employee numbers but to efficiency and added value. Until these different perspectives are acknowledged and understood through trust and communication, then there will always be an undercurrent of contention.

It can also be argued that the 'Anglo-American model' of governance is more for the benefit of shareholders, who tend towards short-termism and risk aversion, as opposed to the longer-term stance adopted in other countries.[29] It is also argued that traditional governance and corporate structures are at odds with mechanisms of modern hi-tech, fast-moving, innovative companies. Companies such as Netflix or Google, for example, are ascribed by modern scholars as having 'founder centrism'. These, it is argued, are better suited to a much stronger, personality-driven 'cult', formed from charismatic entrepreneurs or, say, family owners with high percentage shareholdings. There is evidence of historic familial success in the Japanese *zaibatsu* system or in successful global companies such as Walmart, BMW, Samsung or Tata. Hence, while improved corporate governance might help to rein in the type of behaviours that brought down some of Britain's oldest and biggest companies, it might also now be that these frameworks are not the type of leadership needed in the new industrial landscape, and that Britain's publicly owned and traded corporations are also anachronistic and old fashioned.

Innovation, Research and Development

To have any chance of being the most technically advanced, a business needs science and research. ERA Technology, for example, are developing landmine detection using advanced electromagnetic equipment and ground-penetrating radar. Similarly, Litelok is using a newly developed metal polymer composite called Boaflexicore to develop a better theft-resistant bike lock. The material has a tensile strength of 177kN but also works to reinforce fractures rather than cracking, making cutting a much harder proposition. Security products as a whole have grown by 65 per cent since 2010, and the country is now the sixth-largest exporter of security equipment, employing 76,000 people. ioLight are releasing high-resolution and portable digital microscopes, while Fuel3D is a company developing organic 3D medical scanning. However, industry tends to spend less on research and development than other developed and OECD nations, although there was a 5.6 per cent increase in R & D spending in 2016, which does at least reflect an upward trend from 1984 onwards, and the nation does perform comparatively well in pharmaceuticals and aerospace.

In general, however, Britain is not always good at turning its science into global industrial leadership. Ask yourself this: of the companies around you right now, or the companies you and your friends and family work for, how many are going beyond just doing well and are actually producing or planning to produce groundbreaking goods for the future? A survey of global innovation lists only five British companies, two fewer than China and considerably less than the US, which provides half of the listings.[30] Other surveys include similar results, with US companies including Apple, Netflix, Amazon and SpaceX among the big-name hitters. As an example, 3D printing and additive manufacture have revolutionised the world of design and production, and have had some impact on specialist small-scale production, such as for aerospace, but uptake has been slower than it should have been and it is usually overseas rather than British companies that are behind these technologies. There are, nevertheless, some green shoots. Renishaw, for example, is a traditional metrology company that employs 4,000 people and has been moving more successfully into additive manufacture, where it specialises in metal 3D print. Similarly, Britain's nascent reborn transport industry also looks to have been in the slow lane with respect to electric power and autonomous drive. There are 250 companies exploring autonomous vehicles, but British companies are notably absent from the front of this queue. Perkins and Ricardo are global experts in diesel engines, but where are Britain's battery specialists, particularly as the days of the internal combustion engine appear to be numbered. New car giants will be technology companies, not traditional car producers. Cheers then for Riversimple's bold attempt to lead with a hydrogen fuel cell eco car, and for Dyson. Dyson is planning to open a new 210-hectare (517-acre) campus that will double its UK workforce to over 3,500 as part of a £2.5 billion investment that will support its research, including the development of AI, new battery technologies and robotics. Britain's space ventures have also been far behind the US, Russia, China and Europe, but it retains a positive future through its satellite expertise and emerging blue-sky thinkers, including Surrey Satellite

Technology Ltd, which is developing a partnership for far side of the moon communication, Oxford Space Systems and Foster + Partners.

While there are then mixed outcomes from traditional industries, the country has done better in emerging and future sectors, where the picture is more promising for 'future shapers'. Research from the London Mayor's Office shows that London is the Artificial Intelligence (AI) capital, with twice as many firms as Berlin and Paris combined. AI and virtual reality (VR) start-ups, for example, include HoloMe, Valkyrie Industries, Zappar, FloorSwitch, Blippar and DigitalBridge. Companies that are providing advanced technical know-how for practical purposes are referred to as 'grown-up' technologies and include flexiOPS, InVMA and FundamentalVR, the latter of which provides VR training for surgeons. The UK is also the world's leading country behind the emerging blending of technology and finance known as fintech. Typical fintech technologies include cryptocurrency, blockchain, robo-advisors and cybersecurity. Fintech unicorn company TransferWise is one example. Development in the UK is helped by the co-location of finance, technology and governance within London, whereas in the US, for example, these domains are spread across New York, Silicon Valley and Washington. In future, though, such businesses do need to be less London-centric, and less solely reliant on emerging technology trends that could become tomorrow's dot.com fads.

Many of the examples given emphasise the growing convergence between goods and services. Rolls-Royce, for example, is not just a jet engine manufacturing company but one that provides operational, servicing and consulting support. In respect of the trend for individualisation, Caterham Cars can today tailor each vehicle specifically to the needs of the buyer under its Signature scheme; McLaren has its in-house customisation brand MSO; and Aston Martin has recently launched the Q. There needs to be more of this. The key behind industrial servisitation is to ensure that the business is customer focused and integrates all domains from design and manufacture through to retail, finance and transport. It should draw on big data and skilled staff. The most important key, however, is to focus on problems and R & D rather than on products – think new and revolutionary.

Innovation and Investment

The Industrial Revolution would not have taken place without investment funding. For example, Baron Ferdinand de Rothschild was pivotal in providing finance and helped to establish the shipping, banking industry and financial services that today are so critical to the economy. He was able to build forty-five houses, ending with Waddesdon Manor in Buckinghamshire, which today provides much pleasure to National Trust visitors.

Nowadays, £1 spent on research needs a further £100 to develop a prototype and a further £100 to get to manufacture. How easy is it to access the finance needed for this, and how likely are British businesses to make these financial commitments? Britain can no longer rely on rich aristocrats, its empire or oil for finance and must therefore look to other funding sources.

In fact, 90 per cent of companies report finding access to finance easy.[31] However, the problem is finding funding for innovation, viewed as risky by money lenders, banks and the City, which are notoriously short-termist and risk averse.[32] For traditional industries:

> The net picture is that innovation in Britain is somewhat held back by the financial system. Financial challenges for the sector include a shortage of risk capital. This is particularly evident as a funding gap between research and early development and the funding for proof of concept that is usually required before the market steps in. There is also a shortage of funding for applied research and development in some areas such as the development of advanced green energy sources.[33]

Even though interest rates are at a record low – which should be encouraging industry to invest and step up their gearing – alternative funding sources to banks have risen by 10 per cent since 2011.

Lady Lucy Houston once donated £100,000 (around £3 million to £4 million today) to keep research going at Supermarine for the S.6 seaplane, which influenced the design of the Spitfire. What would the world look like without this? For start-up investments today, there is still too much reliance on unregulated and non-financial sources, such as family or crowdfunding, for start-ups. There are award competitions such as Chairs in Emerging Technology sponsored by the Royal Academy of Engineering (RAE) and supported by the UK's National Productivity Investment Fund for bioelectronics, batteries, robotic safety and AI. The RAE Launchpad and enterprise fellowships are competitions for innovation and enterprise, producing innovations such as aerograft material (silicates plus calcium and phosphate) for 3D dental bone grafting. The RAE's MacRobert Award was recently won by Owlstone for innovation in non-invasive disease diagnosis. In some cases, innovation is charity funded. Donations from Lillian Howell and the Henry Ford Charitable Foundation have funded recent IVF fertility development. Business angels have partially filled the gap, providing both finance and business support for start-ups and smaller businesses. UK technology companies have performed well with this level of investment, with a 31 per cent increase in funds raised between 2014 and 2016. It does, however, seem that important future industrial financing should not be left to charity, competitions or public lotteries – particularly in competing against the state-sponsored operations of companies in China and Russia.

For those who get funding, enterprise might be seen as the drive needed to turn research into innovative products, and here Britain is strong. The UK scores very highly on the 'ease of doing business' indices, and the Inc. 5000 Europe List named London as the No. 1 place for fast-growing private companies (2017). Around 100,000 businesses are consequently started each year in the UK, and many of these are seen to be successful, too. In 1989, 57 per cent of people on The Sunday Times Rich List belonged to old money, such as titled landowners, but by 2018, 94 per cent would be on the list through entrepreneurial activity.[34] One area of concern is the increasing difficulty that young people will have in being entrepreneurial. They were seen as the drivers behind Morris, de Havilland, Armstrong and Vickers, and were later global movers such as Steve Jobs or Bill Gates. British students are, however, now graduating with average debts of £50,800 – more for poorer students – with interest rates extending up to and beyond 6 per cent. Entrepreneurs should not be restricted only to the richer students who can pay off their debts or afford to take on more debt through business propositions rather than those with drive and ideas who are mired in debt.

For entrepreneurs who grow, and existing larger businesses with larger investments and projects, professional investors have arisen since the war through venture capital (VC), which has differed from traditional lending by investing in businesses in exchange for equity that is then rewarded through growth as opposed to traditional interest repayments on a loan. Venture capital can be risky for entrepreneurial activity as any slowdown in growth projections can lead to the project being subsumed by the venture capitalist. To some extent, venture capitalism has also been closely associated with the dot-com failures of the 1990s, with asset-stripping private equity funds that followed and increasingly with similar difficulties in obtaining funds from banks. However, Its emergence in the US is said to have played a significant role in the development of Silicon Valley, and its relationship with British technology looks to be very strong. Some £1.3 billion of VC money was invested in the UK tech sector between January and June 2017, higher than any other period in the previous decade and four times the amount invested during 2013. About £1.1 billion of this was in London, which has received more than double the VC investment in Berlin, and more than Paris and Amsterdam. This is typically in VR companies such as Improbable or fintech companies such as Zopa or Monzo.[35] The Alternative Investment Market (AIM) launched in 1995 has also proved to be successful for innovative, fast-moving technology companies. Starting with ten companies, by 2017 it would list over 1,000, including ASOS, Hutchison China MediTech, Burford, Fevertree, Boohoo, Abcam and Clinigen. Many AIM-listed companies are foreign, and Britain is also one of the most popular countries for direct foreign investment (DFI).[36]

Government and Research

The government made £8.75 billion available for R & D in 2015, with a similar yearly investment level planned for 2022–25 ($39.8 billion). Combined public and private spending on R & D in Britain that year was 1.7 per cent of GDP, compared to 2.9 per cent in Germany and 2.8 per cent in the US. There are, however, many studies that show the economic sense of investing in research because of the returns that are accumulated.

Typically, £1 invested in medical research yields a return on investment of 25p every year, broken down as 7p savings in healthcare and 15p to 18p in economic gains.[37] The government therefore committed £4.7 billion for additional research and development in the UK between 2016 and 2021, to increase public spending and bring this combined R & D spend to £12.5 billion or 2.4 per cent of GDP by 2021 as part of its Industrial Strategy. The government sees the industrial priorities as healthcare, robotics, clean energy, driverless vehicles, future materials and space technology. Cyber safety and the Fourth Industrial Revolution might be specific, too.

Notwithstanding the effects of the Covid-19 pandemic, the government trend for investment has therefore been upwards. This is good, although still behind Japan and South Korea, which spend over 4 per cent of GDP on research. In addition to research, there should also be further investment in development support. An 'Industrial Strategy Challenge Fund' is set to back priority technologies such as robotics and biotechnology, and the Annual Investment Allowance (AIA) provides tax breaks for businesses investing in up to £200,000 on plant and machinery. These are, however, pretty small-scale activities and Thatcherite laissez-faire policy in favour of private rather than public investment looks dated and inadequate given the difficulties businesses have in terms of confidence, measuring ROI and raising finance. The feeling is that more government investment in grants and loans is necessary, particularly around automation. Given the returns, the investment made into the economy and the banking system, and the support seen in other countries, it does not look an unreasonable consideration.

One of the problems is, of course, resourcing. The North Sea oil that helped to stop some of the economic decline is no longer an option. Oil flow peaked in 1999 and has fallen at around 5 per cent annually since, so that Britain is now a net oil importer. Sadly, the money accrued from the oil was not maximised. In terms of revenues raised, in the 1980s the government privatised the rights for oil exploration in favour of a £1 billion profit and future taxation of the companies that assumed the mantle of Britain's oil-producing industry. Concerns were raised that this would look cheap in the future when the value of oil increased, and this proved to be the case. The UK generated $470 billion in oil revenue in real terms up to 2014, while Norway, with a nationalised approach to its oil production with largely equal access to the same-sized oil reserves, would accrue $1,197 billion.[38] Nor was money saved for the long term, as Margaret Thatcher failed to establish an oil fund for further investment as Norway did. Investment in research now comes from other government sources.

It also leads to the question as to whether big-ticket government spending is value for money. It is estimated that the new *Queen Elizabeth* aircraft carrier and its sister ship have cost around £6.2 billion. The Russians have described these as convenient targets, and while this project has been modular in design, allowing many shipyards to stay alive, it has to be questioned whether this money could have been better invested in other industries – or where the spin-outs exist? Some £2 billion has been stated as the cost of the Tempest fighter project that is scheduled to replace the Typhoon in 2035. Again, this is great for consortium companies, including BAE Systems, Rolls-Royce, Italy's Leonardo and the EU missile group MBDA, which includes British Matra BAe Dynamics, but like the aircraft carriers, it seems likely the cost forecasts will escalate; so would this money be better spent on wider industry where the spin-offs would be more transparent? There have also been doubts raised about the technical claims that the Tempest will be a genuine sixth-generation fighter, and with it questions about its global relevance. The figure, sometimes stated to be as high as £167 billion for the cost of Vanguard nuclear-missile submarines, looks even more eye-watering at a time when other forms of electronic warfare and dirty bombs look much cheaper, and the need for environmental spend to avoid global catastrophe looks to be more important than nuclear weapons.

From 1915 through to 1965, industrial research was encouraged through the Department of Scientific and Industrial Research (DSIR), which included the National Physical Laboratory (NPL), National Engineering Laboratory (NEL) and the Road (now Transport) Research Laboratory. On its dissolution, industrial functions were taken over by the Department of Education and Science and the Science Research Council and the Ministry of Technology (MinTech), which later merged in 1970 with the Board of Trade to create the Department of Trade and Industry. Several further iterations have led to the current Department for Business, Energy and Industrial Strategy (BEIS). BEIS oversees the seven UK research councils, Innovate UK and Research England. Whether any of this has made an improvement is a moot point. BEIS is a place described by some of its employees as 'lacking enthusiasm' and it has a very formulaic and political feel to it, rather than being an exciting and dynamic fuse for research inspiration. A newly formed UK Research and Innovation (UKRI) is intended to better manage the research programme, while it remains to be seen whether or not an £800 million Advanced Research and Invention Agency (ARIA) becomes a dynamo of innovation or a government white elephant.

In 2016, the government announced its plans to invest £26.3 billion in academic-based science research over a five-year period. Within the domain of academia, Britain does have some of the world's best research institutions. £1 put into higher education via the catalyst investment fund to support academic and industrial collaboration yields a £12 return.[39] Oxford and Cambridge Universities regularly top the list of global overall university performance. Oxford University Innovation (OUI), for example, reports that since its creation in 1997 it has been responsible for spinning out a new company based on the university's research every two months. Summit Plc is one example, specialising in therapeutics and one of five OUI spin outs listed on the Alternative Investment Market (AIM).

Despite being up against a host of US institutions, Imperial, UCL, LSE, Edinburgh, King's College and Manchester universities all score highly for research, and around 50 per cent of the research of these top institutions is recorded in the Research Excellence Framework as being world-leading. For example, carbon can be arranged into many different forms (allotropes) giving it a wide variety of formats from coal, graphite and diamond to nanotubes and fullerenes. In 2004, scientists at the University of Manchester were able to isolate and test single layers of carbon arranged in a lattice that is known as graphene. Graphene is a semi-metal with an overlap between valence and conduction bands, allowing it to efficiently conduct heat and electricity. It is also a polycyclic aromatic hydrocarbon molecule consisting of a single hexagonal lattice layer, giving it a transparent appearance – and strength. It is the strongest material ever tested. As such, it has huge potential as a supermaterial that could reshape the world, although it has yet to fulfil that potential. The trick is being able to use it, particularly incorporating it into other materials, and here a number of recent British organisations are investigating, including the Graphene Application Centre, the National

Graphene Institute, the Graphene Engineering Innovation Centre, the National Physical Laboratory, 2-DTech, Haydale Composite Solutions, Composites Evolution, Bromley Technologies, Paragraf, Precision Varionic International and Johnson Matthey. Johnson Matthey is a good example of a traditional engineering company, rooted in 1817, but with over 12,000 staff working in forward industries such as advanced materials, environmental, battery and medical products.

This performance is, however, much less apparent at other top-performing universities. Within academia in general, academics are good at turning their research funding into academic papers, but they are less effective at turning papers back into money. Oxford and Cambridge are also supported by £21 billion endowments – more than the other Russell Group universities combined – and this lopsided funding model is not healthy for the nation in enabling the broader academic base.

Government and Business

The free-market, non-interventionist approach introduced by Margaret Thatcher and maintained by subsequent governments looks set to continue. Conservative free traders argue that our past might was forged on free trade rather than empire, which should therefore continue,[40] and there are plenty of enthusiasts for this position, including Friedrich Hayek, Milton Friedman, the WTO and the International Monetary Fund (IMF). The problem is that free-market economics is never truly free. It is always bound by rules, manipulated and distorted. Karl Marx knew this, as did John Maynard Keynes, and even Adam Smith, the father of economics and advocate of free markets, recognised this. An increasing number of modern economists are agreeing too, including Thomas Piketty, Joseph Stiglitz and Paul Krugman. Given the troubles of global supply chains during the Covid-19 pandemic and the increasing levels of environmental uncertainty caused by global transport systems, there is even an argument for increasing levels of industrial self-dependency and commercial isolationism, known as autarky. The end results for unfettered capitalism, however, are large corporations in unhealthy positions of power, production tending towards only low-quality, mass-demand goods, the abandonment of citizens seen as less employable and the degradation of the planet as secondary to the principle of winning and making money. For Britain, the free-market approach may have helped see off some companies that were long past their prime, but it almost certainly failed to save companies that should not have been allowed to fold, and the nation's debts seem an incredibly high price to pay. Many other economies around the globe, forced by WTO conditions to adopt these free-market principles, have come painfully unstuck. France and Germany, by contrast, have been seen to play and do well in the post-war era by not adhering completely to free-market rules.

Unfortunately, the British government does not seem to have learned those lessons, and in the most recent economic depression it chose to repeat the same mistakes. Again citing Ted Heath's interventionist mantra that banks were too big and too important to fail, it invested heavily and chose to merge financial institutions, irrespective of whether the institution deserved to survive or not, creating bigger but not necessarily better organisations. Despite the bail out, there were few reforms of the finance sector despite the appearance that some were playing hard and fast with business rules of taxation and money laundering, or that they were paying too much money to top employees while not providing an efficient lending service. The government also needs to learn the lessons of private versus public control. The abject failure of PFI (Private Finance Initiative)[41] and the confusing and costly mess of reprivatised rail travel in Britain today exemplify the failure of applying political dogma instead of cogent, analytical consideration. Building more airport runways, high-speed trains, motorways and housing flies in the face of common sense – which includes the need for environmental reduction and the creation of proper jobs in a managed economy.

With respect to industrial management, BEIS is continuing the approach of its forebears of developing industrial policies in different industrial sectors, but manufacturing is distributed throughout these sectors rather than appearing as a field in its own right. This bitty, iterative and fractured development of control is highly unsatisfactory. The government's Industrial Strategy document released in 2017 is a step in the right direction.

It has a wide range of ideas around innovation, people, infrastructure, places and the business environment to help fix productivity problems. Ideas include more research money, more maths and tech teaching funds, funds for a better digital infrastructure and (at last) a National Industrial Strategy Council. While these are all positive, there are issues. Despite its 255 pages, it is only a start and lacks the detail and depth needed to tackle the scale of the problems. Its funding proposals are too small-scale and weak in seeking the better release of private funding. It continues to fund research through tax breaks, which only really support big business that would have spent on research anyway. More direct spending is needed for SMEs. For example, the £75 million for developing post-graduate AI and online AI testing is not enough to help the UK develop world-leading AI. Other criticisms of the document include a confusing mix of old and new initiatives and a perception that it is poor in helping SMEs with productivity and supply chain issues. Moreover, it does not really address the issues of productivity – or Brexit!

Many companies would simply like more basic support. Seventy per cent of businesses, for example, see their export potential as good but 30 per cent report not knowing how to achieve this.[42] Innovate UK is the body aiming to support and grow home-based innovation as part of the government's UK Research and Innovation body (UKRI). Innovate UK supports 'catapult' centres – organisations and facilities that are intended to fire research towards commercial success, including centres in digital, satellite, semiconductor, cell and gene therapy, energy systems, future cities, medicine, transport, offshore energy and High Value Manufacturing (HVM, which has a number of Advanced Manufacturing Research Centres [AMRCs] around the country). These look to be providing the kind of innovation support that the Royal Aircraft Establishment and the National Physical Laboratory provided to companies such as de Havilland and ICL. However, the catapults are said to have no clear objectives, with inconsistent performance, and are difficult for smaller companies to access. The transport, future cities and digital catapults look likely to be scrapped, and only manufacturing and bio provide any kind of real value. Exporting itself seems to be supported by a hodgepodge of Innovate UK, chambers of commerce and an on-the-ground old boys' network. The government's

Export Credits Guarantee Department (ECGD) provides further support and encouragement to export through the UK's Export Finance (UKEF). It is the world's oldest export credit agency, winning some accolades but also mired in controversial claims as a promoter of arms, bribery and environmental damage.[43]

Infrastructure is also important to industry. The UK's largest carmaker, Jaguar Land Rover, has asked the government to agree to £450 million of infrastructure improvements in the West Midlands before it will commit to building its next generation of electric cars in Britain. However, infrastructure is a difficult problem because while it helps to drive industry forward, and provides jobs and growth through inward investment, it can be controversial and expensive. The High Speed 2 train line proposal (HS2) will, for example, triple line capacity and might start a revitalisation of the entire train network. It is, however, damaging to some residents and the environment, set to provide a modest improvement in running time, and likely to cost around £55 billion. This may seem pointless and remote to many of Britain's businesses that are found shunted into sheds and outhouses on dreary estates or in farmyards. The third runway proposed for Heathrow is even more contentious, affecting even more people, causing even more damage to the environment and costing something like £14 billion. The benefits of better connectivity it will provide range somewhere between £5.5 billion and £30 billion. Better support of regionalisation and the environment would somehow seem not to have won the argument here.

With respect to staffing, there is seemingly an ongoing reported shortfall of 200,000 engineers, around 59,000 per year. For the future, it is estimated that there are only half as many graduates as employees need, and the shortfall will soon rise to 257,000.[44] Fewer than 10 per cent of engineers entering industry are women. In fact, the number of students taking A-levels in science, technology or maths is in decline.[45] There has been some action by the government and relevant professional bodies to address this imbalance between education and industry, for example, by increasing the emphasis on STEM subjects at school through the EBacc system (including soon-to-appear new Design Engineering A-levels) and increasing STEM outreach to school-aged children.[46] This has led to an increase of 11 per cent (to 51 per cent) in school children who would consider an engineering career (Engineering UK, 2017). There are increased apprenticeship schemes, including degree apprenticeships and increased technical qualifications, including BTEC and HND. However, only 5 per cent of businesses have confidence that the Apprenticeship Levy system will achieve its goals, and it has already started to decline. It is a good idea, but it needs revamping.

Alongside this shortfall in engineering graduates, however, there is widespread criticism of the capabilities of the engineering graduates that are produced. More than half of employers say that recruits do not reach the expected standard and nearly two-thirds think skills gaps are a threat to their business.[47] These skills failings include poor work experience, poor soft skills, poor career-path mapping, poor creative capabilities and weak synaptic knowledge.[48] One of the problems for education is that the Engineering Council, via its professional bodies such as the Institution of Mechanical Engineers, prescribes a long list of competencies and skills that engineering courses are required to impart in order for the courses and their graduates to be recognised as professional, chartered engineers. The Accreditation of Higher Education Programmes (AHEP) requires radical overhauling if engineering academics are to develop interesting and future-looking degree courses that will excite and inform the nation's future industrial innovators.

In summary, it can be said that the picture is much changed in relation to the mistakes involving strategy, operations, leadership, innovation and national governance that hammered industry in the past. The economy is weak and efficiency is problematic, but there are positives. Britain is set to exploit new growing markets, is producing higher-value goods, and is starting to move forward in terms of research spend, automation and higher-technology industries. The main barriers seem to be a need for some better governmental housekeeping, and a change in the disposition towards hi-tech at the expense of traditional industry. The environment is also a critical factor since industrial production simply cannot keep moving as it does. Economists, politicians and business leaders need to find new models of working. As the country that introduced industry to the world and which now has to change to rebuild the shape of industry, Britain should once again lead the world by example.

16

Brexit

Britain prevaricated from the start in joining with France and Germany as they worked towards economic co-operation after the Second World War. It was a position the Europeans found difficult to fathom. France's Jean Monnet, who helped to build the ECSC, stated, 'I never understood why the British did not join [the ECSC]. I came to the conclusion that it must have been because of the price of victory [in the war] – the illusion that you could maintain what you had done, without change.'[1] As co-operation led to the European Economic Community (EEC), Britain instead proposed a free-trade area around the EEC, which was rejected. In its place it formed the European Free Trade Association (EFTA) with other European but non-EEC countries, but this proved to be an ineffective failure. After much hand-wringing on all sides, Britain finally joined Europe in 1973, with the EEC itself morphing into the European Union (EU). The relationship between Britain and the EU was, however, never an easy marriage and forty-three years later, on 23 June 2016, 51.9 per cent of British people who voted in the referendum on Britain's membership of the EU voted to leave; it was the British exit, or Brexit.

Declinism

A significant proportion of the older generation voted to leave. They still seemed to remember Britain as an industrial powerhouse and global leader, recalling its troubled joining and the disagreements Britain had had with its

EU partners over social, industrial and monetary policies. Some seemed, ironically, to actually blame the EU, with a perceived expensive administration and hindering bureaucracy as being part of the reason for the nation's industrial demise; 'declinism', being the term used to describe a belief that Europe had somehow played a role in Britain's economic and political decline.

Echoing colonial attitudes, this sector of society pushing for Brexit seemed unwilling to acknowledge that the reality of the industrial collapse and loss of jobs and status was a mixture of home-grown incompetence coupled with increasing global factors and US hegemony rather than a result of European collaboration. They also seemed to ignore the benefits that the EU had brought, in terms of peace, stabilisation and increased industrial efficiency, forgetting that the EU is part of the reason that British Industry stabilised from the 1970s onwards. British companies were forced to recognise they could no longer rely on Commonwealth customers, but they now had to innovate, become more customer-focused and become more efficient. Within the EU, GDP per person in Britain has grown faster than in Italy, Germany and France in its forty-year membership, and by 2013 Britain was more prosperous than these economies for the first time since 1965. Without the EU, it is estimated that Britain's economy would have been 23 per cent worse off, more similar to that of New Zealand and Argentina.[2]

It could even be said that this aged generation should look closer to home for the decline of the country. After all, is this the same generation who bought foreign cars in the 1960s, who managed firms poorly and fought union battles in the 1970s, who spent their money overseas on package holidays and invested in Margaret Thatcher's policies in the 1980s and who retired on full, unaffordable pensions in the 1990s and 2000s? This generation more than any other should also not forget that the EU brought a peace dividend to countries that had previously been at war regularly during the Industrial Revolutions.

In Control?

Many younger Britons seemed to vote leave for more economic reasons, arguing on the theme that independence would give more flexibility for the British government to implement the tools needed to steer the economy more effectively. It would, for example, be in a better position to implement its own monetary and fiscal control, implement tariffs or not, nationalise or privatise at will, support more direct inward industry investment, and unencumber itself and industry with EU-generated bureaucracy. Additionally, it would be able to adjust its corporation tax to support industrial growth, to make inward investment more attractive and to encourage more overseas companies to set up in the UK. It could also encourage some companies to look closer at manufacturing back at home ('reshoring') for shorter supply lines, strike its own trade deals outside of the EU framework, and trade globally and not locally with a belief that future growth markets lie outside of the EU. As an indicator of this increased control, the government temporarily extended zero tariffs from 80 per cent of imports to 87 per cent of imports, leaving some protection still in place for primarily agriculture products but now including some cars and ceramics.

This tariff change might raise the percentage of imports from around the world coming into Britain that do not pay tax from 56 per cent to 92 per cent while reducing the percentage of EU imports paying tariffs from 100 per cent to 82 per cent. The move to lower import tariffs does help to keep costs lower for some businesses and does keep import costs low for consumers. It does, however, remove the protection that tariffs provided for some industries in much the same way the Corn Laws developed. Removing 12 per cent on the import of foreign-made bicycles, for example, is a blow for British-made bikes. This position of low tariffs also makes the UK negotiating position harder; Britain cannot agree to a like-for-like tariff drop if it has already done so. It also does not preclude the likelihood of import taxes being set in overseas countries, is hastily contrived without business consultation, and is likely to be against WTO rules, so not sustainable in the long run.

The argument that being outside of the EU allows Britain to be more relaxed in meeting EU legislative requirements, enabling an increase in competitiveness, also looks flawed. The government's ability to influence Britain's industrial decline with all of these controls before it joined the EU has already been seen to be limited and the additional tweaks it can achieve from being outside after Brexit look respectively minimal. The government is, for example, agreeing to the relevant climate change legislation such as the Paris Accord, outside of the EU framework. With respect to EU legislation itself, business will still need to engage with EU legislation in order to trade there, but will now need to do this individually rather than through the government. It will also have Britain's own trading legislation to consider as well. For example, for many years there has been some confusion about the difference in consumer protection between the British Sale of Goods Act (SOGA) and the European Consumer Rights Act (CRA). SOGA is remedial while CRA is preventative; SOGA covers goods for six years, CRU for two; and so on. SOGA was recently repealed, so can Britain now ignore the CRA? Of course not; it must meet both EU and any British safety requirements. It also follows that EU safety laws may not now need to apply to goods imported into Britain at all. This is but one aspect of trading, and the whole vision of business working to a whole ranch of British-specific legislation while accommodating EU legislation for exports to the EU as well is somewhat scary. The argument that bureaucracy will reduce then looks particularly thin.

There is a further issue with respect to research. Companies like de Havilland showed that modern large-scale technology and innovation need partnerships. Between 2007 and 2013, the UK contributed €5.4 billion to EU science and received €8.8 billion in return. It was, therefore, a net recipient of EU funding for research and development, which it will lose. It will also be hard to engage with large-scale innovation projects that are facilitated by the EU: space, planes, nuclear. The threats to technological co-operation include Galileo, the EU's £9 billion rival to GPS; Copernicus observation satellites; Euratom nuclear safety and research; Framework Nine (a successor to Horizon of which the UK is a net recipient); and the European Medicines Agency, which is now likely to go to Amsterdam.

A Global Not European Player

For some leavers, the argument is that Britain has not benefitted from the EU as much as other EU countries. The most protected EU tariffs, for example, are in the food and vehicle industries where France and Germany are strong, and these stable home markets help them. Meanwhile, the trade deficit in goods for the UK has grown from £6 billion in the 1990s to £29 billion in 2021, mostly to the EU. Service performance is better, but these are not liberalised within the EU, and Britain therefore has not benefitted as much from EU membership. Consequently, only 12 per cent of British UK GDP is derived from exports to the EU, and over the past twenty years, goods exported by the UK to the EU have grown by only 2 per cent, whereas it has been 3.3 per cent to the rest of the world. James Dyson made the point about emerging markets: 'We have got the opportunity to export globally – Europe is only 15 per cent of global trade and declining. The world outside Europe is expanding faster than Europe, and that is the same for Dyson.'[3] J.C. Bamford Excavators (JCB), with a staff base of 11,000 and global revenues of around £2.75 billion, argued that the benefits of global trade would outweigh any additional tariffs arising from Brexit. India and China, for example, jointly represent one-third of the global market. Being globally rather than EU-focused has been a key argument for some leavers and that leaving Europe without an EU trade deal (a 'hard' exit) is fine.

Despite this argument, the EU is still Britain's biggest market and trading partner, providing a market zone that replicates to some extent its former empire. Without the protection of this 'home market' Britain could become lost, as it did with the loss of its empire market. The EU Rules of Origin also mean that products coming from the EU must have 52 per cent of components made in the EU – and Brexit will exclude British manufacturers from this. Note that US companies invest significantly more in the EU than they do in Asia, while EU companies similarly invest more in the US than they do in India or China.

The argument for increased global trade is also troublesome because without trade agreements in place, this operates under burdensome WTO rules. The WTO replaced the previous General Agreement on Tariffs and Trade (GATT) in 1995 and Britain's trading rules are defined within it based on its EU membership at the time. Leavers dismiss the problem of trading under WTO rules as groundless, identifying the fact that 60 per cent of trade is already under WTO rules and that Britain's trade with 111 countries under WTO rules between 1993 and 2015 still grew at three times the rate of that done with the EU – 2.9 per cent growth as opposed to 0.9 per cent.

These arguments, however, tend to be company- and industry-specific, and increased tariffs and bureaucracy will as a rule make British companies less competitive. Consider a car manufactured in the UK. On average its direct cost base may include up to 42 per cent in materials and components. If 50 per cent of these are brought in from overseas (half of the components for the BMW Mini built in Oxford come from abroad, for example), then roughly a quarter of the car's cost base is liable to increase in both import and/or export tariffs (for example, adding a 4.5 per cent tariff) while exporting the whole car might incur a 10 per cent export tariff. Jaguar Land Rover estimated that without any border agreements, the tariffs alone would cost it an extra £1.2 billion, while the Society of Motor Manufacturers and Traders (SMMT) estimated this will add £2.7 billion to imports and £1.8 billion to exports to the industry as a whole.

Uncertainties and delays in new cross-border supply lines will also add cost, for example, forcing companies to carry more stocks in a reversal of the just-in-time production policies that have helped Britain become more efficient. The interest on this additional investment must be paid, and more stock will be prone to be lost through damage and theft. These issues are particularly difficult for companies striving for efficiency and competitiveness through quality and lean manufacturing. Honda anticipated a hard Brexit would cause an additional three-day delivery time for components, and if this is multiplied out across industry then the whole essence of just-in-time and low-stock inventories will be blown apart. Manufacturers will need to fund three more days' stock and logistics to cover the stock now stuck in customs and to keep production moving. The weaker position of the pound also increases the costs of bringing in raw materials and components from abroad. MI supplies in Teesside quoted costs as rising by £750,000 in the two-year period after the Brexit referendum (against a total turnover of £3 million). Companies using lower-cost labour from Eastern Europe are likely to have to pay more wages and benefits to encourage migrants to stay, or to encourage a greater take-up of employment among home labour sources. There will also be more administrative hassle and more regulations, and more customs activity and more delay. If this direct cost base is multiplied up through the addition of overheads, profit and taxation, then the additional cost to consumers becomes very large. Hence the Confederation of British Industry (CBI) leader Paul Drechler described Brexit as having zero benefits to industry from being outside of the customs union and a death knell for motor manufacturing.[4] Expenditure in the car industry halved in 2016–17 compared to 2015–16 from over £750 million with BMW holding off from investment. Airbus is similarly holding off £80 billion of planned investment in the air industry, and have considered withdrawing all manufacturing from Britain full stop.

Making Trade Agreements

Leavers have contended that becoming a global player under WTO rules is not a problem because trade agreements between nations are easy to achieve. Boris Johnson and the then Trade Secretary Liz Truss claimed that Britain 'have now agreed trade deals covering sixty-two countries plus the EU', apparently forgetting that sixty of these agreements were pre-existing.[5]

In reality, the process is hard. The US and the EU, for example, account for around a third of world trade in goods, and trade agreements, including the adoption of WTO rules, has meant that trade barriers between the two economic zones have been generally kept at under 3 per cent. It has long been argued that a transatlantic free-trade zone that sought to remove any barriers would liberalise trade further and boost growth further – not just in the EU and US but across the globe. The Transatlantic Trade and Investment Partnership (TTIP) is an attempt to formulate – or at least approach – this position. Discussions are, however, protracted, covering at least fifteen rounds of negotiation that have controversially been maintained as confidential, leading opponents to suppose that not everyone will benefit. Particular arguments consider that liberalisation may lead to a reduction in regulatory safeguards – such as welfare or food standards – and will enable transatlantic corporations to put sovereign governments under more economic and political pressure, potentially undermining social models and democratic processes. While the EU and Canada have managed to formulate a deal, it took over ten years to achieve.

Even if deals were easy to cut, are other countries really going to offer Britain terms in a deal that are in Britain's favour rather than in their own?

Did everyone forget the 1962 trade deal with Japan that killed off the British bike industry? To get new trading concessions with other countries, Britain will also have to get agreements approved through the WTO, and any WTO member could object if they feel disadvantaged. Many neutral parties seem to think that cutting deals will not be as easy as leavers have argued. The International Monetary Fund (IMF) has predicted 1 million job losses and a cost to the British economy of $250 billion. Global consultancy firm Oliver Wyman says that, under the most negative scenario of high import tariffs and high regulatory barriers, the cost to the economy could total £27 billion. Households could be left up to £1,000 a year worse off because of Brexit trade barriers.

Reclaiming Britain?

Some leavers seemed to vote to leave in order to achieve a more independent and self-determining Britain, irrespective of the economic cost. This included some ministers, who would seemingly recognise the dangers but wave them away as less important than their own patriotic beliefs: 'F★★★ Business,' as Boris Johnson is reported to have said.[6]

However, the idea of reclaiming Britain even after Brexit seems unlikely. The state-owned organisations of which Britons might once have been proud – British Rail, British Telecom, British Gas, the Central Electricity Generating Boards, and others – were sold off for a free-market ideology that intended to make everyone in the country a financial stakeholder, and which has failed. If you are a football supporter of a major club, then over the same period you may well have seen ownership of your club move overseas. Following the switch to Premier League football, seven top-flight clubs fell into US hands alone, while on the pitch itself, three-quarters of the players are now from overseas. Within the private sector, the initial hesitation to look at British companies because of the uncertainty of the economy diminished once it was clear that the economy had sunk to a level whereby there were bargains to be had. During 2019–21, over £120 billion was spent buying out 1,206 British firms. Many of these organisations are now instead owned by Australian banks, Canadian pension funds, Arabian investment funds and even, with the ultimate irony, by the French and German governments. Using the area of Thanet in Kent as an example, a local school is owned by a Luxembourg-based investment company, while the running of the school is subcontracted to another company. The local airport, Manston, was closed down by Scottish-based internationalist owners. The local company, Hornby, produces much of its output in China, while Pfizer cut its research base by three-quarters. Of fifty-three retail premises in the main shopping centres, only two are local and not chain-owned, and the centre itself is owned by a distant shopping centre chain. The offshore turbines are owned by a Swedish company, and the power lines are run ashore by a Hong Kong business magnate. Hong Kong, Australian and Canadian consortia own the water supplier.

As James Meek points out in his book *Private Island*, local power, pride and accountability have all diminished as a consequence of such changes. It should be remembered that this process did not come from the EU. Germany and France tend to be stunned by Britain's selling-off activities, initiated by Margaret Thatcher on the whim of academic theory and pursued as policy by successive British governments, who seem to have given away British organisations to foreign ownership in a manner that has been described as 'privatisation, jurisdiction hopping, protection of inherited wealth and a shift of taxation from rich to poor'.[7] Leaving the EU will not return these privatised and increasingly foreign-owned aspects of the country to the British people.

Immigration

Similarly, leavers, and particularly the older leaver camp, have also blamed the EU for increasing uncontrollable immigration, which has been perceived to have diluted endemic and historic British culture. This, too, is fallacy. Britain is and always has been an island of immigrants. Immigrants were instrumental parts of the warships that won the famously British victory at the Battle of Trafalgar. Churchill's 'few' – the famous and remarkable Battle of Britain wartime pilots who beat off the Nazi invasion of Britain and saved the world from the terrifying prospect of Nazi domination – was fought by 574 foreign pilots alongside 2,353 British ones. Churchill himself, voted Britain's greatest hero, had an American mother. The British monarchy is of Scando–French descent, and the late queen – that most patriotic of institutions – was of German descent, while the king is of German–Greek origin. Britain's industrial growth has also been built on the back of immigrants and the evidence of this is writ large in the corporate stories told within this book.

The planting of turnips and clover that sparked the British Agricultural Revolution, which then fired Britain's Industrial Revolution, was a concept brought over from France.

In 1496 a water-powered blast furnace was developed at Newbridge in the Ashdown Forest that produced ten times more iron than the incumbent bloomeries and would also help to kick-start the Industrial Revolution. It was an idea imported from the Low Countries along with immigrant workers. Frenchman Pauncelett Symart would take on a seven-year lease from 1498 and start a gun-making revolution that would see Sussex guns lead the world for the next 300 years. Take-up was initially slow, as imported bronze cannon were more reliable, less prone to corrosion and strong and light. Henry VII, however, turned to British-made bronze cannon but made under the expertise of another Frenchman, Peter (Pierre) Baude. This inward-facing switch in purchasing, coupled with the drive for cheaper cannon, stoked the industry. Henry VIII commissioned the first iron foundry in Ashdown Forest, considered to be fifty years after the development of cast iron cannon in Europe. The development fifty years later in Buxted of a bored-out cannon that lifted Britain to the forefront of arms manufacture was again achieved with the expertise of Baude. By 1548, thirty-two furnaces and thirty-eight forges had sprung up, turning the localised Wealden iron industry into an industrial powerhouse. Nearly half of the workers in Britain's industrial heartland of the Weald were, of course, French and Flemish.[8] William III, who later commissioned British-made arms that led to the formation of BSA, was, of course, a Dutchman.

The Barings family were wool traders who became the country's greatest cotton traders and who would become only the second company in the world to establish a merchant bank that helped to finance the Industrial Revolution. The family were descended from Johann Baring, an immigrant from Germany. The silk industry was started in the country by Italian immigrant John Guardivaglio, who set up a silk-throwing enterprise in Stockport. The family behind the founders of the textile giant Courtaulds were immigrant Huguenots. 'Artificial Silk', which would become the rayon that enlivened British textiles, was first patented in Britain by George Audemars of Lausanne. It was Freidrich Lehner arriving from the Chardonnet factory in Switzerland who kick-started Britain's development of rayon, working with Lister and Co of Bradford Ltd to produce cellulose nitrate yarn in 1893. H.G. Tetley at Courtaulds had worked at Listers, and he then brought the technology into Courtaulds.

The roots of ICI were started by foreigners Ludwig Mond and Alfred Nobel. Newcastle's Holzapfel Compositions Company Ltd was founded in 1881 by German brothers Max and Albert Holzapfel, along with friend Charles Petrie, to supply marine coatings to the local shipping industry. This would become International Paint, now operating as part of AkzoNobel based in Gateshead but with 5,500 employees worldwide.

GEC founders, the Binswangers, were German immigrants. Marconi, inventor of the radio and founder of the Marconi Company that formed a large part of GEC, and which today underpins BAE Systems, was of course Italian. J. Lyons & Co., one of the largest food manufacturers in Europe, the first business to use a computer (the LEO), and the organisation behind the quintessentially British tea shops, was also founded by immigrant Germans, the Gluckstein family (Lyons was a 'borrowed' name).

Norwegians and Greeks were behind the engines and styling for Morris Motors. Triumph, founder of the much-loved British Triumph marque now proudly carried forward by Triumph Motorcycles Ltd, was founded originally in 1893 by a German immigrant called Siegfried Bettman, supported later by another German immigrant, Moritz Schulte.

Polish engineer Leo Kuzmicki designed and developed the Featherbed-framed Manx Norton single-cylinder racing models that formed the basis of Britain's world championship-winning motorbikes in the heyday period of the early 1950s. BSA's popular post-war Bantam motorbike was actually based on the German DKW RT100. Germany had refused to continue to supply the Jewish importer of the DKW bikes to Britain, who promptly gave the designs to BSA.

Paul Eugene Louis Angois, a French citizen, set up a small bicycle work-shop with an English colleague to form Raleigh Bikes, one of the oldest bicycle companies in the world and, by 1913, the biggest. Viners cutlery, which contributed to Sheffield's steel-making strength, was started by the German Jewish Viner family. Rothschild, the man who helped to fund the Industrial Revolution and found British banking, was an immigrant. Isambard Kingdom Brunel, voted in the BBC poll as Britain's second great-est ever Briton, was the son of French immigrant Marc Brunel, who was himself instrumental in developing mass production techniques in this country through his work with the production of naval pulleys. He intro-duced to this country the first metal machinery capable of producing the necessary accuracy to do this. Polish cryptographers and radio engineers developed the bombe that was used in cracking the Enigma code machine and computer development by Alan Turing and colleagues. Graphene was discovered in Britain by Russian-born scientist Sir Konstantin Novoselov and Russian-born Dutch–British scientist Sir Andre Geim. Is it necessary to go on?

This view of a British 'race' then completely ignores the role that immi-grants have played in Britain's industrial development, which has helped to define and make Britain what it is. The reduction of migrants will not help Britain's current or future industry either. At the time of writing, thirty-two chairmen of FTSE companies driving forwards Britain's economic recovery are from overseas, and forty-two chief executives were not born in the UK. Lower-skilled workers will be absent, causing production costs to rise. A 2013 Review of Engineering Skills by the government's Chief Scientific Officer showed that around 20 per cent of the engineering sector in areas such as aerospace relies on immigrant expertise, with university engineering sectors relying on 32 per cent of overseas students.[9] The cur-rent Tier 2 visa restrictions will also cut back skilled overseas workers needed for the nascent technology industry – which currently has around 25,000 job vacancies in London alone. It won't help the balance of pay-ments either since wages paid to workers overseas are greater than that paid to foreign workers in the UK and contributes to the balance of payments losses. The government's start-up visa allows tycoons to enter Britain – but only tycoons and not the skilled or those with great ideas but less money.

The Brexit Deal

For many remainers, the arguments in favour of Brexit always looked to be flawed. What exacerbated their angst was that it was well known that the information used in the original debate was flawed and misleading, even though the process was criticised as illegal by the Electoral Commission. Despite this, despite the narrowness of the exit vote at just 51.9 per cent to 48.1 per cent, and despite the importance of the outcome to the nation, the emotion of the debate was too strong for any willingness from too many people to reconsider their positions in favour of entrenched views and opinions. Instead, everyone held their breath, hoping for a good deal, and a good deal might have helped overcome the problems – if Europe was prepared to let Britain have its cake and eat it. How likely was that?

Achieving a Brexit deal was also always going to be difficult, given not just the different perspectives of Britain and the EU, but the different viewpoints within Britain itself. The older leaver camp, for example, was aiming for Britain to return to a land of cream teas and Union flags with independent self-determination, where British workers and research once again do their own bit to rebuild an economic empire. A no-deal, hard exit was fine for this group. The younger leavers were looking for Britain to become an economic powerhouse, a land of multinational companies with foreign manufacturing plants and foreign owners and investors. This view of leaving the EU would contrast in a vastly different way to that of the older generation, a more 'hollow brand' nation where business values and business ethics dominate over cultural values in order to survive. One section of the leavers' camp was thus going to be dissatisfied. Remainers, meanwhile, felt disenfranchised by a referendum voting system that had produced a marginal outcome, that had been unfairly influenced by false claims, that had seen no examination of the possible consequences of the vote and where they felt the outcomes were going to be bad.

Given the internal difference between the leave, remain, hard and soft camps, let alone the dealing with Europe itself, resolving the issue of how to leave Europe presented what engineers would call a 'wicked problem' – one without an obvious solution or even obvious places to start. Former Prime Minister Theresa May's solution was a compromise 'customs partnership' proposal with one set of hard exit rules for services (non-EU compliant) and another softer exit for goods (which would be EU compliant). Most importers would pay UK tariffs, and some would pay EU tariffs on finished articles being re-exported. The UK could then forge trade deals elsewhere while avoiding EU jurisdiction and free movement through a separate mobility framework. This solution was seen by business as complex and prone to fraud, seen by Europe as barmy, and seen by both remainers and leavers as making Brexit pointless. It was unsatisfactory for remainers, too, because business would de facto have to follow EU rules – or do better – with extra cost and extra administration with no more chance of further trade deals. For this reason, and particularly the issues around the Northern Ireland and Irish border, May's deal was rejected, and she resigned.

Boris Johnson's deal was, in some eyes, even worse than May's. It left both the customs union and the single market, meaning that although some agreement was reached on tariffs, hence avoiding WTO rules, there are still border issues, including customs declarations, rules of origin checks, regulatory checks, work permits and health and safety and testing certificates. Border hold-ups are working against the key production efficiency principle of 'just-in-time' production, meaning more investment is needed in stock, administration and time, adding to efficiency woes. In some cases businesses can operate through an export intermediary known as an Authorised Economic Operator, but these add cost and are likely to be EU based. The deal also requires these controls on goods passing from mainland Britain to Northern Ireland. The service industry on which Britain has come to rely was ill considered at all. Agreed at the eleventh hour, without proper scrutiny, the deal was passed.

The Outcomes

It is hard to be exact about the full effects of Brexit on businesses because, at the time of writing, any difficulties are conflated with Covid-19 lockdown problems. The outcomes of Brexit were, however, always likely to be bad and the indications so far are shaping up that way.

As a result of Brexit predictions alone, Britain slipped to sixth place and behind France in the world economy. As global economists and traders forecast problems for Britain, the pound weakened from about $1.50 to $1.20, making British businesses ripe for takeover. Britain's remaining jewel in the technology crown, ARM, was immediately taken over by SoftBank for £24 billion. The takeover of GKN in 2018 marked the end of British ownership of the last great, Victorian British engineering company (noting the exception of BAE Systems, which, while a modern construct, has many historical roots). What stopped a greater number of takeovers was the concern that the British economy was facing such peril that it outweighed any bargains that could be had.

The first financial reports after Brexit, in January 2021, indicate that exports to the EU fell by 41 per cent, valued at around £5.6 billion (ONS). Trade between Germany and Britain has particularly slumped, with British exports down 56 per cent to Germany, and German exports in return down 29 per cent. Exports to other EU countries fell less, by around 6 per cent, and by 10 per cent to non-EU countries but this disproportionately high drop with Europe's leading economy does not look good, and the drop in trade between Germany and other countries is nowhere near as bad.[10]

Some reports forecast a bounce back. However, even at this time, it is clear too that sorting out the 'rules of origin' has become a burdensome task, with more paperwork and delays at borders than expected. Some businesses are choosing not to export because of these problems, and some suppliers are similarly choosing not to import because of the added complexity. Small businesses, which account for one-third of exports, are being hit particularly hard: 'What looks like permanent deterioration in their competitive position due to higher admin, paperwork and shipping costs.'[11]

Brexit has encouraged some companies to look closer to home and to reshore with shorter supply lines, but other companies are already looking to relocate plant overseas, and PwC reports that one-third of manufacturing companies are considering the movement of some manufacturing plant overseas because of Brexit, notably into China and India. Companies including Honda, Nissan, BMW, Toyota and JLR cut jobs and closed plants. Philips closed its only UK factory, and Panasonic and Sony planned to move their headquarters from London to Amsterdam.[12] Within the professional services sector, 43 per cent of companies have or plan to move operations to the EU, including £1.3 trillion assets, while 8,000 jobs in the financial sector have moved abroad since Brexit.[13]

As a result, 86 per cent of people who voted to remain consider Brexit to have gone badly or worse than expected, according to an Opinium 'One year on' Survey among 1,904 adults. Many people and companies who argued in favour of Brexit seemed to do so from self-interested perspectives without consideration of Britain's industry as a whole and many now seem surprised that Brexit does not appear to be turning out as they expected. Forty-two per cent of leavers had a negative view of Brexit, according to the survey, including swathes of farmers and fisherman who voted leave but now awakening to the reality of Brexit.

How bad can it get? Perhaps we can look back to the last time Britain stepped outside of a European-led consortium. In 409 BCE, Britons threw off Roman rule and saw off pagan invaders. However, the victory was short-lived, leading to 'probably the most dramatic period of social and economic collapse in British history',[14] followed by 400 years of the Dark Ages fighting off aggressive invaders and 1,000 years of domination by Norman rules and their descendants. The Vikings may no longer be with us, but China and Russia are potentially just as adversarial.

The best we can say is that it is too early to assess the impact of Brexit; however, it is likely to add to the negative impacts on Britain's economy. What then are the future prospects for industry?

17

Will Britain Make it?

The early part of this book summarised how Britain came to lead the world through innovations that created the Industrial Revolution. If you had lived in the nineteenth century, during Britain's Victorian period, you would have seen the world transformed through remarkable engineering: iron bridges, hydraulic cranes, affordable clothing, and affordable travel through steam trains, all of which are still awesome. Through innovation and enterprise, and business and government practices, sometimes but not always entirely ethical, it stayed ahead of the game. The companies that created these products were technological giants that dominated the industrial scene – the Googles and Amazons of today – but some of Britain's greatest companies were still to come, hewn out of the turbulence of the First, then the Second and Third Industrial Revolutions that stormed the world in the nineteenth and twentieth centuries.

Britain, however, always faced competition from around the globe and its pre-eminence inevitably slipped as more and more countries began to industrialise, including notably the US and Germany, with products that were better, cheaper or could call on bigger markets. The population in the US, for example, was growing, at over 30 per cent each year in the decades prior to the First World War and at 20 per cent thereafter. Homegrown US pioneers in rail, steel and equipment began to exploit the size of this home market and towards the end of the nineteenth century the US overtook Britain as the world's leading manufacturing nation. After the Second World War, Britain's economy was then hit by a perfect storm: the unpredicted loss of its empire and trading partners, war indebtedness that was not felt in the same way by other economies, and a rise in more industrial competition that grasped the Second and Third Industrial Revolutions more efficiently than the British. Industrial decline was held back as the world bounced back from the trauma of the war, but then accelerated rapidly from the 1960s onwards, sparked particularly by the oil crisis of the 1970s.

Most of Britain's leading industrial companies could not escape from this storm, and this book has explored the stories of some of them; how and why they became great and what happened to them during this difficult period. The actual mechanisms for failure have looked at the issues of strategy, organisation, leadership and innovation. Those reasons, it should be noted, were not then due to the sudden appearance of a Chinese manufacturing nation emerging from the shadows to undercut everybody. The other surprising thing is not that companies failed – that is normal – but that so many failed during the same period and that they were not replaced with new and powerful, innovative companies. A succession of British governments impotently failed to halt the decline. They failed to drive the changes that industry needed, or to excise controls that might have helped. They supported companies that needed to change rather than be invested in, they coalesced industries that simply tied together a series of holed boats. Margaret Thatcher then stopped supporting industry in a free-market policy that abandoned companies and industries that needed short-term help. Thatcher and free-market economists argue that this was simply evolution at play within the business world, with companies emerging slimmer and fitter. In many cases though, British industry failed to emerge at all. The car industry, motorbike industry, power generation, aero and computing sectors all failed to achieve the levels of home-owned success that might have been expected of the UK. In 1952, manufacturing had employed 40 per cent of the British workforce, but today it stands at just 8 per cent. In 1952, manufacturing had produced 30 per cent of the nation's GDP, but today that stands at just about 11 per cent. In the 1950s it had produced 20 per cent of world exports, but that is now just 2 per cent, with imports surpassing exports in 1983.

Does this industrial decline matter, being as it is replaced by a much-lauded service economy and much smaller but higher-value technology-based industry? The point has been made, however, that the emergence of a more service-based economy is not enough to keep the economy on a level footing and industrial growth is essential to maintain the country's finances. This has become all the more prescient since the Covid-19 global pandemic. Over £100 billion has been spent on job support alone, and the Office for Budget Responsibility forecasted borrowing of £355 billion in 2020–21 and £244 billion in the year after. These are the highest levels seen outside of wartime, and might just have the same effect as such borrowing. Britain needs an industrial base, not just for economic reasons but for philosophical security, social and cultural reasons, too. The industry of the future will provide the technology that will determine the way we think and the way we live. Britain needs to be a part of that.

There is some hope. The discovery of oil off Britain's shores helped to stabilise the country, and joining the EU and looking towards Far Eastern quality movements helped increase the efficiency of British companies. Some companies survived and changed. Legacy organisations have emerged like phoenixes from the smouldering industrial ashes, while new, fitter and more savvy companies have been born, all helping the industrial base to stabilise and grow again. British industry revived from thirteenth to move up to eighth or ninth in the world rankings. On the whole, the future prospects for British industry are reasonably good. People will always need products and goods, but the environmental position means that in future this must be done through more sustainable means. New technologies, new business models, the increased merging of goods and services and lower energy sources all present opportunities that British firms are capable of taking. It can take a lead in providing the goods we need without costing the planet. They look less likely to fail at doing this than they were in the past but need better auditing systems. There are pockets of excellence in science and research and some improvement across the board in terms of spending on these areas, but there is still a need to do more. There is also more to be done in translating these breakthroughs into innovative new businesses with better cultural support for entrepreneurs and access to less short-term financial support. The big area of weakness is still efficiency. Past businesses tried to ignore inefficiency through diversification; today's business leaders seem to be hiding behind the mantra of hi-tech, advanced engineering – but it is still dodging the issue in much the same way and must be addressed if Britain is to compete.

For the government, the Industrial Strategy document has been a step forward, but it is limited, while Brexit, China, IR4.0 and the environment all seem absent from the country's current industrial thinking and it is vital to get these thoughts right. A government industry office is desperately needed to promote, support and champion this vital area. Industrial policy also needs to be determined through evidence and analysis and not through political agendas and dogma. The policy of free-market operation followed by knee-jerk support when it fails, instead of cogent analysis, needs to be revised. It is clear from the past that government behaviour was critical in developing the textile industry, and then critical in failing to prevent its decline. It would be better to evaluate each industry and company on a case-by-case basis and to act intelligently rather than dogmatically. There is also a lack of credibility in a policy that seeks to encourage start-ups, but not to support them when they grow bigger. What, for example, is the point of investing heavily in R & D, and encouraging conditions for businesses to grow, if they are then allowed to be picked off by overseas competitors. Is Britain to be, in football terms, doomed to stay in the lower leagues while international teams pick off the best players? At the very least the government should: encourage consumers to stop spending on imports and encourage investment; encourage spending on British products rather than those from foreign companies produced overseas; aim for a low exchange rate that makes imports more expensive and exports easier; and get to grips with overseas unicorn businesses that are seemingly too complex, too tax-avoiding, too dangerous, too interrelated, too stressful and too fast for the good of the nation. The government also needs to ensure it addresses the needs of everyday business, and not just hi-tech sectors, while addressing better housekeeping around taxation, pensions and industrial leadership with a particular emphasis on consistency. 'Economic vitality' is the objective and this too looks optimistic.

Brexit casts a long shadow. It highlighted the flaw in thinking in much the same way as thinking was flawed for companies and governments in earlier years. Much of the debate around Brexit was around the wrong questions. The question should not have been whether Britain should be in or out of Europe. The questions to ask should have been how important is industry to Britain? Does it matter if China makes our goods? Does it matter if goods are made in Britain from overseas-owned companies? This book has tried to argue that it does matter, but it really depends on whether you see industry as being based on size and employees, or relative importance to the economy, and whether you see it now in better shape for the future or not. Other questions to ask are what type of Britain do British citizens want? Does it even matter if we are British anymore? What will the effect of Brexit be either way?

The answers to these questions should have been made on informed analysis with decisions and actions determined less than the beliefs, doctrine and dogma that bedevilled Britain's decline and which bedevils debate today. The process of researching a problem, generating wide-ranging creative solutions and evolving ideas into optimised decisions is coincidentally known as 'design thinking'. If only the government practised it; the most disappointing aspect to the Brexit debate was the lack of discussion around substantive evidence in favour of argument based on emotion and beliefs. This point was iterated by Conservative minister Nicky Morgan, who accused her colleagues of having their eyes shut to job losses.[1] Rather than taking on board any comments from manufacturers, the Conservative Jeremy Hunt, for example, simply described negative comments as 'threatening'.[2] Arguments from both camps were based on animal instinct, uninformed opinion and bias. Both sides picked facts only that supported their argument rather than added to the discussion. The debate was foolhardy and has led to bitterness and recrimination. To put this in context, Britain's offhand approach to this question of industry contrasts wildly with the Soviet and Chinese leadership, which implemented some of the worst atrocities in human history in order to try to create what Britain was nonchalantly discarding. But that is another story for another day.

If the Brexit debate was a mess, the conversation around the environment has not yet started. The post-Second World War 'Golden Age of Capitalism', which saw industrialisation surge across the globe, enabled mass production to bring millions of people out of poverty and enjoy unprecedented levels of health and comfort. The downsides were that the global population boomed, from 2.5 billion people in 1950 to 8 billion today, and that population, spurred on by cheaper goods and a thirst for convenience, was demanding more. For example, 14 billion drinks bottles alone are used in Britain each year. Can the planet sustain this level of industrialised consumption? No. Similarly, Britain imports nearly 90 per cent of its products, part of the half a billion containers that are shipped each year. Planned obsolescence, fashion trends and a rise in disposable products were good for business, but have also meant that people were and are throwing away more, too. By 1979, plastic injection moulding had overtaken steel production, but only recently have the impacts of plastic waste been seen in our seas, on our animals and on ourselves. The impact of the 30,000 chemicals industry has available is rarely known, as the effects on people have not been widely examined, but many are proving to be toxic, permanent and damaging. Rising levels of resource utilisations, power and transport requirements, and wastage are having a devastating effect on us, on our flora and fauna and on the planet. The industrialisation that has swept the earth cannot continue, and urgently needs an IR 5.0 – an environmental revolution – but where is the debate and drive to achieve that coming from? Can the planet sustain the current levels of production? No. Does the argument for autarky at least not need discussion?

Can Britain make it? Yes, despite all of these issues, it can. Industrial leaders are sanguine but then industrialists, manufacturers and engineers can be a remarkably stoic lot – heroic even – planning, determined and hard-working and making less noise about Brexit than squawking politicians and journalists. They might make it work, given time. Some people think so, and even among professional economists there is an optimism that British manufacturing is on a faster upward trajectory than its competitors. If current growth continues then Britain is projected to become the world's fifth-biggest industrial nation. Even in the thirty-year-long-term, even as more and more low-cost economies industrialise, it is forecast that the country will remain in the top ten of industrial producers.[3]

The book has outlined some actions that would help industry. Above all else, however, business leaders, employees, citizens and politicians must stop reverting to dogma, making decisions based on entrenched opinion. The book has shown the fallacy of this. The belief that the empire would last forever, that big was best, that money should be thrown at businesses that had no chance of surviving, or that money should be kept from businesses that need tiding over, that tariff-free open markets are always the best, that the planet can keep on delivering resources and absorbing the impact without damage. This lack of objectivity fuelled by fake news looks like a return to the type of pre-Enlightenment thinking where this book started out. The Enlightenment, it may be remembered, 'excoriated fanaticism and superstition and stood for reason, tolerance and debate'.[4] Whether Britain will make it depends on whether it chooses to progress through thought, reason and analysis, or simply return to the Dark Ages.

Appendices

Appendices

Abbreviations and Acronyms

AHEP	Accreditation of Higher Education Programmes
AIA	Annual Investment Allowance
AIM	Alternative Investment Market
BEIS	Department for Business, Energy and Industrial Strategy
BOP	Balance of payments
CEO	Chief executive officer, or chief executive (also known as managing director, or MD)
ECSC	European Coal and Steel Community
EEC	European Economic Community
ECGD	Export Credits Guarantee Department
ERM	Exchange Rate Mechanism
ERP	European Recovery Program
EU	European Union
EPZ	Export Processing Zone
FT 30	Financial News 30-share index
FTSE	Financial Times Share Index
GDP	Gross domestic product
GVA	Gross value added
IMF	International Monetary Fund
IPR	Intellectual property rights
MD	Managing director (see also CEO)
MOOC	Massive Open Online (learning) Course
NHS	National Health Service

OECD	Organisation for Economic Co-operation and Development
ONS	Office for National Statistics
OPEC	Organization of the Petroleum Exporting Countries
PEEK	Polyether ether ketone
PMMA	Polymethyl methacrylate (trade name acrylic)
PPP	Purchasing Power Parity
QE	Quantitative easing
RAE	Royal Academy of Engineering
RAF	Royal Air Force
RPI	Retail Price Index
SME	Small/medium enterprise
UKEF	UK Export Finance
STEM	Science, technology, engineering, mathematics
UKRI	UK Research and Innovation
UNCTAD	United Nations Conference on Trade and Development
VC	Venture capital
WTO	World Trade Organization

Sources of Further Information

Related library subject areas (Dewey Decimal class mark system):

Business	330, 380, 650
Engineering	620
Enterprise	337
History	900
Innovation	600
Manufacturing	338, 670, 680
Science	530, 540

Helpful Organisations

Gauge & Toolmakers Association (GTMA)
Make it British
Newcomen Society
The Manufacturer

Places to Visit

The silk factory of the Lombe Brothers in 1719, the world's first mechanised factory, can still be seen today as a museum alongside the River Derwent in Derby. To gain a sense of early textile factories, however, try visiting the giant Styal Mill (Quarry Bank) in Cheshire to hear the clatter of machinery and the chaos of spinning equipment, dust and focused and frenetic operators. For an even more authentic look at a working mill, try the tiny Brynkir Woollen Mill in South Wales, which has been producing wool products since the 1850s. Even today it can draw on water power (now attached to a turbine rather than the original water wheel) to work its Goldthorpe & Co. (Huddersfield) and Dobcross power looms, two 300-spindle spinning mules and a small collection of spinning wheels, yarn scales, hank winders, sock-knitting machines, carding engines and a willying machine. The National Wool Museum of Wales is another textile treasure.

The Wandle Trail runs along the entire length of south London's River Wandle from Wandle Park near East Croydon train station to the River Thames near Wandsworth Town station. The river is but a shallow shadow of its former glory as the world's 'hardest working' or 'busiest' river, and you have to use much imagination to consider its once frenetic working past, but it's a pleasant, leafy, well-signposted route that still has some relics of industry to be seen; the bleach fields at Beddington Park, a plaque identifying the William Morris factory site, a tobacco factory site at Merton Park now owned by the National Trust and Merton Abbey Mills, still operating a 7hp (5kw) water mill.

For iron-making and foundry work, and a visceral feel to the Industrial Revolution, there is no better place in the world to visit than the English Heritage site at Ironbridge, and the Ironbridge Gorge museums, near Telford. Not too far away would be World of Wedgwood, showcasing Britain's pottery heritage.

W.G. Armstrong spent much of his fortune on his house at Cragside in Northumberland, and restoring Bamburgh Castle on the Northumberland coast. Cragside was one of the first houses in the country to instal electricity and is today a part of the National Trust. Bamburgh is still in the hands of the Armstrong family and, like Cragside, can also be visited by members of the public.

The Bluebell Railway is among a number of excellent historic steam railway preservation sites and is now connected to the mainline network at East Grinstead, in easy reach of London. Historic England also maintains a number of industrial heritage sites, including Ironbridge where the whole shebang started. Check out the English Heritage website for a full list of sites (historicengland.org.uk). For the record, the industrial heritage industry employs 190,000 people and contributes £74 billion to the economy!

The Science Museum houses some of Britain's greatest innovations, including James Watt's steam engine design, George Stephenson's Rocket, the iron lung and the Black Arrow rocket. It also has a valve from the code-breaking Colossus project at Bletchley Park, which fired the fuse for the computer industry. A museum of computing, code-breaking and radio is also housed at Bletchley Park itself.

The famous site of Brooklands in Surrey was the birthplace of both British aviation and motorsport with cars that once thundered round its famous banked curves. It is now home to a museum voted as one of the best in the country, although it now sits, rather ironically, alongside Mercedes-Benz World. A little further down the road in Hampshire is the biennial Farnborough Airshow, which shows off some of the best, more modern aviation developments. The RAF Museum at Cosford provides evidence of the number of prototypes made after the Second World War but often never followed through.

For other more modern insights, many companies offer factory tours and experiences, and these include Land Rover, Triumph, Mini Plant, Brompton Bikes, Amazon and Aston Martin. Other advanced science tours might include the Diamond Light Source, Red Bull F1 Factory and Dungeness Power Station.

References

INTRODUCTION

1. Measuring Worth. 2018. www.measuringworth.com

1. THE FIRST INDUSTRIAL REVOLUTION

1. Geraint (ed)., 1972. *The Wool Textile Industry in Great Britain*. Routledge & Kegan Paul.
2. Beckert, Sven., 2014. *Empire of Cotton. A new history of global Capitalism*. Allen Lane.
3. Francis, A.J., 1977. *The Cement Industry. 1796–1914: A Social History*. David & Charles, Vancouver.
4. Landes, David. S., 1969. *The Unbound Prometheus: Technological Change and Industrial Development in Western Europe from 1750 to the Present*. Cambridge, New York: Press Syndicate of the University of Cambridge. p.46.
5. Gross domestic product (GDP) is the market value of all goods and services produced by a nation. Gross national product (GNP) is the total value of goods and services produced, equivalent to the gross domestic product, plus net income from foreign investments. GDP and GNP are useful economic tools, although it should be noted it can be difficult to equate them between countries if one country has a much lower cost of living than the other. Purchasing Power Parity (PPP) looks at what a country's finances could actually buy within that country, and is hence sometimes used as a better measure of economic well-being.
6. Nester, William, 2020. *Britain's Rise to Global Superpower in the Age of Napoleon*. Frontline Books.
7. Ibid.

2. THE SECOND AND THIRD INDUSTRIAL REVOLUTIONS

1. 'CRIMEAN WAR. SECTION II. LOSS OF MONEY' in *Advocate of Peace*, Vol. 1, No. 8. August 1869, pp. 117–21. www.jstor.org/stable/27904414.
2. Hall, Peter. Prof., 1991. *Structural Transformations in the Regions of the United Kingdom*. Routledge.

3. Rachman, G., 2008. In 'The Bretton Woods Sequel will Flop' by Gideon, Rachman. *The Financial Times*. 11 November 2008.
4. Bown, Chad P., Irwin, Douglas A., December 2015. 'The GATT's Starting Point: Tariff Levels circa 1947'. NBER Working Paper No. 21782.
5. Pembroke, Michael, 2021. *America in Retreat: The Decline of US Leadership from WW2 to Covid-19*. Oneworld.

3. COURTAULD

1. Kerr, Gordon, 2019. *Short History of the Victorian Era*. Oldcastle Books.
2. Ibid.
3. Lomax, K., 1959. Production and Productivity movements in the United Kingdom since 1900. (Read at the University of Manchester for the Royal Statistical Society 21.1.1959. Index of Industrial Production, 1920 = 100).

4. W.G. ARMSTRONG & CO.

1. Hamer, F.E. (ed.), 1931. *The Personal Papers of Lord Rendel*. Ernest Benn.

5. VICKERS LTD

1. Baxter, J., 1946. *Scientists Against Time*. Little, Brown and Company.

6. BIRMINGHAM SMALL ARMS

1. Jackson, Colin, 2013. *The British Motorcycle Story*. The History Press.
2. Bruce-Gardyne, Jock, 1978. *Meriden. Odyssey of a Lame Duck*. Centre for Policy Studies.
3. Ibid.
4. Ryerson, Barry, 1980. *The Giants of Small Heath*. Haynes.
5. Ibid.
6. Lee, Jim. 7 May 2021. 'It was the best of times, it was the worst of times'. *The Classic Motorcycle* (www.pressreader.com/uk/the-classic-motorcycle/20210507/281775632026778).
7. Tiller, Stuart. Reported by Hogan, James. 17 February 2020. 'Norton Motorcycles – was it fraud from the start'. *Superbike* (www.superbike.co.uk/article/norton-was-it-a-fraud-from-the-start).

7. THE GENERAL ELECTRIC COMPANY

1. BBC. 7 September 2001. 'Lord Simpson: The man who broke Marconi'. (news.bbc.co.uk/1/hi/in_depth/uk/2000/newsmakers/1527551.stm)
2. Robinson, Michael. June 2004. 'The men who broke Marconi'. *The Money Programme*. BBC. First transmitted 14 November 2001.
3. Investopedia. Dotcom Bubble. 2018.
4. *Daily Telegraph*, 24 July 2002.

8. Morris Motors Ltd

1. Darley, Gillian, 2003. *Factory (Objekt)*. Reaktion Books.
2. Lewis, David I., 1976. *The Public Image of Henry Ford: An American Folk Hero and His Company*, pp.41–59. Wayne State University Press.
3. Barber, John (BLMC deputy Chairman), 23 October 1973. Mini Sold at a loss. BLMC says. Reported by Webb, Clifford in Honest John Classics archive. (classics. honestjohn.co.uk/news/archive/1973-10/mini-still-sold-at-a-loss-blmc-says)

9. De Havilland Aircraft Co. Ltd

1. Simons, G., 2017. *De Havilland Enterprises*. A History. Pen and Sword.
2. Birtles, Philip J., 1967. *The De Havilland Hornet* (Profile Publications No. 174). Profile Publications Ltd.
3. Brown, Eric (Captain, CBE DSC AFC RN), October 1982. 'Viewed from the Cockpit: Sea Hornet Supreme'. *Air International*, Vol. 23, No. 4, pp.192–199.
4. Martin Sharp, C., 1982. DH; A History of de Havilland. Airlife. P212
5. AP-Dow Jones, 31 October 1991. 'BAE rights flop spoils it for other equity-raisers'. *Financial Review*. (www.afr.com/companies/bae-rights-flop-spoils-it-for-other-equity-raisers-19911031-k4l3y)
6. Wyse, B., 2012. 'Next-Generation 737 Program'. *Boeing Aero Magazine*. Quarter 4.

10. Imperial Chemical Industries

1. Treanor, Jill, 12 April 2003. 'ICI faces inquiry after warning on profits'. *Guardian* (www.theguardian.com/business/2003/apr/12/1).
2. Pfeifer, Sylvia, 20 November 2014. 'Jim Ratcliffe'. *Financial Times Magazine* (www.ft.com/content/9318986c-8ec2-11e3-b6f1-00144feab7de).

11. International Computers Ltd

1. Swade, Doron, 2002. *The Difference Engine: Charles Babbage and the Quest to Build the First Computer*. Penguin.
2. Moralee, Dennis, Nov/Dec 1981. 'Robb Wilmot: the ICL story'. *Electronics & Power* 27. Reported in Wikipedia, retrieved 29 January 2021.

12. Looking Back

1. Comfort, Nicholas, 2013. *The Slow Death of British Industry: A 60-Year Suicide, 1952–2012*, Biteback Publishing.
2. Peters, Tom & Waterman, Robert, 1982 (first published). *In Search of Excellence*. Harperbusiness.
3. Alliance, David, 2015. *A Bazaar Life*. Biteback Publishing.
4. Coleman, D.C., 1969. *Courtaulds, an Economic and Social History Vol. II*. Clarendon Press, Jenkins.
5. Kitson, M. & Michie, J., 1995. 'Britain's Industrial Performance since 1960'. ESRX Centre for Business Research, University of Cambridge working paper 14.
6. Glancey, Jonathan, 2012. *Giants of Steam*. Atlantic Books.

7. Ibid.
8. Andrew, Christopher, 2010. *The Defence of the Realm; the Authorised History of MI5.* Penguin.
9. Attributed to Sir Frank McFadzean, quoted by Sir Keith Joseph. Bruce-Gardyne, Jock, 1978. *Meriden. Odyssey of a Lame Duck.* Centre for Policy Studies.
10. Holliday, Bob, 1978. *The Story of BSA Motor Cycles.* PSL.

13. Does it Really Matter?

1. Resolution Foundation, 2018. Research Foundation of DWP, Households below Average income Family Resources Survey.
2. Elliot, Larry & Atkinson, Dan, 2007. *Fantasy Island.* Constable.
3. Ibid.
4. Thoms, D. & Donnelly, D., 1985. *The Motor Car Industry in Coventry since the 1890s.* Routledge.
5. Brand, C. & Hunt, A., 2018. *The Health Costs of Air Pollution from Cars and Vans.* Global Action Plan.
6. YouGov. 2015. Patriotism in Britain reduces with each Generation, survey. d25d2506sfb94s.cloudfront.net/cumulus_uploads/document/ttknang75q/InternalResults_150331_personality_traits_Website.pdf
7. Klein, Naomi, 2017. *No is Not Enough.* Penguin Books.
8. Williamson, Ian, 2021. *Every Breath You Take: China's New Tyranny.* Birlinn.

14. Where is Britain Now?

1. Alabaster, M. et al., 2009. *The Future of UK Manufacturing.* PricewaterhouseCoopers.
2. Hawksworth, J. (Chief Economist), February 2017. *The World in 2050.* PwC.
3. Office for National Statistics. 30 May 2018. Labour Disputes in the UK:2017. UK Government
4. Neave, S. et al., 2018. 'The State of Engineering. Synopsis and Recommendations'. *Engineering UK.*
5. EEF. 2016. UK Manufacturing 2016/17. 'The Facts'. Engineering Employers Federation (now known as Make UK).
6. Ibisworld, 2016. *Consultant Engineering Services in the UK.*
7. Royal Academy of Engineering, Enterprise Hub. May 2018. enterprisehub.raeng.org.uk/latest/news/poll-compares-us-and-uk-engineers-views-engineering-enterprise
8. ADS (Aircraft, Defence Security) Group figures, reported in the *Manufacturer*, 2017, 'UK aerospace suppliers target doubling of revenues by 2022'. Hennik Research 2021.

15. Britain's Industrial Future

1. Schulten, Thoren, 27 November 1999. Eurofund. www.eurofound.europa.eu/publications/article/1999/vodafones-hostile-takeover-bid-for-mannesmann-highlights-debate-on-the-german-capitalist-model
2. Kuma, Rajesh, 1 January 2019. *Vodafone Acquisition of Mannesmann: Integrated Case Studies. Wealth Creation in the World's Largest Mergers and Acquisitions,* pp.17–29. ResearchGate.

3. CNN Money, 2000. (money.cnn.com/2000/01/17/europe/glaxo_deal).
4. CRAM. GlaxoSmithcline Beecham case Study. (www.cram.com/essay/Difference-Between-Smithkline-Beecham-And-Glaxo-Wellcome/PJDWVSHWU).
5. Croft, Jane, 15 November 2019. 'Lloyds Bank defeats £600m shareholder lawsuit'. *Financial Times*.
6. New City Agenda. (newcityagenda.co.uk/rbs-abn-amro).
7. Larsen, Peter Thal, 22 April 2008. 'RBS discover the true cost of the ABN deal'. *Financial Times*.
8. Blackman, B. (MP), 21 January 2021. Equitable Life. House of Commons debate. Recorded in Hansard Vol. 687.
9. Keizer, G., 8 July 2015. 'Microsoft writes off $7.6 bn, admits failure of Nokia acquisition'.
10. Sayer, P., 11 February 2022. 'The HP-Autonomy lawsuit: timeline of an M & A disaster'. CIO.
11. Kopytoft, V., 30 January 2014. 'Motorola was a gargantuan mistake only Google could afford to make'. *Time*.
12. Fitzpatrick, D., 1 July 2012. 'BofA's Blunder: $40 Billion-Plus'. *The Wall Street Journal*.
13. Patel, K., *The 8 Biggest M & A Failures of All Time*. DealRoom.
14. UNCTAD, 2018. *World Investment Report*. Organisation for Economic Cooperation and Development.
15. Hermes, Jennifer, 2017. Environmental Management in 2017. Environment + Energy leader (www.environmentalleader.com/2017/12/175385)
16. Vezzoli, C. Ceschin, F. Diehl, J.C. et al., 2015. 'Why have Sustainable Product-Service Systems not been widely implemented? Meeting new design challenges to achieve societal sustainability'. Journal of Cleaner Production 35: 288–290.
17. Stacey, N. & Cordes, F., 2017. *Is the UK Ready for the Fourth Industrial Revolution?*. Boston Consultancy Group.
18. Barclays Bank Plc, 2016. *Future Proofing UK Manufacturing*. Reporting on yougov survey.
19. Office for National Statistics, 30 May 2018. *Labour Disputes in the UK:2017*. UK Government.
20. Resolution Foundation, 2018. Research Foundation of DWP, Households below Average Income Family Resources Survey.
21. Fritz Foley, C., 2013. *Impact of Taxation on Location of Manufacturing Activities*. Harvard Business School and NBER.
22. Sargent, Steve, 5.10.2017. Chief Product Officer. Reported in *Bennetts* 'Where was your Triumph motorcycle made? (www.bennetts.co.uk/bikesocial/news-and-views/features/bikes/where-was-your-triumph-motorcycle-made)
23. Ibid.
24. Office of the US Trade Representative. *2017 Special 301 Report*. Executive Office of the President of the US.
25. International Energy Authority, 2008. *World Energy Outlook*.
26. Manufacturing Advisory Service. 2013 'MAS National Manufacturing Barometer Survey', available at www.mymas.org/barometer
27. Bersin, J. McDowell, T. Rahnema, A. Van Durme, Y., 2017. 'Global Human Capital Trends'. Deloitte (reported in Insights, the organisation of the future: Arriving now).

28. Straus, William & Howe, Neil, 1991. *Generations*. Quill.
29. Hutton, Will, 1996. *The State We're In*. Vintage.
30. Forbes, 2018. *The World's Most Innovative Companies*.
31. Peters, Nick (ed.), 2018. *Annual Manufacturing Report 2018*. Hennik Research reported in *The Manufacturer*.
32. Foresight, 2013. *The Future of Manufacturing: A new era of opportunity and challenge for the UK*.
33. Ibid.
34. 'Rich List, 2018. 30th annual guide to wealth in the UK'. *Sunday Times*.
35. London & Partners. 2017. Pitchbook data reported in www.londonandpartners. com/media-centre/press-releases/2017/20170705-record-start-to-2017-for-investment-into-london-and-uk-tech-companies. 30/6/17.
36. Blue Book, 2016. *UK National Accounts*. ONS.
37. Grant, J et al., 2018. 'Estimating the returns to the United Kingdom publicly funded musculo-sketal disease research in terms of net value of improved health outcomes'. *Health Research Policy and Systems*. 16:1.
38. Myers, Keith & Manley, David, 2018. 'Did the UK miss out on £400bn worth of oil revenue?' *Resource Governance*. 2018.
39. Edgerton, David, 2018. *The Rise and Fall of the British Nation: A Twentieth Century History*. Allen Lane.
40. Ibid.
41. HM Treasury 2018. *PFI and PF2 report by the Comptroller and Auditor General, National Audit Office HC718 Session 2017–2019*.
42. Deloitte, 2017. *Catalysts Fund Economic Impact Study*. Summary Report for the Higher Education Funding Council for England.
43. Hawley, S. (Dr), 1 June 2003. *Turning a Blind Eye*. The Corner House.
44. Engineering UK. 2018. Synopsis and Recommendations.
45. Howard, J. (Chair) et al., 2006. *A degree of concern? UK first degrees in science, technology and mathematics*. Royal Society.
46. Gatsby, 2017. *Key Indicators in STEM provision*. Gatsby Charitable Foundation.
47. Institute of Engineering and Technology [1] (2015) *Ones to Watch*. IET.
48. Institute of Engineering and Technology [2] (2015) *Skills and Demand in Industry Survey*. IET.

16. BREXIT

1. The Week, 20 March 2019. 'Why did the UK join the EU?' (www.theweek.co.uk/100313/why-did-the-uk-join-the-eu)
2. Giles, Chris, 2017. 'What has the EU done for the UK'. FT Series: Brexit in or out.
3. Dyson, James, 28 February 2017. Reported in *The Guardian*.
4. Drechsler, Paul (CBI President), June 2018. BBC Radio 4 Today Programme.
5. Sandford, Alasdair, 2021. 'Brexit trade deal; Nine claims by Boris Johnson or his ministers that are untrue'. Euronews.
6. Ross, Tim, 5 October 2021. 'Boris Johnson's "fuck business" approach to the supply chain crisis is a risk for Britain'. *The New Statesman*.
7. Meek, James, 2014. *Private Island: Why Britain Now Belongs to Someone Else*. Verso.

8. Brandon, Peter, 2008. *Kent and Sussex Weald*. Phillimore & Co. Ltd.
9. Perkins, John (Professor), 2013. *Review of Engineering Skills*. Department for Business, Innovation and Skills (DBIS).
10. De Statis, Statistisched Bundesamt (German Federal Statistics body), published 9 March 2021.
11. Matt Griffiths. Spokesperson for the British Chamber of Commerce, reported in *The Guardian*, 29 March 2021.
12. Scott, M., Brexit: 23 February 2021. 'Winners and Losers'. Investopedia.
13. EY, 'Brexit tracker', February 2021.
14. Birley, A.R., 2005. *The Roman Government of Britain*. Oxford. 415–16, 428–9, 430 40.

17. WILL BRITAIN MAKE IT?

1. Morgan, Nicky (Baroness), 29 March 2016. 'Leaving the EU risks a lost generation'. Education Secretary speech reported at www.gov.uk.
2. Smith, Adam, 24 June 2018. 'Jeremy Hunt brands threats by businesses "completely inappropriate"'. *Metro*.
3. Hawksworth, J. (Chief Economist), February 2017. 'The long view: how will the global economic order change by 2050. The World in 2050'. PwC.
4. Williams, David, 2006. *The Enlightenment*. Cambridge University Press.

Bibliography

General

Biography Online (www.biographyonline.net/people/famous/economists.html)

Bown, Chad P., Irwin, Douglas A., December 2015. The GATT's Starting Point: Tariff Levels circa 1947. NBER Working Paper No. 21782.

Broadberry, S. (Prof) Leunig, T. (Dr), 2013. *The impact of Government policies on UK manufacturing since 1945*. Government Office for Science.

Campbell-Smith, Duncan, 2020. *Jet Man*. Apollo Book, first published by Head of Zeus.

CEBR (Centre for Economics and Business Research), 2017. *The Impact of Automation*.

Deloitte, 2015. YouGov survey 29 May–1 June. Reported in the *Deloitte Consumer Review*.

Elliot, Larry and Atkinson, Dan, 2007. *Fantasy Island*. Constable.

Engineering.com, 23 March 2017.

Engineering Council, 2013. UK-Spec 3rd Edition.

Frankopan, Peter, 2018. *The New Silk Roads*. Bloomsbury.

Government Office for Science, 2013. *The Future of Manufacturing. Summary Report*. HMSO London.

Graces Guide (www.awa.uk.com)

Hamilton-Paterson, James, 2018. *What Have we Lost. The Dismantling of Great Britain*. Head of Zeus.

Hutton, Will, 1996. *The State We're In*. Vintage.

Kai Huang, 5 Aug 2017. China SourceLink quoted from Quora.

Lincoln, Margarette, 2021. *London and the 17th Century*. Yale.

Lomax Index of Industrial Production.

Mahbubani, Kishore, 2018. *Has the West Lost It?* Allen Lane.

Maier, J. (Chair), 2017. *Made Smarter 2017*. UK Government.

Moore, Charles. Bazalgette, Edward (producers), 2002. *100 Greatest Britons*. BBC2 Television series.

Peng, S., 2001. *Comparing Industrialisation between Japan and China*. Lund University, School of Economics and Management.

Rachman, G., 11 November 2008. Senior Official of the Bank of England (1944) In 'The Bretton Woods Sequel will Flop' by Gideon, Rachman. *The Financial Times*. Archived from the original on 16 January 2014. Retrieved 25 March 2017.

Snyder, Timothy, 2010. *Bloodlands*. Penguin.

Stewart, J., 18 May 2017. 'All the start-ups and companies working on self-driving cars'. *Wired*.

Trading Economics, 2018, tradingeconomics.com/china/industrial-production

UK Research & Innovation (www.ukri.org)

Unknown, 'CRIMEAN WAR. SECTION II. LOSS OF MONEY' in *Advocate of Peace*, Vol. 1, No. 8. August 1869, pp. 117–21. www.jstor.org/stable/27904414.

Von Tunzelmann, G.N., 1978. *Steam Power and British Industrialisation to 1860*. Clarendon Press, Oxford.

Von Weiseker, 2004. US figures, cited in Willard.

Wackernagel, M., 2018. *Earth Overshoot Day*. Global Footprint Network.

Wakeham, W., 2016. *STEM degree provision and graduate employability*. Department for Business, Innovation & Skills/Higher Education Funding Council for England.

Selected

COURTAULDS

Coleman, D.C., 1969. *Courtaulds an Economic and Social History Vol. I and II*. Clarendon Press, Oxford.

Beckert, Sven, 2014. *Empire of Cotton. A New History of Global Capitalism*. Allen Lane.

Jenkins, Geraint (ed.), 1972. *The Wool Textile Industry in Great Britain*. Routledge & Kegan Paul.

The Funding Universe. (www.fundinguniverse.com/company-histories/courtaulds-plc- history)

Reference for Business. (www.referenceforbusiness.com/history2/25/Courtaulds-plc. html)

ARMSTRONG & CO.

Graces Guide (www.gracesguide.co.uk/W._G._Armstrong_and_Co)

Heald. H., 2012. *William Armstrong: Magician of the North*. McNidder & Grace.

VICKERS

Scott, J.D., 1962. *Vickers, A History*. Weidenfield & Nicolson.

BSA

Bruce-Gardyne, Jock, 1978. *Meriden. Odyssey of a Lame Duck*. Centre for Policy Studies.

Holliday, Bob. *The Story of BSA Motor Cycles*. PSL.

GEC

Bob's Telephone File. History of GEC. (www.britishtelephones.com/histgec.htm)
Graces Guide (www.gracesguide.co.uk/GEC)
The Lawrences.com (www.the-lawrences.com/tl-gechistory)

Morris Motors Ltd

Jackson, Robert, 1964. *Lord Nuffield*. Frederick Muller Limited.
Thoms, D. Donnelly, D., 1985. *The Motor Car Industry in Coventry since the 1890s*. Routledge.
Whisler, Timothy. *The British Motor Industry, 1945–94: A Case Study in Industrial Decline*. Oxford University Press.

De Havilland

Martin Sharp, C., 1982. *DH: A History of de Havilland*. Airlife.
Rivas, B., 2012. *A Very British Sound Barrier*. Red Kite.
Simons, Graham, 2017. *De Havilland Enterprises. A History*. Pen and Sword Aviation.
Johnson, Howard, 1985. *Wings Over Brooklands*. Whittet Books.

ICI

AkzoNobel. www.akzonobel.com/en/about-us/our-history
The Funding Universe. www.fundinguniverse.com/company-histories/imperial-chemical-industries-plc-history
International Directory of Company Histories, Vol. 50. 2003. St James Press,

ICL

Bird, Peter, 2000. *The First Food Empire. A History of J. Lyons & Co*. Phillimore & Co. Ltd.
D. Moralee, 'The ICL story,' in *Electronics and Power*, Vol. 27, No. 11, pp.788–795, November–December 1981, doi: 10.1049/ep.1981.0360.

Looking Back

Dunnet, P.J.S., 1980. *The Decline of the British Motor Industry; The effects of government Policy, 1945–1979*. Croom Helm.

Does it Really Matter

Sainsbury, 2016. *Post-16 skills plan and independent report on technical education*. HMSO. 4 July 2018.

Index